Strategy in Practice

Strategy in Practice

A Practitioner's Guide to Strategic Thinking

Third Edition

George Tovstiga

WILEY

This third edition first published 2015
© 2015 John Wiley & Sons, Ltd
First edition published 2010, second edition published 2013 by John Wiley & Sons, Ltd

Registered office
John Wiley & Sons Ltd, The Atrium, Southern Gate, Chichester, West Sussex, PO19 8SQ,
United Kingdom

For details of our global editorial offices, for customer services and for information about how
to apply for permission to reuse the copyright material in this book please see our website at
www.wiley.com.

Wiley publishes in a variety of print and electronic formats and by print-on-demand. Some
material included with standard print versions of this book may not be included in e-books or
in print-on-demand. If this book refers to media such as a CD or DVD that is not included in the
version you purchased, you may download this material at http://booksupport.wiley.com. For
more information about Wiley products, visit www.wiley.com.

Designations used by companies to distinguish their products are often claimed as trademarks.
All brand names and product names used in this book are trade names, service marks,
trademarks or registered trademarks of their respective owners. The publisher is not associated
with any product or vendor mentioned in this book.

Limit of Liability/Disclaimer of Warranty: While the publisher and author have used their best
efforts in preparing this book, they make no representations or warranties with respect to the
accuracy or completeness of the contents of this book and specifically disclaim any implied
warranties of merchantability or fitness for a particular purpose. It is sold on the understanding
that the publisher is not engaged in rendering professional services and neither the publisher
nor the author shall be liable for damages arising herefrom. If professional advice or other
expert assistance is required, the services of a competent professional should be sought.

A catalogue record for this book is available from the Library of Congress

Tovstiga, George.
    Strategy in practice: a practitioner's guide to strategic thinking/George Tovstiga. — 3rd
Edition.
        pages cm
    Revised edition of the author's Strategy in practice, 2013.
    Includes index.
    ISBN 978-1-119-12164-0 (pbk.) — ISBN 978-1-119-12168-8 (ebk.) — ISBN 978-1-119-12167-1
(ebk) — ISBN 978-1-119-16915-4 (ebk)
    1. Strategic planning.   I. Title.
    HD30.28.T68 2015
    658.4'012--dc23   2015019356

A catalogue record for this book is available from the British Library.

ISBN 978-1-119-12164-0 (paperback) ISBN 978-1-119-12168-8 (ebk)
ISBN 978-1-119-12167-1 (ebk)   ISBN 978-1-119-16915-4 (obk)

Cover design: Wiley
Cover image: ©carlo fornitano/Shutterstock

Set in 11/14pt Trump Mediaeval LT Std-Roman by Thomson Digital, Noida, India

Contents

Preface to the First Edition

S trategy is still a source of contention in most organizations. It seems that since the beginning of time man has associated strategy with mystery and esoteric rituals restricted to only an enlightened inner circle. The ancient Greeks consulted their oracle at Delphi for guidance before moving into battle. Indeed, in preparing for the historic battle at Salamis in 480 BC that pitted the Greek coalition against the might of Xerxes' fearsome Persian army it took the persuasive and cunning "vision" of the Athenian *strategoi* (general) Themistocles, commander of the Greek allied navy, to provide an interpretation of the oracle that ultimately encouraged the Greeks to stay and fight in the face of almost certain defeat against the Persian army. Some had interpreted the oracle's sign to predict defeat. Themistocles skillfully and convincingly interpreted the oracle's omen to mean victory. Little, of course, could he or his Greek compatriots have appreciated the historical significance of their great victory in that battle.[1]

Many managers today still seek out their "oracles" when faced with strategic decision making. The modern manager's oracle often takes on the form of endless reams of essentially meaningless data generated by management information systems. Many

---

[1] Greene, R. (2006) *The 33 Strategies of War*, London: Profile Books.

managers find solace in numbers, just as the early Greeks did in the Delphian oracle's signs.

Strategy need not be enigmatic. It need not be a mystical codex with seven seals. Good strategy is about clarity of thinking; of balancing insight based on well-founded intuition with rational analysis – particularly in the face of incomplete information and complex circumstances. Strategy is practiced in social contexts; that is to say, in organizations and their competitive environments. Admittedly, these represent ambiguous contexts that often defy rational analysis. Andrew Lo of MIT's School of Management has remarked that while in the physical sciences three laws can explain 99% of behavior, 99 laws in finance can at best explain only 3% of the behavior.[2] The latter can be argued for the social sciences in general. However, while the context in which strategy is practiced is complex and fraught with ambiguity, the basic premise of this book is that how we approach strategy need not be. In this book we develop an approach to strategy that seeks to fulfill that purpose. An underpinning element of this approach is the strategic thinking process that leads to the generation of strategically relevant insight, even in highly ambiguous and complex competitive contexts.

This book builds on several relatively simple assumptions. The first is that strategy is a practice discipline. While this extends to the field of management science in general, it is arguably in the strategy area that "getting it wrong" leads to the more serious consequences. Strategy attains meaning only in the practice field; indeed, some strategy thinkers even go so far as to suggest that strategy attains meaning only in the retrospective; that is, after the fact. Strategy may look impressive on paper, but it is in the practice field that it fulfills its ultimate purpose. While this may seem readily apparent to any military commander, it is not necessarily what the strategic management literature would

---

[2] *The Economist*, Schumpeter – The Pedagogy of the Privileged (September 26, 2009).

lead us to believe. Second, strategy is not only about rational analysis and the models that support the analysis. No doubt, analysis is important in strategy. Indeed, as will be argued in this book, appropriately selected frameworks of analysis can generate a lot of useful insight. But as we will see, analysis is only one of several inputs to the strategic thinking process. Intuition, reflection, and above all a predisposition for experimentation and learning are its other important constituents.

This book is about strategy in practice. It draws on strategy theory and current thinking in the field of strategic management. However, this book is written with the practitioner of strategy in mind – the manager who faces strategic decision making in every day management practice. This is where strategy has the potential for making a difference in the business outcome of a firm. In my experience, both as management practitioner and consultant, this is where we often still find substantial gaps in the understanding of even very basic strategy concepts in firms. Managers typically have difficulty in knowing where to begin with strategy. Of those who do succeed in getting started, many quickly get bogged down in the maze of strategic analysis. This book seeks to address those gaps in understanding strategy; it aims to provide the strategy practitioner with a balanced compendium consisting of essential theory and pragmatic, practitioner insight. The strategic thinking approach that forms the core theme of this book delineates the path through the strategy forest.

Setting the right strategy is arguably the most critical managerial challenge facing a firm. Strategy is about making appropriate choices about *why*, *where*, and *how* to compete. Decisions of this type are invariably being made under conditions of incomplete information in increasingly complex contexts. This doesn't make the task any easier. It does, however, reflect the reality of the complex, fast-changing and messy real world we compete in. In that context, strategy is first and foremost about *being different* and *doing things differently* in deliberate response to opportunities in the firm's external competitive environment. This response invariably takes on the form of creating and delivering a superior value offering to the market. However, strategy might also have an inward focus; it might also be thought about as seeking and achieving competitive advantage through differentiation in the strategic (re-) positioning of the firm. This might require a realignment of resources and capabilities to better fit changing circumstances in the external market environment.

Good strategy, whatever its pretext, demands astute and discerning insight – strategic insight which is grounded in a suitably balanced mixture of rational analysis, intuition, healthy skepticism, reflected experience, and the willingness and ability to continually challenge the prevailing logic and paradigms. In this book we explore the strategic thinking process which leads to strategic insight. This may seem a questionable proposition – a systematic approach to understanding a complex context? No doubt, competitive contexts are highly complex. Firms' external competitive environments are continually changing; internal organizational contexts are no less complex. Complexity, we know, inherently defies structure and order.

Why then a book about anything even remotely related to *structure* given the messy real world we are competing in? In this book we clearly differentiate between a firm's reality marked by complex and changing contexts and an appropriate *response* on the part of the firm to that reality. The former, the firm obviously can neither influence nor impose structure onto. The latter, however, clearly lies within the firm's realm of strategic choices. Strategy is about clarity of thinking; about making appropriate choices under conditions of incomplete information. Strategic thinking can be a powerful means to that end.

The strategic thinking approach developed in this book does not seek to achieve simplification of the firm's complex competitive context; rather, it seeks to bring structure to the *thinking* that allows managers not to lose sight of the wood for the trees. Good

structured thinking begins with asking the *right* strategic questions – those that really have potential to make a difference to the
firm's ability to compete in its markets. There might be numerous questions on a manager's plate, but in reality only relatively
few of these have potential for really making a difference to a
business's competitive situation. Managers will want to ensure
that they are indeed focusing on the few high priority issues.
Strategic thinking also continually challenges the prevailing
business logic. It seeks to establish relevant insights and to
understand these in their current strategic context. Insight ultimately leads to the emergence of patterns that reflect the firm's
competitive landscape. Though inevitably incomplete and
spotty, this level of granularity is often the best there is available.
The good news in all of this is that the firm's competitors are no
better off in this regard.

Arguably, strategic thinking leading to an insight-driven approach
to strategy is an increasingly critical strategic capability enabling
those firms that have acquired skill and acumen in its application
to recognize and act on opportunities faster than their competitors;
alternatively, it can help to avert situations that might prove to be
detrimental to the firms' competitive position. Hence, there is a lot
at stake. The purpose of this book is to provide a relatively
accessible guide toward achieving mastery of this important skill.

The strategic thinking process developed and discussed in this
book represents an accumulation of insights, experiences, and
reflections that have evolved as a result of my various roles over
the years as management practitioner in industry, as strategy
consultant, and as professor of strategy. This book represents a
summary of the insights distilled from experiences gained wearing these various hats both in the practice field and in academia.
Boxed inserts throughout the book under the heading "*Strategy in
Practice*" underscore the pragmatic emphasis on strategy. These
provide practical insights and suggestions for applying the key
notions and concepts discussed in the respective chapters.

There is little in this book that is *really* new. It would be equally pretentious to assume that a book of this brevity can exhaustively deal with strategy in its breadth. The focus of this book is on the front end of the strategy process; it is about setting the right strategic direction from the outset. To that end, this book does purport to make a unique contribution; its aim is to provoke a new and different approach to thinking about strategy.

In compiling the book, I have poached without remorse ideas and thinking put forward by fellow scholars. I am particularly indebted to former colleagues in industry and consulting, current colleagues in academia, my MBA, and doctoral students. Particular mention must go to those at Bayer, ABB, Arthur D. Little, Henley Business School, the Private Hochschule Wirtschaft (PHW) in Zurich, Switzerland, and the University of St. Gallen, Switzerland. This book is as much a tribute to their generosity of spirit in sharing insights and experiences as it is to their relentless challenging of my thinking both in the practice field and classroom, respectively.

I am particularly grateful to several individuals who have contributed directly to the book. I am indebted to the following for their reviews of the manuscript, valuable feedback, and endorsement: Professor Peter Lorange, Lorange Institute of Business Zurich (Switzerland); Leif Bergman, Managing Director of Henley Nordic (Denmark); David Wright, MD of AllCloud Networks and formerly a Strategy Director and Business Vice President at Hewlett Packard; Professor John McGee, Warwick University (UK); and Professor David Collis, Harvard Business School (USA). Further, I am grateful to Rosemary Nixon, Senior Commissioning Editor at John Wiley & Sons, for her unwavering support from the outset. Last, but by no means least, I am indebted to my wife, Heidi, for her meticulous scrutiny of several versions of the book's manuscript, and for engaging and challenging discussions on its content as it evolved.

I am grateful to all. It has been a great learning journey and I look forward to sharing some of the insights that have emerged with you in this book.

George Tovstiga
Henley-on-Thames
March 2010

Preface to the Second Edition

The need for clarity and structure in strategic thinking is greater than ever. Since publication of the first edition of this book, companies are facing ever greater challenges in a global economy marked by widespread uncertainty. New worries triggered by the Euro crisis have driven business confidence levels to unprecedented depths. Indeed, there is no end to the recession in sight as the threat of a "triple dip" recession in the foreseeable future appears ever more probable.[1] More than ever, firms are seeking new ways to approach their strategy; if not to achieve strategic growth, then to counter threats with more effective defensive strategies. Strategy, the way we know it, appears to have arrived at an evolutionary crossroads. The current economic crisis has introduced several important changes to the way in which we think about strategy.

The first has to do with our fundamental understanding of competitiveness, the firm's *"right to win."* This has been defined as the ability of the firm to engage in its competitive markets with a better-than-average chance of achieving success – not just in the

---

[1] Not all geographic areas are equally affected, of course; talk of a possible "triple-dip" recession is currently making its rounds primarily in the UK; see, for example, Groom, B. (2012) Companies to Cut Investment and Hiring, *Financial Times* (July 9, 2012).

short term, but consistently. This is being challenged as never before.[2]

Second, the notion of *"sustainable"* competitive advantage, while still conceptually interesting, is being seriously challenged in the practice field. Traditionally, the achievement of "sustainable" advantage has been the Holy Grail in strategy. Increasingly, however, firms are finding themselves pursuing not "sustainable" competitive advantage, but punctuated situations of *"unsustainable temporary"* advantage. Once achieved, these position the firm favorably only until the competition has caught up or markets have moved on – at which point the search for new advantage continues.[3] If anything, this new mantra has heightened the awareness that firms' strategy increasingly revolves around gaining relevant insight, rapid experimentation, and evolutionary learning.[4] Kelly's[5] prescient assertion of firms engaging in ever more frequent cycles of *"find, nurture, destroy"* resonates closely to what we are, indeed, experiencing in the practice field.

This second edition of *Strategy in Practice* pursues the same purpose as its earlier edition: it seeks to provide the practitioner of strategy with a compendium that balances current thinking in the field of strategic management and pragmatic guidance for putting that thinking into practice.

This new edition, however, substantially extends the section on strategic sense making and analysis. Following on an introductory chapter on strategic analysis, two new chapters have been added; these elaborate on *high-level* and *supporting-level* strategic analyses. The distinction between the two levels of analysis is critical to strategic sense making and thinking; it is also a unique

---

[2] Mainardi, C. and Kleiner, A. (2010) The Right to Win, *Strategy + Business* (Booz&Co), Issue 61 (Winter 2010).
[3] Stern, S. (2010) Get Your Strategy Right Now before the Dust Settles, *Financial Times* (July 21, 2009).
[4] McGrath, R.G. (2010) Business Models: A Discovery Driven Approach, *Long Range Planning*, Vol. 43, pp. 247–261.
[5] Kelly, K. (1997) The New Rules of the New Economy: Twelve Dependable Principles for Thriving in a Turbulent World, *Wired*, September 1997.

contribution of this book to the current thinking in strategic analysis. The *unique competing space* concept and analysis framework, a unique contribution introduced in the first edition, is also dealt with much more thoroughly in one of the new chapters (Chapter 5). Finally, this new edition of *Strategy in Practice* introduces some practical exercises in Appendices A and B for putting the thinking, concepts, and frameworks introduced throughout the book into practice. These exercises have been used effectively in Executive Strategy seminar workshops around the world, and in consultancy work with both small start-ups as well as multinational firms.

I am sincerely grateful to fellow scholars, management practitioners, and MBA students around the world whose generous feedback and suggestions on the first edition have contributed directly to this new edition. I am particularly indebted to my Henley DBA research associates, Henning Grossmann and Jacob Bruun-Jensen, for engaging discourse on a number of the key themes and concepts elaborated on in this edition; these have contributed significantly to their advancement. Further, I am grateful to Rosemary Nixon, Senior Commissioning Editor at John Wiley & Sons, for her continuing support for this edition.

Lastly, but by no means least, I am once again indebted to my wife, Heidi, for her careful scrutiny of the manuscript of this second edition, and for her numerous invaluable suggestions for clarification and structuring of its content.

The learning journey continues; with this second edition I look forward to sharing new insights and learning with you.

George Tovstiga
Henley-on-Thames
August 2012

Preface to the Third Edition

This third edition of *Strategy in Practice* is being published in the aftermath of what has been an exceptionally prolonged economic crisis. By most accounts, the difficult period marked by double- and triple-dip relapses of the economy is over. Once again buoyant Wall Street earnings appear to support that view.[1]

Nonetheless, the global business environment has changed, even as business is returning to "normal." But it is an unprecedented "new normal" that businesses are facing in the wake of the crisis; one characterized by continuing uncertainty, disappearing industry boundaries, and new spheres of economic activity, against a backdrop of ever shortening time horizons. Has the economic crisis been at the root of the changed business context? No doubt, the crisis has had an impact; as to its extent, we really don't know.

Fact is, however, that several new global mega factors appear to be changing how and where we compete in rather fundamental ways. A recent report by the McKinsey Global Institute[2] identifies four of the mega drivers to be: (1) a shift of economic activity,

---

[1] Braithwaite, T. and McLannahan, B. (2015) Buoyant Wall Street Earnings Lift Cloud of Crisis, *Financial Times* (April 16, 2015).
[2] Dobbs, R., Manyika, J. and Woetzel, J. (2015) The Four Global Forces Breaking all the Trends, *McKinsey Global Institute* (April 2015) (accessed online at http://www.mckinsey.com/insights/strategy/ on April 30, 2015).

globally, to emerging markets, and within these, to urban centers; (2) accelerating technological change resulting in an unprecedented scope, scale, and economic impact of technology; (3) an aging human population against a backdrop of falling fertility rates; and (4) greater global flow and connections through trade, movements of capital, people, and information extending to a complex, intricate, and sprawling global economic web.

According to the McKinsey authors, these four factors are disrupting long-established paradigms of competition across virtually all sectors of the global economy. This is causing familiar patterns to break down, to break up, or to break altogether. The impact of the macro-scale disruption is quickly trickling down to the business level. The evolving "new normal" is asserting itself in a number of ways relevant to management practice. Disruption is playing havoc with the intuitions that in the past have underpinned much of our business decision making.

For one, the competitive game has changed – and is continuing to change. New rules of competition are emerging. These demand that we think differently about how we compete. Traditional, static approaches to strategy are being challenged as never before, particularly as they are proving to be far too inept in the face of the changing nature of competition. "Practice-relevance" has become the new business criterion.

If anything, these developments reaffirm the need for strategic thinking at all stages of the strategy process. To that end, the core theme and emphasis on strategic thinking established in the earlier editions prove to be as compelling as ever. The notion of strategic thinking, therefore, serves as the unifying theme and "red thread" connecting the chapters of this new edition as it has in the earlier editions. Strategic thinking is shown to pervade the strategy process throughout its stages – regardless of whether at the sense making stage, the strategic option formation and evaluation phase, or the stage in which the deployment of a preferred strategic response occurs.

The third edition has been thoroughly revised, updated, and substantially extended. Conceptual notions introduced in the earlier editions, such as the *strategy building blocks*, and the *unique competing space* concept and framework, have been substantially elaborated in several thematic areas. For example, the notion of the unique competing space, particularly from the perspective of its respective strategic boundaries, is shown to provide a cogent, rational basis for the formation of strategic options. Similarly, the strategy building blocks are used to develop insightful criteria for evaluating the appropriateness of strategic options. Two entirely new topics have been added: *strategy execution* and *strategic performance appraisal* are explored in a new chapter. With the inclusion of strategy execution this third edition now thematically embraces the entire strategy process.

Finally, this new edition features an accompanying website holding additional resources for tutors (this can be located via www.wiley.com/go/strategyinpractice3e). I look forward to more interaction with users via this new online functionality.

For this third edition, I remain indebted to a multitude of people, in particular my Henley MBA students, for whom previous editions of the book have constituted the syllabus of the core Strategy module of the Henley MBA program. I am grateful for their relentless challenging of the concepts and thinking; this has contributed immensely to sharpening the thinking reflected in the book. I am also indebted to my Russian students at the Graduate School of Management (GSOM) of the University of St. Petersburg, with whom I first used the material on strategy execution and strategic performance appraisal (unbeknownst to them!) in the core CEMS "Strategy in Practice" core course in December 2014, for invaluable impulses that helped shape the new Chapter 8 in the book.

Further, I am grateful to Holly Bennion, Sam Hartley and Jenny Ng at John Wiley & Sons for their continuing support in preparing this edition.

Finally, I remain indebted to my son, Matthew, and my wife, Heidi, for their careful scrutiny of the manuscript of this third edition, numerous invaluable suggestions for clarification and structuring of its content – and above all, to Heidi for her endless understanding and unwavering support throughout the endeavor.

This third edition thus marks a further milestone along a learning journey that has yielded new thinking and new perspectives on strategy in practice. I am keen to share these with you in this new edition!

George Tovstiga
Henley-on-Thames
May 2015

About the Author

George Tovstiga is Professor of Strategy and Innovation Management at Henley Business School at the University of Reading where he is Director of the Henley Executive Strategy Programme and Lead Tutor for Strategic Management in Henley's MBA programs. He teaches, researches, and consults in the areas of strategy and innovation management. George has extensive international experience as management educator, industry management practitioner (including Xerox Research in Canada, Bayer AG in Germany, and ABB Ltd in Switzerland), author, and consultant. Prior to joining Henley, George consulted for Arthur D. Little (Switzerland) Ltd's Strategic Growth and Innovation Practice. He is a consultant to a number of multinationals in the area of strategy and has published extensively in this area.

CHAPTER 1

Introduction to Strategy in Practice

It is important to remember that no one has ever seen a strategy or touched one; every strategy is an invention, a figment of someone's imagination . . .

—Henry Mintzberg

IN THIS INTRODUCTORY CHAPTER, WE:

- define and explore fundamental notions related to strategy and the practice of strategy;
- review and frame key problems and issues contributing to the ongoing dilemma managers face with strategy;
- reflect on the centrality of value creation, delivery, and capture to strategy;
- introduce strategic thinking and the strategic thinking process in the context of strategy in the practice field;

- reflect critically on the differences between *strategic thinking* and *strategic planning*; particularly from the perspective of their relevance to strategy practice;
- introduce the strategy roadmap, and use it to briefly introduce and outline the subsequent chapters of this book;
- close with some caveats and useful pointers on strategy in practice.

Strategy: A Persistent Dilemma

Strategy – is it really a figment of someone's imagination? One would hardly come to that conclusion judging by the popularity of the word in the business media. Scarcely any business word is invoked more frequently and with greater fervor. Business leaders take great pride in referring to "their strategy." A simple search for the word "strategy" in the *Financial Times* online (FT.com) for the 12-month period of 2014 results in 6,506 hits. The term is being used; in fact, it is being used a lot.

Yet many business leaders have difficulty articulating their strategy. Ask a business leader to explain their organization's strategy in simple terms and how it sets them apart from their competitors. More often than not, this simple question elicits an evasive response. Ignorance of the firm's strategy extends down through the ranks; recent research reports that only 55% of middle managers surveyed can name even one of their firm's top five strategic priorities.[1] Simply put, this means that when managers are given the task of explaining strategy to their subordinates, almost half fail to get it right. It doesn't end there; not only are strategic objectives poorly understood, they often appear disconnected from the firm's overall business strategy. The sobering reality is that most business leaders cannot articulate their organization's strategy in a simple, compelling way.

Many boards fail as well in providing appropriate strategic guidance to their companies. A recent survey of non-executive directors indicated that merely 34% of those polled believed that boards on which they served fully understood their companies' strategies. Just 22% were of the opinion that their boards really understood how their firms created value and only 16% affirmed that the boards on which they served had a good understanding of the dynamics of their firms' industries.[2]

This is worrisome when considering that these are the people who are responsible for the strategic course of their company. Although business leaders often see themselves as the architects of their organization's strategy, many rather quickly lose sight of the wood for the trees when it comes to strategy. Many are quickly baffled, if not by the jargon then by not knowing how to approach strategy in the first place. Surely, this cannot be for lack of "cutting edge" management thinking. Time and again, authors of best-selling business books, their publishers, and the media would have us believe that the holy grail of strategy – *the* strategy theory to put all previous ones to rest – has finally been found. And indeed, a number of useful advances in strategic thinking have been made over the years. The fundamental problems facing managers today, however, are related to putting that strategy to work in the field of practice.

Yet, even strategy scholars are still grappling with the notion of strategy. As a concept, strategy still suffers from a lack of precision in its definition. A number of significant gaps in the strategic management literature have left the discipline with a high degree of ambiguity, despite its popularity as a scholarly field of study. Rondo-Pupo and Guerras-Martin[3] in their recent study note the following reasons for this:

1. A paucity of knowledge regarding the evolution of the definition of the evolution of the strategy concept in the field of strategic management;

2. A lack of consensus among scholars leading to significant diversity and ambiguity in definitions of the strategy concept;
3. Ambiguity in terms of the constituent elements of the strategy concept;
4. A lack of analysis and understanding regarding the structural evolution of the strategy concept; and
5. A lack of sufficient evidence supporting the understanding of the evolution of the strategy concept, and its influence on the field of strategic management.

Opposing views, on the other hand, have argued for the need to retain an element of conceptual diversity regarding the definition of the strategy concept. For example, Mintzberg[4] has argued that *" . . . the field of strategic management cannot afford to rely on a single definition of strategy . . . explicit recognition of multiple definitions can help practitioners and researchers alike to maneuver through this difficult field . . . ."*

And so, the debate continues.

What then is "Strategy"?

In view of the proliferation of management publishing on the topic, it would seem reasonable to assume that we might at least begin with a clear and consistent definition of the notion of *strategy*. As has been argued in the previous section, however, this is not the case. Strategy has been defined in many different ways and it is still evolving as a concept. Early definitions of business strategy strongly imply deliberate planning and action, such as Chandler's (1962) classic definition:

> *The determination of the basic long-term goals and objectives of an enterprise, and the adoption of courses of action and the allocation of resources necessary for carrying out these goals.*[5]

A more recent definition of strategy proposed by Rondo-Pupo and Guerras-Martin[3] introduces the notion of responsiveness on the part of the firm to developments in its environment:

> . . . *the dynamics of the firm's relation with its environment for which the necessary actions are taken to achieve its goals and/or to increase performance by means of the rational use of resources.*

This definition, while an improvement on earlier definitions, still lacks clarity regarding *purpose* of the goals. The rational use of the firm's resources in response to opportunities and/or threats in its environment is no doubt important, but no end in itself. Rather, the purpose of any activity on the part of the firm is to fulfill its obligations to its stakeholders through the creation, delivery, and capture of value. Indeed, we argue in this book that the firm's very purpose for being revolves around its value obligations to its stakeholders. The form of that value created and delivered may range from explicit, readily measurable expressions of value to highly intangible, and difficult to measure forms of value. Indeed, the latter form of value is becoming increasingly important; many value offerings today encompass both tangible and intangible components. As a case in point, consider a typical purchase transaction across the counter at a Starbucks coffee shop: no doubt the actual cup of coffee served over the counter has attributes of "measurable" value, the least of which would be the price paid for the beverage. However, according to Starbucks' CEO Howard Schultz the overall "experience" perceived by the customer in the course of the transaction is of primary importance. Attributes of that "experience" encompass a complex amalgamation of numerous tangible and intangible attributes of value delivery associated with the Starbucks visit. These might include the friendliness of the barista preparing and serving the coffee across the counter, the ambience of the store setting, and the impression of cleanliness of the tables and chairs. In Schultz's view these intangible factors, more than the actual cup of coffee, reflect the real value delivered by Starbucks.

Centrality of the "Value" Notion in Strategy

The notion of *value* is indeed a central theme in strategy. In the broadest sense of the word, firms compete on the basis of value. This may relate to the value intrinsic to the firm's basis of competitiveness (such as might be reflected in the uniqueness and superiority of their resource base) as much as it might relate to the value the firm succeeds in creating (for example, by virtue of its superior resource position) and delivering to their stakeholders. In fact, one might argue that the creation of value constitutes the very purpose of an organizations' *raison d'être*, regardless of whether the organization is driven by the profit motive or whether it is a non-profit organization.

However, in a competitive sense, the objective is not simply the creation of *any* value; rather, firms compete on the basis of the *differentiated* value they achieve in creating and capturing. Strategy is therefore ultimately about creating value that is *different* – ideally this difference relates to the *uniqueness* and *superiority* of the value offering at stake. The *value premium* is a measure of that differentiation; it reflects the degree to which a firm succeeds in achieving competitive advantage on the basis of the uniqueness and superiority of its (thereby differentiated) value offering.

However, firms do not create value simply for its own sake. Rather, firms create value in response to stakeholders' needs and expectations. Stakeholders may vary and their needs and expectations might diverge considerably. Therefore, strategy is also about identifying and prioritizing needs and expectations and aligning the firm's efforts on those to be fulfilled. Good strategy is focused; it is as much about where and on whom the firm will focus its value creating efforts as it is about where and on whom it will not.

While much of the focus is on value *creation*, value *capture* is, in fact, equally critical for firms' competitiveness and sustainability. *Value capture* refers to the appropriation of the value *created*; the difference between value created and value captured is referred to as *value slippage*. Organizations do not always capture the full benefit of the value they create. Other organizations or parties may benefit more from the value created than its creating organization. Numerous industries are currently struggling with the issue of value slippage. The music and creative industries sector is a case in point. Ease of accessibility and growing consumer demand for free online content is resulting in traditional revenues streams to its creators drying up. The so-called *freemium* pricing model is currently being deployed by some players in those industries to recapture some of the value created. Social media is another area facing the challenge: Facebook, even with its undisputed ability to create value for its 1.3 billion monthly active users, has yet to ultimately prove its capability for capturing sufficient value to justify its colossal market capitalization and price–earnings ratio – if its highly volatile share price is any indication.

While the notions of value creation and capture are in themselves relatively cogent, there is little consensus among scholars as to what, in fact, value is, how it is created and the mechanisms for its capture.

Box 1.1 The Purpose of the Company: An Old Debate Rekindled

Intrinsic to the notion of the firm's strategy is the question probing its purpose for being. The hotly contested debate as to whether the firm's reason for being is to maximize *shareholder* value or whether its purpose is to pursue the creation of broader social benefit has been going on for decades. Conservatives, primarily proponents of *Anglo-Saxon capitalism* and defenders of the shareholder value position, have been facing off against the progressive camp representing broader stakeholder interests. The socio-economic fallout of the recent recession appeared to have played to the progressives' favor. The collapse of Lehman Brothers that triggered a global economic crisis epitomized the failures of the shareholder model; prompting even one of its champions, Jack Welch, GE's former CEO, to remark that pursuing shareholder value as a strategy was "the dumbest idea ever."

Indeed, the shareholder value model appears to have conceptual as well as practical shortcomings. Despite its proponents' claims that companies are owned by shareholders, this is, strictly speaking, not true. Publicly traded companies are in fact "legal persons" that own themselves; shareholders simply own entitlements such as the right to dividends and to vote on certain occasions. This is a protective measure that provides shareholders with benefit of limited liability. Claims by creditors can be made only against the firm's assets rather than against individual shareholders' assets. Companies thereby also enjoy the freedom of capital "lock-in," enabling them to pursue long-term projects. Shareholders, however, are typically not a homogeneous group sharing collective goals and objectives; they may include speculative investors interested only in short-term gain to those seeking long-term investment opportunity.

Regulatory measures introduced by governments in the aftermath of the recent recession have resulted in a return to more stakeholder oriented constraints on business. For many progressives, this is not enough. Recently, pundits from the progressive camp have called for legislation that would require firms to declare upon incorporation their intention "to deliver particular goods and services that serve a societal or economic need." Other calls have been for companies to "articulate their purposes" and for directors to be held accountable for delivery of these. Firms such as Bosch, Carlsberg, Tata, and Bertelsmann owned by foundations have been held up as notable examples. However, all of these have been experiencing performance issues of one sort or another of late.

Mediating views seeking to reconcile the opposing camps suggest that at the core of a modern company's success is in fact its ability to achieve the best of both worlds. They point to the fact that most companies, far from being enslaved to their share price, in fact continually engage in a process of negotiation over their strategy and time horizons between investors and themselves. Moreover, it appears that both mature companies such as Shell and Nestlé as well as new-economy companies such as Google, Facebook, and Amazon succeed at this. Neither appears to have difficulty in steering shareholders' demands for short-term returns in favor of long-term gain. Notably, this appears to be happening in the absence of any lofty declaration of purpose.

This conciliatory reasoning notwithstanding, it does not appear, however, that either of the two camps will concede their stance significantly anytime soon. Recently reported figures indicate the size of the average Wall Street bonus in 2014 to have been $172,860. This is a 2% increase over 2013 and the highest average payout since 2007. Anglo-Saxon capitalism, it would appear, will not be ceding any ground anytime soon.

Sources: The Economist (2015) Schumpeter/The Business of Business (March 21, 2015); *TIME* Briefing, Vol. 185, No. 11 (March 30, 2015).

Deliberate versus Emergent Strategy

Consensus today appears to be forming around definitions of strategy that allow for the fact that strategy has both deliberate as well as unintended elements; that it is often only recognizable as such in retrospect. On the basis of this frame of reference,

Mintzberg[6] suggests thinking of strategy as a stream of actions, the meaning of which often becomes apparent only after their occurrence. Mintzberg also argues for thinking about strategy as a pretext for action positioned somewhere along a continuum that runs from purely deliberate to purely emergent, though in practice neither extreme is ever really encountered despite claims in the management literature suggesting otherwise.

So, rather than trying to nail down an exact definition of what strategy *is*, it is perhaps more evocative to reflect on what strategy is *about*.

From its earliest military origins, strategy has always been about gaining the competitive edge. We look back on several thousands of years of military history in which strategy has, in essence, always been about *winning*.

BOX 1.2 LORD HORATIO NELSON: STRATEGY LESSONS FROM TRAFALGAR

In the face of increasing complexity and ambiguity in their business environments companies are finding less space than ever for experimentation with their strategy. Competitive advantage, when gained, is often transient at best. However, while competitive contexts may be complex, the firm's approach to strategy needn't be. "Good" strategy needn't be the exception it mostly is; but it does demand both creativity and courage. We can derive lessons on what constitutes "good" strategy from Lord Horatio Nelson's winning naval engagement at Trafalgar in the autumn of 1805. At the time, England's sovereignty was under threat. Napoleon had conquered large parts of Europe and the invasion of England was next on his agenda. Napoleon's great hurdle was wresting control of the sea away from England in order to cross the Channel. Both sides met in a stand-off near the southwest coast of Spain.

The French/Spanish combined fleet had 33 ships and the English 27. Lord Horatio Nelson commanded the outnumbered English fleet in that fateful naval face-off off the southwest coast of Spain at a point called Cape Trafalgar. Conventional battle strategy of the day dictated that opposing fleets stay in line firing broadsides at each other but Lord Horatio Nelson had another idea. Instead of lining up ships broadside, he broke the English fleet into two columns and drove these perpendicularly into the French/Spanish fleet. The accompanying element of surprise and the superior ability of the English were asymmetries Nelson was banking on.

Nelson's gamble was that the less-trained French/Spanish gunners would not be able to compensate for the heavy swell that day. The outcome of the Battle of Trafalgar is well known: the French/Spanish lost 22 ships; the English lost none though Nelson himself was mortally wounded. Nelson's courageous strategy was that, although outnumbered, he risked his lead ships in an unexpected maneuver in order to break the coherence of the enemy ships. As this case nicely illustrates, good strategy is often deceptively simple; it revolves around the three key elements:

1. Grasping a few critical issues in the situation; this demands astute sense making, analysis, and, thereby, identification of potential asymmetries to be exploited.
2. Identifying appropriate pivot points by which the asymmetries identified can multiply the effectiveness of effort.
3. Focusing and concentrating coherent and cohesive action and resources to exploit the advantage offered through the asymmetries.

In practice, contexts and situations, of course, vary considerably. Nonetheless, the learning derived from Nelson's victory at Trafalgar applies aptly to strategy in a modern business context.

In a modern business context winning involves setting the right direction for an organization through periods of change and securing its competitive well-being over time. By extension, a central research question that has emerged alongside the notion of *strategy as winning* is focused on why some organizations persistently outperform others. Strategic performance is assessed in terms of the value created and captured by relevant stakeholders. An organization's competitive well-being rests on its ability to *differentiate* itself – that is, being *different* – from its competitors in how it does this. This was the basis of Nelson's victory. It is equally valid in a modern business context: firms *win* on the basis of their ability to both differentiate themselves and create and capture superior value.

Indeed, we may extend the lessons learnt from the Nelson example even further to develop a perspective of the strategy process that underpins the series of steps taken to create and deliver value. In reconstructing Nelson's strategy, we recognize three distinct stages comprising *sense making, strategizing,* and *executing.* Viewed in a more generic way, a three-stage iterative strategy process consisting of *strategic analysis, strategic option formation,* and *strategy execution* can be derived from these, as suggested in Figure 1.1. In this book, each of the three stages of the strategy process is explored in greater detail.

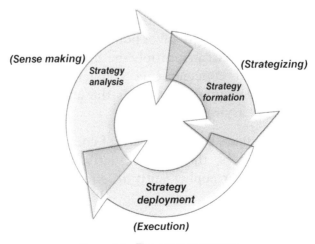

Figure 1.1 The strategy process

Box 1.3 The "Building Blocks" of Competitive Strategy

Strategy is inherently complex. We can nonetheless single out simple components of a good strategy as we have seen earlier in this chapter. The essence of a sound strategy is captured by the following few and deceptively simple questions; these comprise the basic building blocks of strategy:

1. Given our understanding of the external context, our internal basis of competitiveness, and ability to create and deliver a uniquely superior value offering in response to stakeholders' needs, what is our window of opportunity for creating unique differentiated value – our *unique competing space*? Where will we compete, where not? How is our window of opportunity changing?

2. Who are our stakeholders, recipients of that unique and differentiated value we seek to create, today? Who will they be tomorrow? What do they/will they "need" and demand?

3. What is the competitive economic environment in which we are competing? What are the key drivers of change? How are these changing?

4. What is our internal basis of competitiveness? On the basis of which resources, capabilities, and practices are we competing? How do these provide us with an advantage relative to competitors? How is our competitive basis changing?

5. How do we align and orchestrate our organization's resources and capabilities to deliver uniquely superior value in response to our customers' needs; in other words, how do we "get our organizational act together"?

When considered individually, the five building blocks appear to be relatively straightforward. In practice, the complex nature of strategy is reflected by the fact that the notions intrinsic to the questions are changing at variable rates at any point in time; moreover, they are often inextricably linked in real business contexts.

Aspirations are Important, but they are not "Strategy"

When discussing their strategy, business executives often allude to their *vision* and *mission* – and erroneously take these to be their strategy. No doubt a firm's aspirations and guiding principles, often expressed as the firm's vision and mission, are important. However, neither should be mistaken for a strategy. They are *part* of a strategy; as we will see in Chapter 5, they address the "why?" question of a firm's purpose, but not more than that. Aspirations and guiding principles serve to energize and inspire the firm; they may provide a means to mobilize and challenge a firm during critical periods. However, they do not provide the firm with a strategy; they do not address the much more fundamental, and difficult, questions prompted, for example, by the five building blocks of strategy. These, rather than the firm's aspirations, encompass the real substance of the firm's strategy – that of making deliberate and decisive choices about *where* to play and *how*.

Why, then, is Strategy so Difficult?

On the basis of the foregoing, we might be forgiven for thinking that strategy is rather straightforward: simply find responses to the five basic questions outlined in Box 1.2 and the firm's strategy falls neatly into place. Why, then, do managers struggle with strategy? There appear to be several plausible reasons for this. And, as is often the case in complex contexts, these are not entirely unrelated.

First, strategy is not *only* about rational analysis. Recent decades that have seen strategy evolve through a number of schools of thinking have ultimately put to rest the perception that strategy is simply an analytical problem to be solved with left-brain dexterity. Many of the approaches to "strategy" in the past have been shown not to have had much to do with strategy at all. In their place we find a growing number of diametrically opposed perspectives that underscore the paradoxical nature of strategy. Moreover, in messy, real-time strategy making there is no single "right" response. This insight has encouraged thinking and the search for insight "beyond the numbers" in strategy making. It has also given rise to a much more comprehensive understanding of the roles and importance of knowledge, intuition, and the human condition and involvement in strategy. If nothing else, we have come to realize that strategic responses, no matter how seemingly appropriate, always remain shrouded in uncertainty introduced through complex environmental factors and the irrationality of human behavior.

Second, strategy is ultimately a practice discipline – as much as management is intrinsically a practice discipline. Many strategy scholars appear to neglect this. Strategy may start out as a paper exercise, but its ultimate test of validity occurs in the practice field. Practice fields are beset by complexity and ambiguity. In the practice field, we find an additional factor that often stands in the way of good strategy: many managers prefer *acting* (indeed, this is often a criterion for promotion) over *thinking*. In many corporate environments it is better to be seen doing something – *anything*, really – rather than to fall under the suspicion of inactivity (see Box 1.4 "A Bias for Action?"). Mintzberg[7] argues that managers often simply do not have or take the time to think. He points to studies showing that managers dislike reflective activities, and are strongly oriented to action. One particular study of British middle and top managers indicates that they worked without interruption for a half hour or more only about once every two days. Levy[8] points out, though, that deep reflection cannot be hurried and that insights cannot be forced; that both generally require substantial investments of time and sustained attention.

BOX 1.4 A BIAS FOR ACTION?

Topping the list of their "eight basic principles to stay on top of the heap" in the bestselling book entitled *In Search of Excellence*[9] by authors Peters and Waterman, we find "*A bias for action: a preference for doing something – anything – rather than sending a question through cycles and cycles of analysis. . . .*" That advice appears to have resonated well with Percy Barnevik, former CEO of ABB. Barnevik believed in taking decisive action. He is said to have argued that: "*1. To take action (and stick one's neck out) and do the right things is obviously the best behaviour; 2. To take action and do the wrong things is next best (within reason and a limited number of times); 3. Not to take action (and lose opportunities) is the only unacceptable behaviour.*" Barnevik elaborated in an interview with the *Financial Times*, asserting that "*. . . if you do 50 things, it is enough if 35 go in the right direction; . . . the only thing we cannot accept is people who do nothing.*"[10] This ethos involving action, initiative, and risk-taking characterized ABB's culture and was often cited as a prime reason for its mercurial ascent in the 1990s. However, it was also at the root of a near-fatal business decision made in that same period. One of the companies acquired by ABB on its global acquisition spree was Combustion Engineering, a Stamford, Connecticut-based, reactor vessel manufacturer. ABB acquired the firm in 1989; unfortunately, though, its due diligence failed to flag Combustion Engineering's history of using asbestos in its reactor linings. The resulting messy asbestos litigation almost nudged ABB over the brink of bankruptcy in the early 2000s. ABB was able to resolve the asbestos claims in a $1.43 billion settlement agreement only in 2006.[11]

Third, many managers are deeply uncomfortable with having to make strategic decisions under circumstances of incomplete information. There is still a persistent attitude in management circles that decisions need to be backed up with numbers – any numbers, even if these are often largely meaningless and effectively irrelevant to the issue in question. Business environments are complex and ambiguous, invariably non-quantifiable and continually changing. Therefore, only in a relatively few cases are numbers of even marginal significance available. Causality is all too often not apparent and the available information is therefore incomplete and asymmetric. Seldom does the "bigger picture" present itself in a cohesive manner. Yet, despite the lack of factual data, important strategic decisions often cannot wait. Business leaders must make decisions even in the face of inherent uncertainty and risk. That, after all, is their managerial task.

The list of circumstances and factors contributing to the strategy dilemma faced by managers today is long. Hence, we will only mention a final one for the sake of this argument: increasingly dynamic business environments are forcing managers to make decisions ever more quickly and on the run. This throws up a number of dilemmas: how can high-quality decisions be made quickly when critical information is incomplete or missing entirely, analysis is limited to a minimum, and debate and discourse – both necessary elements of good decision making – are suppressed in view of time constraints?

Given these circumstances, how should managers approach strategy in practice? This is the question we seek to address in this book. We propose approaching strategy from the strategic thinking angle. The strategic thinking approach developed in this book is theoretically and conceptually rigorous while allowing for a contribution of intuition to decision making. It is about strategy *in practice*; it is about strategizing under circumstances of uncertainty and unpredictability.

Ultimately, strategy in practice is about achieving the right balance between *relevance* and *rigor*. Relevance, inasfar as strategic thinking generates insights of strategic relevance and potential impact; rigor through proper grounding in current strategy theory. The approach to strategy taken in this book is largely consistent with the "strategy as process perspective" – yet without any presumption that strategy can or should be approached in a mechanistic way.

Indeed, the strategy process needs to capture and take into consideration all that is available to the manager – the "soft" insights coupled with collective experience that informs intuition from throughout the organization as well as any relevant "hard" data from analysis of the organization's external competitive context. Strategy making then involves synthesizing the collective learning through appropriate techniques of sense making and deriving from these insights suitable strategic options. To that end, strategic thinking is a complex process that, in Mintzberg's words, "*. . . involves the most sophisticated, subtle, and at times, subconscious elements of human thinking.*"[12]

STRATEGY IN PRACTICE: POINTS FOR REFLECTION

- What are the tensions and dilemmas that typically surface when your organization engages in strategy?
- How are uncertainty, ambiguity, and complexity dealt with in your organization?
- How much of the strategic insight in your organization is based on *rational* analysis (i.e. how much of it is largely numbers driven); how much is based on intuition and "soft" information?
- What role does *strategic thinking* play in your organization's strategy process?

Where Does this Leave "Strategic Planning"?

There is general agreement among strategy scholars that *strategic planning* had little if anything to do with strategy at all. When it arrived on the scene in the 1960s, it was embraced by business leaders as *the* way to "make strategy." At the height of its popularity in the 1970s, corporations employed legions of strategic planners. Since then the realization has hit home that strategic planning really was little more than a controlling exercise that served the purpose of streamlining the rollout of strategies that were already in place. In essence it was about strategy programming and often stood in the way of strategic thinking.

More than that, though, strategic planning represented a managerial mindset that sought the "one right answer" through purely rational analysis based on hard data. Managers seeking comfort in numbers recognized in it a way to mechanistically break a strategic objective down into manageable steps. The probability of the predictable was thought to be thereby maximized, the realization of desirable objectives assured.

Understandably, few business leaders today would be prepared to admit to traditional strategic planning. This doesn't mean, however, that strategic thinking has taken its place. Strategic thinking is still not a core managerial capability in most companies.[13] In many firms the strategic planning function has been replaced by *corporate development and planning*. These functions, however, do not substitute good strategic thinking.

> BOX 1.5 ROBERT McNAMARA: THE "ENLIGHTENED RATIONALIST"
>
> Few senior managers have epitomized strategic planning more than the late Robert McNamara (1916–2009), one of the 10 "Whiz Kids" Ford Motor Company hired in 1946 to shake up its business. McNamara was later plucked from

Ford by John F. Kennedy to be US Secretary of Defense. A former Harvard economics professor, he loved numbers. Things that could be counted, McNamara maintained, ought to be counted. He was an iconic planning manager who could use facts, numbers, and analyses to solve any problem, even to wage wars in far-off Vietnam. There were the four McNamara steps to running an organization: first, stating an objective; second, working out how to get there; third, costing out everything; and lastly, systematically monitoring progress against plan. The Vietnam War became widely known as "McNamara's War." McNamara didn't know anything about Vietnam – nor did those around him. But then, the American attitude in that era was that one didn't have to know the culture or history of a place in order to engage in successful warfare in the respective theater. What was needed was the right data, a proper analysis of the information, and an application of military superiority to win the war. McNamara spearheaded the Pentagon's effort in Vietnam until 1968. McNamara applied all the right metrics – bombing missions flown, targets hit, captives taken, weapons seized, the enemy's body-count. Another metric, the American troops' own body-count, at some point began informing him with equal certainty that America was losing the war. Initially this baffled McNamara. Things began unraveling seriously in 1965. Ordered to win the war, McNamara stepped up his statistical war of attrition by approving ever more troop increases. On the home front, resistance to the war grew. At the height of the conflict he was denounced as a baby-burner; his own son joined in the protest marches against him. As he later admitted in his penitent memoirs, he had learned the hard way that he had not understood the variables of war itself – the most important of which was that numbers capture neither the human condition nor human activity. As McNamara came to realize, hard quantitative data can have a decidedly soft and qualitative underbelly. In the case of the Vietnam War, human factors played a decisive role – the enemy Vietcong made every single person count. Of the 11 lessons to be learned from McNamara's war in Vietnam, regrettably, this and most of the others occurred to him too late to be of much help.

Sources: The Economist, Obituary on Robert McNamara, July 11, 2009; *TIME (Europe)*, L.H. Gelb: Remembrance – Robert McNamara, July 20, 2009.

Insight-Driven Strategy

Insight plays a key role in the strategic thinking process. While we explore the notion of insight in greater detail in Chapter 3, suffice it to say here that insight formation involves a complex combination of analysis, intuition, and heuristics. That is not to suggest that all insight is equally relevant or useful to strategic thinking. The key to good strategic thinking lies in knowing what insight to seek and use. Collis and Montgomery[14] argue that two potentially powerful insights relate to the organization's capabilities and the competition it faces. Insight on stakeholder needs and how these evolve is also critical. Together, insights such as these help determine where opportunities exist for creating and positioning new differentiated value offerings.

Strategic insight is an outcome of the strategic thinking process; hence, the emphasis in this book on an *insight-driven* approach to strategy. Strategic thinking is the vehicle for delivering insight. It provides the systematic and structured approach that draws on sense making to bring into balance rational analysis and intuition, experienced-derived judgment and knowledge. Leonard and Swap[15] refer to the collective outcome of these components as "deep smarts." Strategic insights serve a number of purposes. They are outcomes of sense making at individual stages of the strategic thinking process. However, they also help to guide and align the thinking process through its various stages.

Ultimately, individual strategic insights, when collated like pieces of a puzzle, contribute to the emergence of a reconstructed "bigger picture" of the firm's competitive landscape. Inevitably, this picture is never complete. However, if properly executed, the strategic thinking process ensures that the pattern that emerges is sufficient to identify potentially suitable options for strategic action. To that end, strategic insights collectively contribute to and enable the formation of potentially suitable strategic options in the emerging competitive context. Strategy formation is a dynamic process that presents the strategist with a range of options, of which one represents the most suitable option. Seldom, however, does a single "right" strategic response emerge as an outcome of this activity. In practice, the selection of a strategic option involves some degree of compromise. Insight supports the process whereby options are evaluated and ultimately selected.

Real competitive environments are highly complex and messy. This presents limits to the degree to which strategy making can be formalized. We need to allow for circumstances under which strategies emerge inadvertently, without deliberate intention on the part of the organization's management. The premise of this book is that while real strategy is not programmable as such, it does not mean that our approach to strategy needs to be haphazard. The purpose of this book is to provide strategy practitioners with the strategic wherewithal to successfully navigate complex and ambiguous business contexts, whereby strategic thinking forms the basis of that capability.

STRATEGY IN PRACTICE: INSIGHT-DRIVEN STRATEGY VERSUS STRATEGIC PLANNING

- Today's fast-paced, continually changing competitive environment leaves little room for the strategic planning approaches practiced in many companies throughout the 1970s and 1980s; few companies today enjoy environments that allow any meaningful planning by numbers in time frames of five and more years into the future.

- Insight-driven strategy enables a very different approach; while offering a systematic and structured strategic thinking framework, it draws on multiple inputs and variable time frames; it balances the hard numbers (where available) with the "soft" indicators emerging from complex contexts.
- The key to implementing an insight-driven approach to strategy begins with a mindset that is prepared to challenge assumptions and that is comfortable with non-quantifiable measures and inputs.
- Paraphrasing Kevin Kelly,[16] insight-driven strategy "seeks not so much to perfect the known, rather to imperfectly seize the unknown"; it is congruent with an organizational culture that embraces experimentation and learning.
- What is your organization's mindset? One that is more in tune with strategic planning or one that is amenable to insight-driven strategy?

"Strategy in Practice" or "Strategy as Practice"?

This book is about "strategy *in* practice." It aims to provide guidance to the management practitioner engaging with strategy in the practice field. Hence, it is about how strategy should be approached by practitioners of strategy. How, then, is the focus on strategy practice pursued in this book different from the school of thought that has emerged in recent years known as "strategy *as* practice"? To the extent that the latter focuses on bringing the *thinking* element back into strategy[17],[18] the approach developed in this book is largely consistent with the underlying conceptual thrust of the "strategy as practice" school. However, this book neither purports nor aspires to contribute to the institutionalization of any particular school of strategy, including the "strategy as practice" approach (which has been critiqued for adopting an unclear and contradictory definition of "strategy practice"[19]).

The purpose of this book is first and foremost to provide the strategy practitioner with appropriate guidance when engaging with strategy and strategizing in the practice field.

Summary and Structuring of the Book

This chapter began with a review of the current dilemma most business leaders face when confronted with strategy and strategy making, despite the proliferation of strategy theory in recent years. Given the ongoing discourse on what strategy *is*, it is probably more meaningful to focus on what strategy is *about*. It is about winning; about achieving superior performance relative to competitors in creating and delivering a superior value offering. Ultimately, however, strategy is a *practice discipline*. Indeed, many of the difficulties experienced by managers in dealing with strategy relate to the sheer complexity, ambiguity, and messiness of management practice in the competitive environments of organizations. This requires a strategic thinking process that draws on a balanced combination of systematic analysis and intuition leading to insights relevant to strategy making, hence the centrality of the theme *insight-driven* strategy.

The following chapters of this book (shown schematically in Figure 1.2) lead through the insight-driven strategic thinking process.

We begin with the process of *strategic thinking* in Chapter 2. Strategic thinking focuses particular attention on the "fuzzy front end" of the strategy process. A lot is at stake at this stage. The objective at this stage is to scope and articulate the relevant strategic challenge at stake. Strategic challenges (with might be either opportunity or threat-driven) are triggered by external changes to the competitive environment, internal factors, or combinations of the two. We begin by scoping the strategic problem (or challenge), ensuring that it is indeed a challenge

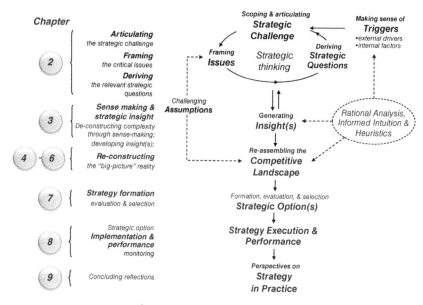

Figure 1.2   Strategy process and outline of the book

worthy of the effort to be spent on it. The scoping process is an iterative process; the first "draft" version of problem's articulation may be vague. Through successive iterations involving framing of issues and the derivation of questions from these, the articulation of the strategic challenge is gradually sharpened. The objective is to end up with those relatively few strategic questions, which, if resolved, really will enable a resolution of the strategic challenge at stake. At any one point in time, there may be numerous seemingly important questions demanding to be addressed by a business leader – yet, arguably, only relatively few will really make a disproportionate difference to the company's competitive positioning if appropriately resolved.

Failure to get those relatively few really critical strategic questions "right" inevitably leads to severe consequences for the business. Questions prompt responses; we refer to the responses to the strategic questions as *strategic insights*; these form the basis of the insight-driven approach to strategy.

The next stage consequently involves generating those insights prompted by the strategic questions through sense making of one sort or another. In Chapter 3 we therefore explore the notions of sense making and its role in generating strategic insight. We examine how sense making helps us to deconstruct the complexity of the current reality through selective and judicious generation of insights relevant to the strategic challenge at hand. Sense making might be supported by informed (i.e. challenged) intuition, appropriate heuristics, or rational analysis.

Chapters 4 through 6 are devoted to the subject of rational strategic analysis. In Chapter 4 we set the general context for strategic analysis. We examine how analysis is used to generate insights required for strategic sense making. This is followed by an introduction to *high-level*, "big-picture" strategic analysis in Chapter 5. In Chapter 6 we introduce the *supporting level* of strategic analysis and derive its purpose and application in the context of strategic sense making. A basic premise of this book is that relatively few apt frameworks applied appropriately to support strategic thinking can yield a disproportionate amount of insight. It is important to know which frameworks to use and how to use them. In this chapter we review some of the more useful frameworks, their application, and their limitations. In this chapter we also explore how the insights generated during the sense making stage are subsequently assembled – not unlike pieces of a puzzle in the reconstruction of a bigger picture that represents the competitive landscape of the organization in question, albeit an incomplete one. Intuition and heuristics again play an important complementary role during this stage. Research on intuition suggests that its usefulness at this stage derives from insight related to reflected experience[20] – experience in knowing what to look for, where to look, and how to integrate the new insights into an existing pattern of understanding. Management reality is riddled with ambiguity and complexity. It is in this context that intuition and heuristics provide the basis for strategic decision making.

Sense making and analysis are not ends in themselves. Strategic thinking and sense making, properly executed, enable us to identify the strategic landscape or "big picture" relevant to that challenge that triggered the need to engage with strategy in the first place. However, strategizing is ultimately about decision making; it is about coming up with an appropriate response to that strategic challenge. In Chapter 7 we explore how we use the outcome of strategic thinking and sense making to form strategic options. This second stage of the strategy process thus focuses on the *formation* of strategic options, their *evaluation*, and, ultimately, the *selection* of one preferred option for implementation. The preferred option represents the *most suitable* response to the strategic challenge that triggered the strategy exercise. We emphasize "most suitable" because we recognize that there is no such thing as a perfect strategic option. Every option, even the most suitable one, has liabilities and trade-offs associated with it. We close Chapter 7 with a reflection on the implications of the imperfections of strategic option for the organization.

The third and final stage of the strategy process focuses on the *execution* of the selected strategic option. We examine strategy execution in Chapter 8. The execution of strategic options invariably demands changes to the organization, hence strategy execution is about changing the organization to align with the requirements of the strategic option selected for deployment. Successful execution furthermore requires metrics that provide a meaningful and actionable measure of the strategy's performance at any point in time. Hence, we introduce some key thinking on strategic performance metrics in this chapter as well.

In Chapter 9, the final chapter of the book, we close with reflections on strategic thinking and insight-driven strategy from various practice field perspectives. We explore why organizational configurations show variations in their predisposition for strategy making. We derive implications for the organization by exploring both the scope and limitations of strategic thinking set against constraints imposed by the reality of firms' competitive context and dynamics. In this way, the book ends with a reality check and some recommendations for enhancing the impact of strategic thinking.

The Appendix section of this book presents some practical applications of the concepts and approaches introduced and discussed throughout the book. The templates suggest structured approaches for putting concepts introduced in the book into practice.

It is only appropriate that we review some final caveats and pointers before delving into the strategic thinking framework that is examined in the subsequent chapters – the final boxed insert below summarizes these.

STRATEGY IN PRACTICE: SOME PRACTICAL POINTERS ON THE STRATEGY PROCESS

- The strategy process mapped in Figure 1.2 is not intended to be used mechanistically. Management reality is intrinsically complex and riddled with ambiguity. Any approach to strategy making must reflect this reality. Therefore, the purpose of the strategic thinking process proposed in this book is to guide and challenge the strategy practitioner's thinking and reasoning process from the articulation of compelling strategic questions through to their appropriate resolution.
- Although the structure of the framework would suggest a series of "top-down" activities, the strategic thinking process is, in fact, highly iterative and features multiple feedback loops throughout.
- There is neither a "silver bullet" nor a single "right" answer in strategy. Management contexts and situations are highly dependent on context. A response that addresses the circumstances of the complex contexts in question

typically demands a degree of compromise between possible solution approaches. Therefore, the outcome of the strategic thinking process should be viewed in terms of strategic options that range from "suitable" to those that are clearly "less than appropriate." The framework enables the strategy practitioner to develop substantive arguments in support of the most suitable strategy option.

- The framework relegates strategic tools of analysis to where they belong – in a supportive role, to be drawn on very selectively to develop relevant insight where required. Managers often find themselves entangled in the dense undergrowth of strategy frameworks, thereby losing sight of the wood for the undergrowth. There is no end to the sophistication of strategy tools nowadays.
- Used appropriately, however, even simple frameworks can deliver useful pieces of the puzzle to be constructed. We will see in Chapters 4 through 6 how some relatively simple models can be integrated into more comprehensive, integrated frameworks that in turn can be used to generate powerful insights.

Notes

1. Sull, D., Homkes, R. and Sull, C. (2015) Why Strategy Execution Unravels – and What to Do about It, *Harvard Business Review*, March 2015 Issue, pp. 58–66.
2. Barton, D. and Wiseman, M. (2015) Where Boards Fall Short, *Harvard Business Review*, January–February Issue, pp. 99–104.
3. Rondo-Pupo, G.A. and Guerras-Martin, L.A. (2012) Dynamics of the Evolution of the Strategy Concept 1962–2008: A Co-Word Analysis, *Strategic Management Journal*, Vol. 33, pp. 162–188.
4. Mintzberg, H. (1995) Five Ps for Strategy, in Mintzberg, H., Quinn, J.B. and Ghoshal, S. (eds) *The Strategy Process, European Edition*, London: Prentice Hall, pp. 13–21.
5. Chandler, A.D. (1962) *Strategy and Structure*, Cambridge, MA: MIT Press.

6. Mintzberg, H. (2009) *Tracking Strategies – Toward a General Theory*, Oxford: Oxford University Press.
7. Mintzberg, H. (1990) The Manager's Job: Folklore and Fact, *Harvard Business Review*, March–April.
8. Levy, D.M. (2008) Wanted: Time to Think, *MIT Sloan Management Review*, Fall, pp. 21–24.
9. Peters, T.J. and Waterman Jr, R.H. (1982) *In Search of Excellence*, New York: Warner Books.
10. Rosenzweig, P. (2007) *The Halo Effect*, New York: Free Press.
11. *Boston Globe* (1 September 2006): ABB says Lummus Asbestos Claims Resolved (Reuters).
12. Mintzberg, H. (1994) The Fall and Rise of Strategic Planning, *Harvard Business Review*, January–February, pp. 107–114.
13. Christensen, C.M. (1997) Making Strategy: Learning by Doing, *Harvard Business Review*, November–December.
14. Collis, D.J. and Montgomery, C.A. (2008) Competing on Resources, *Harvard Business Review*, July–August, pp. 140–150.
15. Leonard, D.L. and Swap, W. (2005) *Deep Smarts: Experience-Based Wisdom*, Boston: Harvard Business School Press.
16. Kelly, K. (1998) *New Rules for the New Economy*, New York: Viking.
17. Whittington, R. (2002) Practice Perspectives on Strategy: Unifying and Developing a Field, *Best Paper Proceedings*, Academy of Management, Denver.
18. Balogun, J.P., Jarzabkowski, P. and Seidl, D. (2007) Strategy as Practice Perspective, in Jenkins, M., Ambrosini, V. and Collier, N. (eds) *Advanced Strategic Management*, 2nd edn, Basingstoke: Palgrave Macmillan.
19. Carter, C.S., Clegg, R. and Kornberger, M. (2008) *A Very Short, Fairly Interesting and Reasonably Cheap Book About Studying Strategy*, London: Sage Publications Ltd.
20. Eisenhardt, K.M. (2008) Speed and Strategic Choice: How Managers Accelerate Decision Making, *California Management Review*, Vol. 50 (Winter Issue), pp. 102–116.

CHAPTER 2

Strategic Thinking

The most serious mistakes are not being made as a result of wrong answers. The truly dangerous thing is asking the wrong questions.

—Peter F. Drucker

IN THIS CHAPTER, WE:

- introduce the concept of strategic thinking in the strategy process and the critical role of strategic questions in strategic thinking;
- explore strategic challenges and how they are triggered by events in the firm's external environment, factors internal to the firm, or combinations of both;
- examine how strategic challenges are scoped and articulated to ensure they are, indeed, of strategic relevance and worthy of consideration;

- show the strategic thinking process comprising the framing of relevant issues and the derivation of strategic questions;
- reflect on the importance of articulating the "right" strategic questions, and how these are derived;
- close with a reflection on the importance of challenging assumptions and the prevailing industry logic.

What's in a question? A lot, potentially. The German theoretical physicist and philosopher Werner Heisenberg[1] argued that nature reveals itself to us by virtue of the questions we ask. Nature does not reveal itself by asking just any question; hence, it is critical that appropriate questions are asked.

Asking the "right" questions is an integral element of *strategic thinking*. But what, exactly, *is* strategic thinking? Strategic thinking has become a favorite expression in management circles; one that is increasingly being used by managers. However, the notion remains to be defined precisely. Strategic thinking, in the way it is used in this book, implies first and foremost a way of thinking; a mindset that underpins a deliberate, intent-driven approach to strategy. Its purpose is to ultimately provide guidance and direction to decision making in circumstances relevant to a specific strategic challenge. According to Sloan[2] strategic thinking is supported by critical–reflective processes (such as critical inquiry, reflection, and dialogue) and complex cognitive functions such as conceptual, intuitive, and creative thinking. Strategic thinking requires suspending judgment, rather than engaging in a rigorous and challenging examination of underlying premises relevant to the strategic challenge at hand. Ultimately, the purpose of strategic thinking is to support the process of generating a suitable strategic response to the strategic challenge that evoked its necessity in the first place.

Returning to the notion of questions: How do we arrive at the *right* questions? How do we go about identifying those questions,

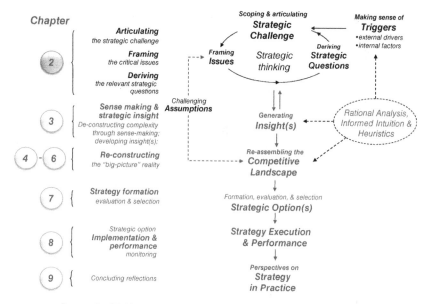

Figure 2.1 Strategic thinking: articulating the strategic challenge, framing issues, and deriving strategic questions

which if answered, will enable us to resolve the bigger strategic challenge facing the organization?

In this chapter we explore the origins of strategic challenges, and how these are scoped and articulated through an iterative process of strategic thinking. We examine the importance of getting the strategic questions "right" at the outset, and how these are derived from the framing of relevant issues as shown schematically in Figure 2.1.

Scoping and Articulating the Strategic Challenge

Strategic challenges are often confused with *symptoms* – at least initially, when they first emerge. For example, falling market share or gradual loss of profitability are not strategic challenges *per se,* rather they are symptoms of challenges facing a firm. These might be a firm's inability to respond appropriately to changes in its competitive environment; these, in turn, might be triggered by a combination of changing technological, societal, and economic conditions.

But what is it that makes a challenge a *strategic* one? Alternatively, one might ask: What makes a problem or opportunity *strategically relevant?* As a basic premise, we tie the notion of strategic relevance to the core purpose of the firm – and that is to create and deliver *differentiated value* to its stakeholders. The greater the potential impact of the challenge on the firm's ability and disposition to create and capture the differentiated value at stake, the greater its strategic relevance; regardless of whether the challenge reflects an opportunity or a threat. An alternative way of ascertaining the strategic relevance of a challenge is to ask: What would be the implications of *not* resolving the particular challenge in question? What would be the opportunity cost of an opportunity not acted upon? Or, what would be the potential loss incurred by neglecting to successfully deal with a threat?

The strategic thinking schematic (Figure 2.2) indicates three basic elements. The first is the *challenge space,* in which the strategic challenge is scrutinized for strategic relevance by framing associated issues and deriving relevant strategic questions from these. The objective at this stage is to ascertain the strategic relevance of the challenge. Once the strategic relevance of the challenge has been established, the second element comprises the *sense making space,* in which insights prompted by the strategic questions are generated through combinations of rational analysis, intuition, and heuristics. Finally, the third element comprises the *relevant strategic context,* which emerges from an aggregation and consolidation of insights generated through sense making, leading to a reconstruction of the firm's strategic landscape (i.e. context) relevant to the challenge at stake. Important to note is that not all insights prompted by strategic questions posed are necessarily attainable. Inevitably, as competitive contexts

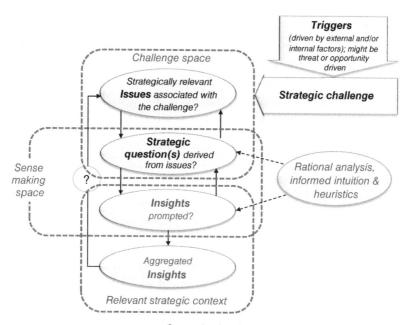

Figure 2.2 Strategic thinking process

emerge and evolve, certain insights deemed important are not available. This is typically the case in emergent, highly dynamic markets. The objective is nonetheless to garner as many insights as possible, and to reconstruct the competitive landscape relevant to the strategic challenge – even if the emerging picture reflecting the relevant strategic context features gaps.

In this chapter, we focus on the challenge space.

Triggers

Strategic challenges may be triggered by a variety of triggers. Very often these have their origin in the organization's external competitive context. Invariably, these reflect changes to that competitive environment, such as the appearance of new competitors in markets currently served by the firm in question. Triggers may also have their origin within the firm; this might be a growing awareness of a lack of key resources to maintain a competitive edge established and held in the past. Most often, triggers are combinations of factors. Often, they do not present themselves coherently to the firm. Thus, implications of the triggers for the firm's competitive position are often not clearly grasped at the outset, as these, as often as not, manifest themselves as symptoms rather than expressions of actual root causes.

Changes in the Organization's External Competitive Environment

Strategic challenges may be triggered by events in the firm's *external environment*. These might reflect changes in the competitive environment. Changes of this type might be driven by any number, or even combinations, of external factors such as sociopolitical change, technological advances, increasing competition through new competitors, demographic changes in the firm's customer base and markets, and other external macroeconomic drivers. As a rule, external factors such as these lie beyond the control of any individual firm. There is little any individual firm can do to influence these external factors. Not all drivers are equally important; not all have the same potential impact on the organization's competitive position. However, organizations nonetheless need to understand the relevant drivers of change in their external environment. More than that, they need to understand the dynamics of the relevant drivers. Not all change at the same rate; some change more than others. Organizations need to understand and track the dynamics of those external drivers with the greatest potential competitive impact.

Changes in Internal Competing Factors

Strategic challenges might also arise as a result of strategically relevant problems that have their source within the organization. These are factors that the organization, as a rule, *can* influence. Such problems might be the result of negligence or failure on the part of the firm to engage in appropriate and timely activities.

These might include, for example, failure on the part of the organization to develop strategic resources over a period of time, or when an organization becomes complacent and neglects to nurture an organizational culture that supports a strategically critical capability, such as an innovation capability. The problem may have multiple dimensions, all of which are internal to the organization. In the case of an inferior innovation capability these might include a missing managerial systems infrastructure, a culture that punishes trying and failing, or a lack of cutting edge knowledge. The problem might manifest itself in multiple ways as well – continual failure to bring new products to market might be one such expression of the problem that might lead to follow-on problems, one of which might be the inability to subsequently attract the best talent as a result of a tarnished reputation in the market place.

Very often strategic challenges are not well articulated; often they fail to capture the essence of the organization's current dilemma altogether. A good articulation of a strategic challenge positions the challenge in question in the context of the organization's core strategic purpose.

Let's examine the articulation of the strategic challenge more deeply with a concrete example: Swiss coffee maker Nespresso's current strategic situation in view of expiring patents on its highly successful single-serve coffee pod machine concept.

Box 2.1 Nespresso – What Next?

Nespresso, one of those companies that have succeeded in generating eye-wateringly lucrative returns to its investors, is currently at a critical crossroads. In the quarter century since an admittedly shaky launch, the company has managed to protect its near-monopoly position with an array of patents – in total about 1,700. The period of exclusivity by patent protection came to an end with the expiry of many of those patents in 2012. Not that this came as a surprise to the coffee maker, of course. Nonetheless, it does mean that its exclusive system consisting of coffee capsules and machine delivery system that produces a high-quality cup of espresso featuring a perfect crema (foam) is now being contested by a number of competitors.

The Nestlé subsidiary has been extraordinarily successful since the business took off in the early 1990s. Margins, estimated to be in excess of 25%, derived from the capsulized coffee pods, for which consumers pay about five times the price of what they would normally pay for the same amount of regular roasted coffee.

No doubt Nespresso's success, supported by astute market positioning of its coffee pod, is "the closest thing to a luxury brand within fast-moving consumer goods," and clever advertising featuring US actor George Clooney has enabled the company to build a formidable competitive position.

However, its success has also attracted considerable competition. Recently, Starbucks announced its intentions to enter into this space. Currently, there are an estimated 50 mimicking systems in the market. Though clearly not all of these are targeting the premium segment currently served by Nespresso, a number nonetheless pose direct threats.

A lot is currently at stake for Nespresso as it seeks suitable responses to competitors' encroachment into its competitive territory. What Nespresso might well fear most at this point is the emergence of a potentially irresistible alternative to the question posed in its provocative advertising slogan: *"Nespresso, what else?"*

Sources: Bond, S. (2014) Nespresso has Shot at Larger Coffee Sale, *Financial Times* (February 19, 2014); Lucas, L. and Simonian, H. (2012) Rivals Eye Nestlé's Captive Market, *Financial Times* (March 10–11, 2012).

Framing the Issues

Triggers, we argued in the previous section, give rise for the need to engage in strategic thinking. Once triggers have been scrutinized and made sense of, the next task is to scope their relevance for the firm's competitive position. Strategic challenges, when they arise, are often complex and multi-layered. Issues framing and analysis are the first step towards deconstructing a complex strategic challenge into its more manageable component parts. Clusters of issues that emerge from a framing of issues reflect the triggers that have given rise to the strategic problem in the first place. The objective at this stage is to ascertain their potential impact and to derive strategic questions that need to be addressed and ultimately resolved. In other words, the objective is to scope the potential strategic challenge that presents itself as a result of those changes indicated by the triggers. We do this by framing relevant issues associated with the challenge. The objective is to narrow these down to those relatively few that are really critical to the challenge – in other words, the strategically relevant issues. Strategic issues prompt questions; here also, the objective is to narrow these to those relatively few strategic questions that, if answered, ultimately enable us to develop clarity and understanding of the greater context relevant to the strategic challenge.

Issue analyses involve a further refinement of high-level strategic questions. A high-level strategic question always consists of multiple components. These reflect the complexity of the problem requiring analysis. A framing of the issues helps us to segment a strategic question into its more manageable component parts. Clusters of issues that emerge from the framing exercise relate to the various triggers that have given rise to the strategic problem in the first place. Figure 2.3 suggests how this might be approached by drawing on the Nespresso case introduced in the previous section.

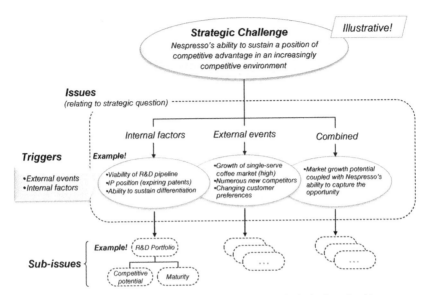

Figure 2.3   Framing the issues; subordinate issues analysis (using the Nespresso case for illustration)

Issues arising for Nespresso (shown illustratively in Figure 2.3) result from:

1. Changes in Nespresso's *internal factors*, such as the viability of its current R&D pipeline and implications of its expiring patents.
2. *External events* triggering changes in its *external competitive environment*, reflecting *the* socio-economic impact of the recent recession, increasing numbers of competitors with (increasingly) comparable product and service offerings.

Issues can be further broken down into clusters of subordinate issues as shown in Figure 2.3; these, in turn, can be extended even further. The point at which the issues cascade is determined largely by the level at which a strategic response eventually needs to be generated. Experience ultimately provides guidance on where the cut-off is most appropriate.

Articulating Strategic Questions

Good strategic questions probe challenges that have a potential impact on the core purpose of an organization – its ability to create and deliver value to its stakeholders. As argued earlier, the challenge typically reflects changes in the organization's competitive ability to do so. Perhaps a new competitor in the market is threatening the organization's competitive position. Possibly, the organization has lost its ability to compete in its markets due to neglect of its strategic resource base. Perhaps it has lost its sense of direction in terms of its shared sense of purpose and guiding values. All of these are challenges of a competitive nature. Problems and challenges, however, need not necessarily be negatively loaded. They might relate to an emerging opportunity in the market that calls for clarification and possibly action. Problems, in order to merit our attention, must be strategically relevant, meaning they must fall into the category of the "important few" that have a potentially high business impact. These are the ones that have an important long-term positive impact on the competitive position of the organization in question. Failure to achieve resolution will have a potentially significant negative impact on the competitive well-being of the firm in question.

Problems and challenges have "owners." We call these owners *stakeholders*. These are the people or institutions that stand to gain (or lose) most by a problem's successful (or failed) resolution. Stakeholders' needs, power, and legitimacy of claim relative to the problem vary. Hence, we differentiate between stakeholders with high legitimacy and a strong position to influence, and those with marginal legitimacy and less power to influence the out-come of the problem's resolution. The first group is important; they are the *key stakeholders*.

Returning to the strategic thinking process, strategic questions are prompted by issues relevant to the strategic challenge.

Returning to the Nespresso case, specific questions arise from the relevant clusters of issues identified. For example, issues related to external factors, questions that might arise include: Who are the competitors threatening to encroach on the competitive niche (premium, single serve coffee capsule/machine concept) long held by Nespresso? Another question arising from the same issues cluster might be: How do competitors' offerings in this niche compare to Nespresso's offering, and how much of a threat do these really present to Nespresso?

The importance of articulating the "right" questions for the physical sciences alluded to earlier in this chapter is easily extended to the social context: contexts relevant to the firm's competitive well-being also reveal themselves by our manner of questioning. Getting to the point of asking the "right" questions is therefore critical to any strategic thinking exercise. What are "right" strategic questions? Simply stated, the "right" questions are those that address problems and issues that are of strategic relevance and importance to an organization. They might be strategically relevant in the near or long term. Good strategic questions are prompted by those relatively few high-level, high-priority issues facing the business that have the greatest potential for competitive impact.

Often, strategic questions are deceptively simple. There might even be some commonality of the strategic questions among competitors. Typically, there are relatively few really critical strategic questions. A review of the basic building blocks of strategy introduced in Chapter 1 provides a good method for ensuring that those questions emerging from the strategic thinking exercise introduced in the previous sections do, indeed, cover the important strategic angles relevant to the challenge at stake (Chapter 1, Box 1.2).

STRATEGY IN PRACTICE: THE BUILDING BLOCKS OF STRATEGY

Invariably, questions of strategic relevance address one or more of the building blocks of strategy introduced in the previous chapter:

- Given our understanding of the external context, our internal basis of competitiveness, and ability to create and deliver a uniquely superior value offering in response to our stakeholders' needs, what is our window of opportunity for creating unique value – our *unique competing space*? How is it changing?
- Who are the important stakeholders relevant to the challenge? How are their needs changing and what are the implications for us as an organization?
- What is the competitive economic environment relevant to the strategic challenge? What are the key drivers of change – and what are the implications of these changes to our competitive position?
- What is our basis of competitiveness relevant to the strategic challenge at stake? On the basis of which resources, capabilities, and practices are we competing? How do these provide us with an advantage relative to competitors? How is our competitive basis changing?
- With a view to the strategic challenge at stake, what are the implications for how we need to align and orchestrate our organization's resources and capabilities; what changes are required – and what do we need to do to "get our organizational act together" in order to respond appropriately to the strategic challenge?

Inevitably, there are a number of problems and challenges facing an organization at any one point in time. Only relatively few, however, are of disproportionate importance – that is, of real strategic relevance. Arguably, therefore, the high-level task of a senior manager is a relatively simple one: it is to identify the two or three really top priority strategic problems (or possibly opportunities) facing the organization and to get on with the task of resolving (or exploiting) these. Failure on the part of the senior manager to get a handle on the few really important questions leads to strategic drift and loss of competitive focus. In management we talk about the "Pareto"[3] principle. Also known as the "80–20 rule," it suggests that 80% of the impact comes from 20% of the causes – for example, that 80% of an enterprise's profitability stems from 20% of its products. In the context of the strategic question, the Pareto principle suggests that it makes good sense to focus one's efforts on those few things that really make a difference. The real crux of this stage in the strategic thinking process, of course, lies in identifying those few really critical high-level strategic questions. This is not a trivial task.

Strategically relevant problems invariably arise as a result of *changes* in the firm's competitive context and ability to respond to these. Broadly categorized, these might lie in any of the three areas listed in the box below.

STRATEGY IN PRACTICE: GETTING THE HIGH-LEVEL STRATEGIC QUESTIONS "RIGHT"

How does one get the strategic questions "right"? While there are no hard and fast rules for articulating the right high-level strategic questions, these typically emerge from diligent and continual effort in the following three activity clusters:

1. *Continual monitoring of the external environment* for developments that might lead to changes in the competitive playing field. Strategic questions, when they arise, are inevitably triggered by changing conditions. Most often these will be externally driven. A simple *PESTEL* (political, economic, societal, technological, environmental,

and legal) factor scan is always a good starting point. Changing conditions of competition prompt strategic questions of the type: What has changed, and why?

2. *Scrutinizing the changing conditions for their strategic (competitive) relevance.* Changes in the competitive environment may have implications for the organization's ability to compete. Multiple changes (change on various fronts), which are becoming ever more the rule, may have a coupled and synergetic overall impact on the organization's competitive position. Strategic questions prompted by scrutiny of change are of the type: What are the implications of the changes for the organization, and why so?

3. *Probing for appropriate responses on the part of the organization to the changing competitive condition.* Changing conditions that have strategic relevance for the organization demand appropriate response. While external factors prompting the changing conditions of competition generally cannot be influenced, these will prompt high-level strategic questions within the organization of the type: What should the organization be doing; what can it do in response to the changing conditions?

Assumptions, Paradigms, and Prevailing Logic

Assumptions are beliefs that are taken for granted; they may be based on intuition or they may comprise facets of an organization's paradigm. In strategic thinking, assumptions play an important role early in the process of making sense of triggers that are potentially of strategic relevance.

Every organization operates on a more or less shared cluster of assumptions and beliefs. Assumptions reflect the firm's deep beliefs and the paradigm it identifies with. Schein[4] defines assumptions as being close to the core of an organization's culture. Their origin lies deep within the organization's substrata characterized by the unconscious and tacit frames that shape the organization's values and paradigm in the subconscious realm. Assumptions are therefore often difficult to discern. Assumptions may be about markets, customers, the competition, and what it takes to compete successfully. Collectively, they comprise the organization's legacy thinking. These may become liabilities when the firm's competitive environment changes. Hence, assumptions need to be challenged and ultimately validated. Where found dated, assumptions must be adapted or even refuted outright.

Our assumptions reveal a lot about how we think, our past experiences and biases. The assumptions business leaders make when thinking about their competitive situation reflect the prevailing mindset within the organization. By extension, the assumptions shared across an industry reflect the prevailing *industry logic*. The prevailing mindset expresses itself in terms of the *business paradigm*. The business paradigm, in turn, is a coherent set of assumptions and perceptions that finds expression in the business's practices, values, and norms. An organization's business paradigm reflects its take on reality, where it perceives opportunities and threats in its market place. Paradigms can constrain and restrict strategic thinking to the point where they lead to flawed conclusions and decisions.

Box 2.2 Fateful French Assumptions

The German invasion of France in May 1940 should not have been the pushover it ended up being. The French military was invincible. Their officer corps was battle hardened from the Great War. French defenses included the impenetrable Maginot Line and the French military's intelligence gathering was superb – or so the French thought. In fact, not only the French but others at the time thought so as well. The German general staff is said to have plotted a coup against Hitler already in late 1939 because they thought his plan to attack France was absolutely insane.

So, what went wrong? Military historian Ernest May[5] suggests that the French failed to challenge a number of very basic assumptions concerning their defenses and an impending German assault. Although the French were clearly aware of the German threat, particularly following the blitzkrieg assault on Poland, they were prepared for every scenario except the one that actually took place. The French assumption was that since the Ardennes Forest was impassable to heavy tanks the Germans would attack France through Belgium. Consequently, this was where the French concentrated their defenses. Another unchallenged assumption of the French was that their forces were better trained and disciplined than the Polish forces, hence the French assumed the blitzkrieg scenario to be irrelevant. A final assumption that proved fatal to the French was that the German high command would behave rationally and not attempt an assault through the Ardennes. In this respect the French reacted no differently than many organizations today: they were blinded by their almost religious faith that the past is a prologue to all futures.

In retrospect we know that events unfolded very differently: the Germans did the unexpected, the Ardennes turned out to be passable after all. The extraordinary success of the invasion of France was largely due to the efforts of Generals Erich von Manstein and Heinz Guderian, who perfected and deployed the so-called "sickle-cut" (the metaphor is said to have originated with Churchill) offensive to outmaneuver French fortifications and reduce any potential impact the French military's superior numbers in men and material might have had.

The German blitzkrieg strategy worked just as well in the West as it had in the East. Despite their smaller size,

German forces overwhelmed France within a matter of weeks. The Allies had simply not anticipated a disciplined and swift offensive by the Germans through the Ardennes Forest. In his treatise, May argues that the German general staff, moreover, correctly anticipated that the French high command would (a) dispatch most of the first-line forces to Belgium; (b) not recognize for several days that this was an error; and lastly (c) react only slowly in making sense of and reacting to the new circumstances.

Another historical footnote of strategic relevance: Hitler, showing surprising lack of nerve in view of the phenomenal success of the assault three days into the campaign, actually ordered General Guderian to halt his Panzer at the River Meuse to wait for the infantry to catch up. It would have been a major tactical mistake – one that quite possibly would have bogged down the German invasion in World War I-style trench warfare. Guderian knew that every day lost would give the Allies time to withdraw and regroup. He chose to defy Hitler's directives and acted in accordance with the nineteenth-century Prussian principle of *Auftragstaktik* (mission command) that confined headquarters to setting objectives while commanders in the field were given freedom to decide how best to achieve the objectives. Hitler subsequently awarded Guderian with a promotion to lieutenant-general for his boldness and initiative, despite his defiance of the Führer's order. The question has been raised: would Guderian have got away with his defiance of an order in the British Army? Likely not. Roberts[6] has argued that this anecdote shows the persistent belief in Britain that German soldiers acted like automatons, blindly obeying orders, for the myth it is.

Managers often get locked into set thinking patterns. Managers' paradigms often keep them from dealing effectively with unprecedented challenges when they arise. Achi and Berger[7] suggest that managers need to move from "managing the probable" to "leading the possible." This requires challenging the prevailing paradigm – and asking very different questions. Questions that prompt a very different perspective on a problem include:

- What would we expect not to find – and why?
- What might we be discounting or explaining away too readily?
- What would happen if we shifted one of our core assumptions on an issue, just as an experiment?

Achi and Berger further recommend the following antidotes to break out of set thinking patterns:

- Playing the *advocatus diaboli* by taking the perspective of someone who frustrates or irritates us while reflecting on what this person may have to teach us.
- Seeking out opinions of people beyond our own comfort zone – particularly those individuals outside of our normal sphere of decision making.
- Listening very carefully to what other people are trying to tell us and withholding judgment until we have really understood their position.

Returning to the Nespresso case, assumptions need to be carefully reviewed at the issues and subissues level. A simple example to illustrate the point: ecological sensitivities have changed over the past quarter century since Nespresso first launched its aluminum pod. While concerns over the recyclability of aluminum and energy consumption associated with its manufacturing have always existed, they were hardly mainstream concerns in the early 1980s. That has changed. Nespresso would be well advised to carefully review the acceptability of aluminum to substantial segments of its markets. Competitors capable of providing alternative solutions (such as a biodegradable version of the pod) have emerged and pose a direct serious threat to Nespresso's product offering.

Assumptions and the prevailing business logic must be continually challenged. Changing competitive environments invariably relegate assumptions that have been formed by past successes to obsolescence. Key success factors change as do conditions in the organization's markets. Whatever the source of the firm's strategic problems, organizations are well advised to examine these in light of their current business paradigm. Past successes are often the greatest hindrance to this exercise. Determinants of past success are all too often assumed to hold invariably for the future. Particularly in rapidly evolving competitive environments this is a perilous assumption. Even great industry players are prone to fail when led by obsolete industry logic.

It would appear that the automotive industry is particularly prone to misguided industry logic. Henry Ford's famous statement in 1922 that " . . . *any customer can have a car painted any color that he wants as long as it is black"* is testimony to the fact that even a pioneering visionary like Ford could end up missing obvious signs of changing consumer tastes. While his sturdy black Model T had made him rich, automobile buyers by 1920 were developing a taste for different cars and models. Ford's refusal to budge brought the Ford Motor Company to the brink of bankruptcy by the end of World War II. Toyota is a much more recent case in point. Its relatively recent difficulties in the face of massive recalls have been attributed to its management's reluctance to accept that the company could build faulty cars.[8]

STRATEGY IN PRACTICE: THE ROLE OF INTUITION IN FRAMING ISSUES

We will examine the role of intuition in strategy more thoroughly in the next chapter when we examine it in the context of sense making and the formation of insight. However, in the context of framing issues, intuition also plays an important role. Intuition helps us frame views that in turn help us identify issues. Intuition also helps shape our assumptions. It draws on the subconscious and is linked to perception and insight, though it may be detached from any immediate conscious or rational deduction. Hence, it is so important that we take a few steps back every so often and challenge the views and perceptions that form the basis of our intuition.

Intuition expresses itself in a variety of ways. Whether we call it "gut feeling," *Fingerspitzengefühl*, [9] or a hunch, intuition is grounded in experience and derived from insights gained from reflection, learning, and experiential knowledge, often gathered over a long period of time. Intuition can be very helpful in identifying and framing issues, particularly when these relate to complex contexts.

However, there is an important proviso to this: intuition is useful only if it is continually challenged and adapted to a continually changing reality. Intuition that fails to reflect current reality can be misleading at best. At worst, it can be fatal for the business when senior management fails to challenge its intuition and blindly adheres to obsolete industry logic.

Reality is highly complex. Numerous forces work inextricably alongside one another so that the effect and impact of any single factor remains inextricable. Synergetic effects between factors may trigger amplifications of outcomes in which the resulting impact is greater than the sum of its parts. Serendipity can also play a critical role, leading to probabilities of outcomes that simply cannot be computed. Problems arise when managers begin making seemingly convincing claims about the likelihood of the occurrence of these outcomes, when in reality it is impossible to establish any level of certainty concerning the likelihood of events.

Box 2.3 Black Swans and the Thanksgiving Turkey

In his recent bestseller, Nassim Nicholas Taleb[10] talks about "black swans," those highly improbable occurrences with potentially devastating impact. Examples of "black swans" include the September 11, 2001 terrorist attacks on the twin towers and the current global financial markets crisis. Taleb argues, for example, that contrary to conventional wisdom, almost none of the world's great discoveries were the result of design and planning. Rather, these were entirely serendipity-driven "black swans" and hence unpredictable.

Taleb elaborates on the dangers of making seemingly logical predictions about the future on the basis of assumptions that, in fact, bear no relevance to the ultimate occurrence. He illustrates this point by tracking the life of an American turkey up to the point of its fateful demise on the Wednesday before Thanksgiving. Nothing happening in the many days prior to the fateful day on which the turkey gets slaughtered could possibly prepare it for its ultimate surprise ending. The friendly daily feedings, if at all, reinforce the turkey's sense of well-being. In fact, one might imagine that the turkey's feeling of security is greatest when the risk has reached its pinnacle – on the day before the slaughter, the turkey's "black swan."

Taleb extends this illustration to general observations about the nature of empirical knowledge and our learning from past events – the notion that if something has worked in the past it may, in fact, turn out to be at best irrelevant, and at worst fatally misleading in changing circumstances.

SUMMARIZING THE CHAPTER . . .

- The strategic thinking process provides the strategy practitioner with a means of approaching strategic challenges in a systematic and purposeful way.
- Strategic challenges are triggered by events and changes in the firm's competitive context (which might reflect external and/or internal factors).
- The first task is to ascertain the strategic relevance of the implications of those triggers for the firm's competitive position.
- Strategic challenges are those that have potential for significant impact on the organization's competitive position.
- The strategic thinking process guides the practitioner through an iterative process of framing issues and deriving strategic questions relevant to the challenge.
- Relevant strategic questions typically are relatively few in number; getting these few wrong, however, can have devastating implications for the organization's competitive position.
- Assumptions underpinning the prevailing business logic and paradigm must be challenged at each stage of the strategic thinking process; this requires intellectual curiosity and willingness to abandon legacy thinking.

Notes

1. Heisenberg, W. (1958) *Physics and Philosophy: The Revolution in Modern Science*, New York: Harper and Row.
2. Sloan, J. (2014) *Learning to Think Strategically*, Second Edition, Abingdon: Routledge (Taylor & Francis Group).
3. The Pareto principle has been attributed to the Italian economist Vilfredo Federico Damaso Pareto (1848–1923) who observed that 80% of the income in Italy ended up with 20% of the population.
4. Schein, E.H. (1992) *Organisational Culture and Leadership*, Second Edition, San Francisco: Jossey-Bass Publishers.

5. May, E.R. (2000) *Strange Victory: Hitler's Conquest of France*, New York: Hill and Wang; referenced in Light, P.C. (2005) *The Four Pillars of High Performance*, New York: McGraw-Hill.
6. Roberts, A. (2003) *Hitler and Churchill*, London: Phoenix, pp. 101–104.
7. Saporito, B. (2008) Is This Detroit's Last Winter? *TIME Europe*, December 15, 2008.
8. Achi, Z. and Berger, J.G. (2015) Delighting in the Possible, *McKinsey Quarterly*, March 2015 Issue.
9. *Fingerspitzengefühl* translates literally from the German as "finger-tip feeling" or the English expression "keeping a finger on the pulse"; it suggests an instinctive sixth sense; in a military context, this might be a field commander's instinctive grasp of an ever-changing operational and tactical situation on the battlefield.
10. Taleb, N.N. (2007) *The Black Swan*, London: Penguin; see also *The Independent on Sunday* (October 19, 2008): "The Visionaries: It's not Easy Being Right."

CHAPTER 3

Sense Making and Strategic Insight

Any fool can **know**. *The point is to* **understand**.

—Albert Einstein

IN THIS CHAPTER, WE:

- examine the role of sense making and the formation of insight in the greater context of the strategic thinking process;
- explore philosophical underpinnings of sense making and show how and why these matter;
- explore sense making from both the spatial and process perspectives:
  - in the spatial perspective we examine a framework for sense making that relates analysis, intuition, heuristics, and interpretation to the generation of insight;

- from a process perspective we examine how sense making occurs in complex organization contexts; the roles of triggers, rational analysis, intuition and heuristics – and how these are linked to learning, interpretation, and the ascription of meaning in complex contexts;
  - examine sense making from a learning perspective;
- close with a review of the formation of insight – and a critical reflection on limitations to sense making in strategy practice.

Organizations and their competitive environments resemble a perplexing terrain. Our perceptions regarding that terrain are based on numerous inputs of information. Some of this information might be incomplete and unclear; some information might be outright misleading. That this is so has long been recognized in military contexts. The great Prussian military philosopher Carl von Clausewitz pointed out in his treatise *On War* that a *"great part of the information obtained in war is contradictory, a greater part is false, and by far the greater part is of a doubtful character."*[1] Some of the contradiction no doubt stems from ambiguous circumstances typically encountered in situations of conflict. Some, however, is deliberate. Deliberate distortion of information, or deception, has always played an important role in military strategy. In the military context, deception is about subtle manipulation and distortion of identity and purpose. This is used to influence the enemy's perception of reality and to instigate the enemy to act on their misperceptions. Greene argues that in war, where the stakes are high, there is no moral stigma in using deception.[2]

The stakes in business environments, though of a different character, are not any less high. As in war, we also encounter both deliberate and unintentional ambiguity in business environments. Our perception of the ambiguity encountered may be subject to multiple and potentially conflicting interpretations, all of which may appear plausible from some point of argumentation. Kay[3] has argued that business organizations, being the complex political organizations that they are, tend to be influenced by individuals and groups with diverse and potentially conflicting agendas. In this context, weighty and careful analysis of the rationale for decisions is most often possible only after these, in fact, have been taken. However, even then, social and political organizational contexts often lead to situations that defy rational analysis of any sort.

Sense making is about creating coherence and order against this confusing backdrop of multiple possible "realities." The purpose of sense making is to introduce some degree of objectivity towards creating a better understanding of how events are linked; of the roles of actors and parties in complex competitive relationships.[4] It involves a deconstruction and reassembling of reality into bits of insight. Its purpose in strategy is to identify those insights that are most relevant to the problem or task at hand. In the strategic thinking context sense making is really an activity that takes place in the organization's realm of knowledge. It is part of the organization's higher-level knowledge and learning processes. The underpinning theory falls broadly in the field of cognitive dynamics and is rich and deep in its own right. It is therefore the purpose of this chapter to draw on only a few of the notions relevant to sense making in strategy practice.

Much of what happens in organizations on an ongoing basis entails some element of sense making. Sense making takes on a particularly critical role in strategy. Sense making and formation of insight are fundamentally critical elements of the strategic thinking process. Schematically, sense making and the formation of insight are shown following the articulation of strategic questions and framing of relevant issues (Figure 3.1).

Sense making involves a deconstruction of complexity through judicious combinations of analysis, intuition, and interpretation. This process leads to the *derivation of meaning*, which in turn enables greater lucidity of the specific context under examination.

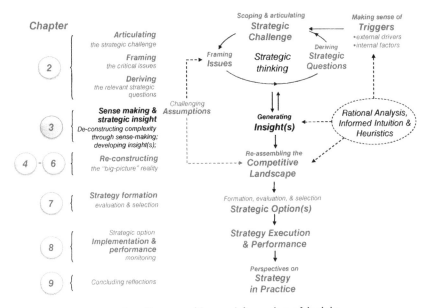

Figure 3.1   Sense making and formation of insight

Sense making is a process that ultimately allows components elements of a particular context (for example, one relevant to the strategic challenge at hand) to be assembled into the relevant "bigger picture" or pattern.

Therefore, the purpose of sense making is to generate a sufficient number of insights and to connect these in such a way that they create a coherent and connected picture. However, given that real business contexts are typically complex and ambiguous, the resulting "big picture" will inevitably be incomplete. Seldom are *all* insights that are prompted by strategic questions obtainable. Therefore, the objective of sense making is to generate a sufficiently complete "big picture" that enables the emergence of patterns sufficiently discernible to enable subsequent decision making to occur. In the first section of this chapter we explore sense making; in the second part we examine the notion of insight.

Perspectives on Sense Making

Sense making has been dealt with from a variety of perspectives in the management literature. Philosophically, sense making is positioned between two contrasting views of how social science research should be approached. Two traditions, *positivism* and *social constructionism*, represent fundamentally different approaches to sense making. Positivism builds on the idea that reality exists in the external environment and is to be deduced through objective reasoning and measurement. In social constructionism, on the other hand, reality is derived through inferred interpretation of sensation, reflection, and intuition. The tension arising between the two approaches in the context of sense making is explained by the respective differences in their *ontological* (relating to the philosophical assumptions about the nature of reality) and *epistemological* (relating to the general set of assumptions about the best ways of enquiring into the nature of reality) underpinnings.[5] Table 3.1 summarizes the fundamental

Table 3.1 Positivism and social constructionism: contrasting approaches to sense making and implications[6]

	Positivist approach	Social constructionist approach
Points of departure	Hypotheses	Meanings
Designs	Experimentation and deduction	Reflection and intuition
Techniques	Measurement	Discourse
Analysis	Verification of facts	Interpretation; derivation of meaning
Units of analysis	Reduction to simplest possible terms and elements	Seeks to capture complexity of the collective "whole"
Explanations	Must establish and demonstrate objective causality	Serves to increase overall general understanding of the situation
Outcomes	Causality	Understanding

differences. While the former leaves the analyst entirely out of the picture and aims to establish objective, causal explanations for circumstances and occurrences, the latter seeks to infer meaning and better understanding through reflection and interpretation of events and circumstances. Both approaches find application in sense making. Indeed, in sense making, we need contributions from both rational analyses as well as from intuition. This is why a pragmatic view that deliberately draws on both approaches for insight is the preferred mode in management practice.

Weick[7,8] bases his perspective on sense making on a conceptualization of organizations as "loosely coupled" systems. Individuals play an important role in interpreting and assigning meaning to stimuli originating in the firm's external environment. Ultimately, though, the purpose of sense making is to reduce the *equivocality* of information in the organization's environment. Management thinkers such as Mintzberg *et al.*[9] and Choo[10] view sense making as contributing to the strategy process through its process of constructing meaning and the creation of knowledge. These subsequently lead to decision making that drives responsive action. This perspective is consistent with the *emergent* school of strategy thinking. Not entirely unrelated to this perspective, sense making has also been viewed as an organizational learning process by thinkers such as Nonaka and Takeuchi[11] and Baumard.[12]

In this chapter we develop a dual perspective on sense making that draws mainly on the work of Weick, Mintzberg, and Nonaka and Takeuchi. We first explore sense making as it occurs in the organizational *sense making space* depicted in Figure 3.2; including a brief review of some of the elements contributing ultimately to the *ascription of meaning*. A subsequent section delves into how individual elements of the sense making space collectively contribute to the formation of insight; an important perspective that views sense making as a *process*. This section explores sense making from a process perspective. The sense making process is inextricably linked to the organizational learning process; hence,

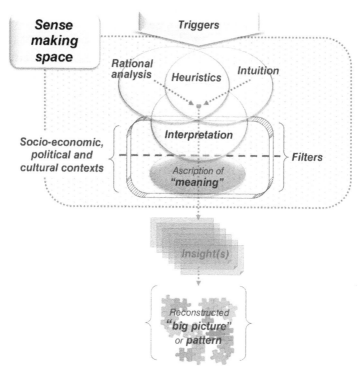

Figure 3.2 Sense making and the formation of insight

organizational learning is an important extension of the process perspective of sense making.

Though shown as a relatively systematic and orderly set of activities in Figure 3.2, the schematic at best reflects an approximation only of what in reality is a highly complex and iterative process.

Sense Making: A Spatial Perspective

Organizations are often viewed as "black boxes." Black boxes imply that only inputs and outputs are apparent. And yet, in real business contexts, constant and diverse inputs consisting of stimuli of all sorts are processed and transformed into action within the box. Hence, a fundamental premise of this book is that organizations need not be viewed as "black boxes"; that managers in fact can and should play a central role in manipulating outcomes through informed action. In order to do so, however, they must be able to peer into the box representing the organization, and understand its inner workings and how these are impacted by external factors. Sense making is a key element in that process.

To be clear, organizations are complex entities. We will never have complete understanding of their inner functioning, if only because organizations change continually and function at multiple levels not discernible to the visible eye. Hence, without any pretense of a complete understanding of its functioning, we can nonetheless glean some understanding of the sense making process, and how it contributes to the formation of insight.

Broadly speaking, sense making is triggered by events, circumstances, or other stimuli that threaten to change the status quo or perhaps offer entirely new opportunities of some sort. Sense making then involves a combination of analysis, intuition, and interpretation of the stimuli. These are shaped and filtered by the sociopolitical and cultural context within which the sense making occurs. Context influences our perception; the stimuli that triggered the sense making thereby attain meaning. Meaning leads to bits and pieces of insight that collectively contribute to the formation of a bigger picture relevant to the circumstances that triggered the need for sense making in the first place. Thus, the outcome of the sense making exercise is insight, which collectively enables the reconstruction of the relevant bigger picture. But how is insight formed – what actually happens in the sense making space that ultimately yields insight? We really don't know. Much of what happens in the process evades our scrutiny due to the complex and subliminal nature of sense making. We may surmise that a significant part of sense making plays out at the subconscious levels of our thinking; hence, at best we can observe the phenomenon and draw limited conclusions accordingly.

STRATEGY IN PRACTICE: REFLECTIONS ON SENSE MAKING MECHANISMS

- Sense making, Clegg et al.[13] remind us, is what people in organizations do all the time, whether they are aware of it or not.
- Both individuals in organizations and organizations in the collective (for example, teams and groups) engage in this exercise through reflection and exchange of thinking and experiences.
- Organizations use a variety of mechanisms for sense making; analogies, mental models, metaphors, concepts, and hypotheses can be very powerful mechanisms for capturing the spatial dimensions in organizational sense making.
- Nonaka and Takeuchi[14] discuss the critical role of such mechanisms in terms of quintessential knowledge creation processes that support organizational sense making; in this way, sense making is inextricably linked to the organization's learning processes (this is discussed in greater detail further on in this chapter).
- These mechanisms help to frame the numerous clues, cues, and signals that are continually emerging in organizational contexts, some of which might be only short-lived; they enable us to "connect the dots," thereby helping us to frame our understanding within a greater rational context.

Insight has traditionally played a crucial role in the natural sciences throughout the ages. Insight in the form of "Eureka!" moments have brought forth important breakthroughs in scientific thinking, hence it is a logical field of endeavor to examine from a sense making perspective. Consider the following account of one such momentous event that resulted in Kekulé's discovery of the ring formula for the benzene molecule.

Box 3.1 Swirling Serpents and Molecules

The German chemist Friedrich August Kekulé von Strado-nitz (1829–1896) had been puzzling over the structure of the six-carbon structure of benzene for some time. At the time it had been assumed that all organic compounds had an open chain of carbon atoms as backbone. Yet, a number of the properties exhibited by certain molecules such as benzene simply couldn't be accounted for by the prevailing assumption of a straight carbon chain structure. Kekulé's flash of insight occurred in a vision while he was dozing in front of the fire; this is his account of that momentous discovery[15]:

"I was sitting writing on my textbook, but the work did not progress; my thoughts were elsewhere. I turned my chair to the fire and dozed. Again the atoms were gamboling before my eyes. This time the smaller groups kept modestly in the background. My mental eye, rendered more acute by the repeated visions of the kind, could now distinguish larger structures of manifold conformation; long rows sometimes more closely fitted together all twining and twisting in snake-like motion. But look! What was that? One of the snakes had seized hold of its own tail, and the form whirled mockingly before my eyes. As if by a flash of lightning I awoke; and this time also I spent the rest of the night in working out the consequences of the hypothesis."

What were the elements that ultimately contributed to Kekulé's flash of insight? We'll never know exactly, of course. Scientific research findings[16] recently published in the *Journal of Cognitive Neuroscience* suggest that although people may not be aware of it, their brains nonetheless have to be in a certain state of readiness in order for an insight to occur. The work reports, furthermore, that the state of the brain can be detected electrically several seconds in advance of the enlightening moment itself. Conscious thought, it appears, does not lead to insight; rather, unconscious processing happens in the background and only delivers the insight to the conscious once it has been arrived at.

In Kekulé's case we can safely assume that it was a combination of several factors – his factual expertise in chemistry, a lively imagination that played off his subconscious, and his ability to envisage three-dimensional shapes and forms in the abstract – that appears to have transpired in the subconscious at the critical moment. From a managerial perspective, we shouldn't overlook the importance of the setting: relaxed musing while snoozing in front of a fire. To think that napping on the job is still viewed as an infraction of the employment contract in most organizations!

Sense Making: A Process Perspective

How does sense making occur? In this section we begin by looking at how sense making is initiated. Key elements (depicted in Figure 3.2) are examined in the context of the sense making process. Next, we look at the sense making process from several angles: we look at the role of interpretation and how this leads to the ascription of meaning; how it relates to learning. Sense making is subsequently examined in the context of complex organizational environments.

Triggers

We've already looked at triggers in the previous chapter. We saw that, broadly speaking, these can be allocated to three areas: external drivers or stimuli, internal occurrences, or a combination of both. Sense making is triggered when there is a discrepancy between the assumed or expected, and what is actually encountered. Sense making is triggered by interruptions to ongoing routine activities. Weick[17] emphasizes the importance of novelty in triggering sense making: novelty might find its origins in dissonance, performance gaps, unanticipated disruptions, unexpected failure, and uncertainty brought on by external events. These create the need for explanation. The purpose of sense making is to produce explanations for the novelty. In practice we talk about "reality checking." This proceeds through reciprocal interaction between information seeking and the attempt to ascribe meaning and causality.

Rational Analysis and Sense Making

One of the formal subprocesses within the sense making space is pure rational analysis. It delivers a rational contribution to sense making. It can be assumed that this activity occurs largely in the conscious realm. It is predominantly a "left brain" activity that focuses on the objective analysis of facts, information, and figures. But this form of conscious sense making also includes the application of heuristics – simple rules of thumb or the deliberate application of lessons learned – which may have an element of experiential knowledge. Conscious, rational analysis deals mainly with codified, explicit stimuli. This may represent a limitation to sense making if only restricted to pure analysis since important intangible stimuli may be overlooked.

Intuition

Intuition, or *gut feeling*, has always played an important part in managerial decision making. A recent study sponsored by the Economist Intelligence Unit[18] confirms the importance of gut feeling in day-to-day management practice. Another recent study conducted by PwC,[19] a management consultancy, points to the importance of experience and intuition; it proposes that these "soft" elements are more important than fact-based analysis when it comes to making important strategic decisions. These and similar studies reflect the growing awareness within managerial circles of the importance of intuition in practice-oriented approaches to managerial decision making.

Intuition is an ethereal subactivity that occurs in the absence of any rational processes. Parikh et al. [20] argue that intuition might be thought of as a process by which perception is formed on various levels of consciousness ranging from logical consciousness to the subconscious. Intuition is an internally experienced phenomenon that may also be influenced by external elements. Two components of intuition particularly relevant to sense making are the logical conscious and subconscious levels.

At the *conscious* level we find pattern recognition through rapid inference typified by "if . . . then" reasoning, the rapid retrieval of which occurs without the conscious application of logic or analysis. At the *subconscious* level the intuition process consists of tapping into the internal reservoir of cumulative experience and expertise developed over perhaps many years; distilling from this deeply embedded knowledge a response, insight, or alternative without a conscious understanding of how we arrived at the particular insight. Sense making in practice draws on both the selective conscious mind and the more unorganized, holistic subconscious. Parikh et al. argue that sensitivity to resonances occurring from subconscious thought can be useful to our conscious thinking and can endow a subtle edge to our thinking. Subconscious thought draws on a vast amount of information that is largely disorganized and significantly more complex than that which we access in our conscious minds. We are consciously inhibited by what we perceive to be real whereas the subconscious encompasses the vast spectrum of the possible.

Intuition most effectively contributes to sense making when we are in a relaxed and reflective state of mind; when we relax, we momentarily suspend the deliberate organization of thought (such might also be the case when we engage in rhythmic physical activity such as jogging). This allows the subconscious to emerge in all its richness of experience and deeply embedded knowledge. New patterns and causal relationships between hitherto unconnected factors suddenly become apparent, much like

Kekulé's flash of insight concerning the ring structure of the benzene molecule.

Heuristics

Heuristics are "rules of thumb" that are derived from experiential learning. The question of how firms explicitly learn from experience, and how this learning is then applied in sense making and in subsequent decision making, has engaged the interest of strategy scholars and practitioners for a long time. The question becomes all the more compelling in situations when time and information are limited, and the future uncertain, such as in what Eisenhardt and Martin[21] have described as *high-velocity markets.* Current strategy theory largely ignores actual approaches used by managers to develop strategies under such circumstances. Recognized as a gap in the strategic management literature, this has led to recent calls for a better understanding of "rules of thumb" – or *heuristic* – approaches to strategic decision making.[22]

Notwithstanding a lack of theory, heuristics have long played an important role in managerial decision making. Heuristics relate to how people actually make decisions in day-to-day situations requiring rapid responses under conditions of incomplete or intractable information. Gigerenzer[23,24] argues that heuristics are more immune to errors in (the often limited) available data because they draw on a complex interplay between evolved capacities in a person's brain and contextual structures. This generally enables judgment that (1) appears rapidly in the decision maker's consciousness; (2) of which the underlying rationale may not be readily apparent; and (3) is nonetheless sufficiently strong to act on. Gigerenzer further suggests that the larger the uncertainty, the number of variables, and the less the amount of data available, the greater the advantage of the heuristic over purely rational approaches. In a similar way, Bingham and Eisenhardt[25] argue that heuristics, in fact, constitute "rational" strategy in uncertain and unpredictable environments, and that they form the primary basis for strategic value creation in circumstances in which information-intensive, cognitively demanding approaches break down for lack of reliable data. Despite often being viewed as dysfunctional, Bingham and Eisenhardt argue that simple heuristics can outperform analytically sophisticated and information-intensive approaches even when time and information are available because they draw on an individual's intuitive grasp of a relevant context. They require less information, simplify cognitive processes, and thereby lead to more rapid decision making. Heuristics are therefore a potentially important element in decision making – provided, of course, that assumptions are continually scrutinized for potential bias.

Interpretation and the Ascription of Meaning

Analysis, intuition, and interpretation occur simultaneously in sense making space. Analysis and intuition provide data that subsequently needs to be interpreted for meaning. Weick[26] tells us that interpretation is that process by which inputs delivered to the organization (e.g. through analysis or intuition) are translated, developed into models for understanding and meaning, and put into context. Weick points out the role of the retrospective and "relating to" in sense making; that meaning is derived from experience and association with the known often only after the fact. As a social activity, sense making is a process in which people co-create, or enact their environment through discourse, conversation, and the narrative. In engaging in these activities, people notice, extract, and embellish cues; these are the familiar structures from which a larger sense of what is occurring is then derived. Finally, not surprisingly, Weick describes sense making as a process that involves emotion and that might provoke confusion.

The meaning derived through interpretation may be strongly influenced by the sociopolitical or cultural context within which the interpretation occurs. We differentiate between high and low context settings. *High context* settings are characterized by an internalized, "closed-society" and implicit understanding of values, norms, and communication. Knowledge is relevant largely "here and now"; it is situational and relational. *Low context* is universal, rule-oriented, and based on codified knowledge that is transferable and widely applicable. Sequencing of time, space, activities, and relationships is separated in low context settings.

Context shapes sense making; contexts impose filters on interpretation that reflect the sociopolitical and cultural attributes of the environment. A specific context may even result in a gross "distortion" of sense making in certain settings and circumstances as the example in Box 3.2 illustrates.

BOX 3.2 TRIAL BY RED-HOT IRON[27]

Picture the scene: Röthenbach in the Black Forest in the year 1485. An assembly of clergy at the signorial court of the Count of Fürstenberg. A woman accused of witchcraft has been arraigned before the signorial court. The Count has decided to place the matter of justice in the hands of God. The suspected witch is to be subjected to the "trial by red-hot iron" ordeal. The accused, by this procedure, is required to take a red-hot iron from a furnace and carry it for three paces. The suspect's hand would then be bound for three days upon which the wound would be inspected. A cleanly healed wound would lead to a declaration of innocence; a weeping or discolored wound would be grounds for condemnation. The woman accused of witchcraft submits to the trial with confidence (not that she is given much choice in the matter). According to one account, she carries the glowing iron not only for the stipulated three paces; she carries it for six. She is eventually acquitted and freed. In a strange twist of justice, the case is brought to the attention of the two Dominican friars Heinrich Krämer and Jakob Sprenger, who condemn the verdict in their influential treatise on witchcraft entitled *Malleus Maleficarium* (1486) on the grounds that the procedure is potentially open to demonic manipulation – conceivable on the grounds that the devil, a master of natural science, may have protected the woman's hand by invisibly placing something between her hand and the hot iron. Judges are warned to avoid using the ordeal in future trials.

Making sense of this case in a modern societal and judicial context leaves us shaking our heads. The woman is first accused of a crime now regarded as impossible (was it possibly her red hair that had triggered the persecution in the first place?) and then set free by a process that appears entirely arbitrary and random. Were her judges irrational, their attitudes and behavior derived from stupidity or hysteria, or possibly a combination of both? Evidence gathered by scholars of medieval and Renaissance history suggests otherwise. Writings from this period indicate an extensive and high level of learning. Even the allegations against witches – suggesting they congregated at night to kill infants and worship the devil – are found in the writings of scholars who rooted their works in the Bible and the philosophy of the Church fathers. The practice of the ordeal, until its decline in the thirteenth century, was endorsed by some of the most thoughtful and scholarly Christians in Western Europe.

Sense making is shaped by sociopolitical and cultural context. Have we made significant and substantial progress in our sociopolitical and culture thinking and practices since the middle ages? In many ways we have, indeed; nonetheless we needn't look far in some organizations today to find examples of outcomes of "sense making" that, while not carried to the extreme described in this case, leave us shaking our heads no less.

Sense making as described in the illustration (Box 3.2) often goes hand in hand with what Baumard[28] describes as a *territorialization* of knowledge and cognition in organizations (or even societies) driven in part by the bounded rationality of key actors, but also in an effort to protect their knowledge, which they associate with their power and authority.

Sense Making and Learning

Sense making serves to help identify bits and pieces of strategically relevant information related to a particular strategic problem; to sort and filter these and reassemble them into bundles of insight that might be relevant to that particular problem. In so doing, it is an activity that involves both conscious analysis and intuition in creating order, sorting out paradox, and making retrospective sense of situations in which the organization finds itself.[29] Ideally, sense making is a collective activity, involving interaction and discourse among individuals in the organization.

STRATEGY IN PRACTICE: SENSE MAKING AND SOME BASIC UNDERLYING ASSUMPTIONS

We draw on Weick[30] for a summary of some of the basic assumptions underpinning the notion of sense making:

- Sense making is about interpreting reality which is ongoing even as we try to make sense of it; sense making is about capturing flows, a continually changing environment, variations in choice, and irrevocability in an organizational context that is evolving even as it makes sense of itself and its environment.[31]
- Sense making is a retrospective process; reminiscing a primary source of derived meaning.
- Symbols and symbolic processes are central features of the sense making exercise; they help associate conscious and

subconscious ideas, thereby endowing meaning and significance to complex phenomena.

- Sense making draws on images and maps to help rationalize complex relationships; these in turn help establish plausible patterns that support the interpretation of complex reality.
- Ultimately, sense making is a mechanism for reducing equivocality (multiple meanings) of an ambiguous context into a more manageable and relevant set of meanings.[32]
- Sense making can be viewed as a learning process in the complex environment of an organization.

Sense Making in Complex Environments

The greater the complexity of an organizational context, the greater we expect the demands on sense making to be. But what do we mean by *complexity*? What is complexity in a business context? Though we intuitively understand what the term implies, complexity is actually difficult to define. The original Latin word *complexus* infers things that are entwined or twisted together. This suggests that complexity involves numerous elements linked in some intricate arrangement. The component elements may be events as such or parties external to the organization. In an organizational context complexity relates to the importance that tacit structures and processes play in the functioning of the particular organization in question. That is to say, complex organizations depend heavily on interactions and transactions within the organization that are not readily obvious to the casual observer.

It has been suggested that organizations can be viewed as intricate interpretation and sense making systems,[33] whereby interpretation and sense making occur in three stages[34]:

1. *Scrutiny* against a complex combination of signals, stimuli, and impulses;

2. *Conferral* of meaning to the information thus gathered; and
3. *Translation* of this information into actionable knowledge by way of organizational learning.

A number of organizational learning theories have been proposed for explaining how these stages actually happen in organizations. Generally, these theories draw on sociocultural psychological perspectives of the organization in which learning involves socially mediated cognitive processes of interpretation and sense making. These theories seek to explain the roles of the individual as well as those of the collective in this process. One of these is the *SECI* (Socialization, Externalization, Combination, and Internalization) model proposed by Nonaka and Takeuchi.[35] Their model emphasizes the social nature of organizational learning; it explains how knowledge is transformed between the tacit and explicit knowledge modes.

Nonaka and Takeuchi's framework reflects a Japanese perspective that views the organization as a living entity that encompasses a collective sense of identity and purpose – as opposed to a typically Western view of the organization as a machine. Perhaps what lends it particular credence for sense making is that it accounts for intangible as well as the more readily visible tangible elements. Sense making can be viewed as one of the multiple knowledge processes explained by the SECI model. This framework furthermore identifies appropriate enabling conditions that support organizational sense making:

1. *Intention* – ensures the strategic underpinning of the sense making process, linking the purpose of the activity to value creation.
2. *Autonomy* – ensures the appropriate flexibility in acquiring, interpreting, and relating information through a system of "minimum critical specification," thereby setting parameters for internal sense making.
3. *Fluctuation/creative chaos* – ensures appropriate stimulation of the interaction between the organization and its external environment, thereby setting parameters for making sense of external factors.

4. *Redundancy* – supports internal organizational knowledge processes by provision of information that might go beyond the immediate requirements of the organization, but which may be relevant in the future.
5. *Requisite variety* – ensures sufficient variety of information to match the organization's internal diversity and the complexity of its external environment; seeks also to reduce any information differentials across the organization.

Although Nonaka and Takeuchi's knowledge creation process begins with the individual, learning is viewed as occurring largely in teams – in an organizational collective sense. Personal knowledge becomes available to the organization through appropriate transformation mechanisms.

Tovstiga *et al.*[36] have proposed a framework for sense making that draws on Baumard's model of knowledge transitions, the Nonaka and Takeuchi SECI model and the *Intuiting-Interpreting-Integrating-Institutionalization (4I)* framework of organizational learning proposed by Crossan *et al.*[37] The framework suggests how sense making occurs in an organizational context (Figure 3.3)

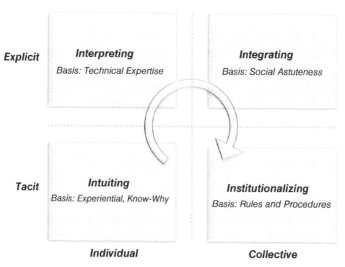

Figure 3.3 Sense making in an organizational context

through interaction between the organization's individuals and the collective, and the organization's tacit and explicit processes.

Intuiting is associated with the highly tacit process of pattern recognition on the basis of an individual's deep expertise in a field. This is the capability, for example, of an expert to recognize a pattern in a problem that a novice may not. Often this reflects deep expertise acquired over many years of practice. At the root of intuiting is the process of transferring explicit knowledge into tacit knowledge. Experiential knowledge is internalized by the individual in the form of shared mental models and know-why.

Positioned in the upper left quadrant, *interpreting* is the process by which individuals share and explain insights on the basis of their own knowledge and expertise. They do so through words and actions; these may be in the form of metaphors, analogies, concepts, hypotheses, or models. Differences in perceived reality and experiential context within an organization, however, may lead to potentially conflicting situations. This is sometimes observed in post-merger integration phases when the merging organizational cultures clash. Interpreting is a quintessential knowledge creation step, occurring largely through externalization.

Integrating, positioned in the upper right quadrant, is associated primarily with developing shared understanding and taking coordinated action through mutual adjustment. Knowledge sharing occurs through social interaction; group dialogue and storytelling. New tacit knowledge such as shared mental models may emerge from this learning interaction. This mode of knowledge creation is most often associated with the theories of group processes and sociocultural interaction. It is also associated with the evolution of social astuteness.

Finally, *institutionalizing* ensures that accepted knowledge and insights are embedded in the organization. Institutionalizing involves combining different bodies of explicit knowledge. This process may support the operationalization of a visionary strategy, product concepts, and organizational routines and procedures. The process may involve explicating written instructions or embedding unwritten rules. Institutionalizing contributes significantly to the formalization of an organization's identity.

Mintzberg *et al.*[38] lend support to this view; they suggest that intuiting is a subconscious (tacit) process occurring at the level of the individual and that this represents the start of the learning process. Interpreting then follows on the conscious (explicit) elements of the individual learning and from the individual to the collective while transitioning through a group-level positioned between the individual and the organizational collective (featured in the Crossan *et al.* model), where integrating of the explicated insights changes the collective understanding. Finally, institutionalizing embeds that learning in the firm's collective memory, an expression of which might be found in the organization's corporate culture.

STRATEGY IN PRACTICE: SENSE MAKING IN THE ORGANIZATIONAL CONTEXT

Organizational contexts represent complex settings for sense making. Various factors contributing to the complexity of this task have been discussed in the preceding section. Sense making, however, is a critical organizational mechanism for generating strategic insight. Weick[39] proposes the following seven practical questions for fathoming the organization's wherewithal for sense making:

- *Social context:* Does the organizational context encourage conversation?
- *Identity:* Does the organizational context provide its people with a definitive sense of who they are and what they represent?
- *Retrospect:* Is there sufficient data to reconstruct past events; how quickly does the organization "forget" past relevant events?

- *Salient clues, cues, and evidence:* Does the organizational context enhance the visibility of important inputs to its sense making process?
- *Ongoing projects:* Does the organizational context encourage overall continuity even in the event of interruption?
- *Plausibility:* Does the organizational context encourage coherent and credible reflection and exchange relating to events?
- *Enactment:* Does the organizational context encourage action or hesitation?

Box 3.3 Cultural "Branding" at Bayer AG

[**cultural:** with reference to the complex of typical behaviour or standardized social characteristics peculiar to a specific group, occupation, profession . . . ; **branding:** to mark with a brand; a mark of a simple easily recognized pattern made by burning with a hot iron . . . ; based on *Webster's Third New International Dictionary*]

Organizations deal with their cultures in different ways. Legacy-rich companies tend to nurture strong corporate cultures. I am reminded of my early days in the venerable Zentrale Forschung (central research laboratory) of Bayer AG in Leverkusen, Germany. A freshly minted chemical engineering PhD, I was joining what was at the time one of the largest industrial research laboratories in Europe. The year was 1986 and Bayer was still an archetypal German industrial behemoth deeply entrenched in the "Rhineland Model" mindset.

One of my more poignant impressions from those early days was being informed by one of the mentors charged with my cultural induction that considerable effort would be invested by the company over the next five years on my assimilation into the "Bayer family"; an experience, he added – and this only half in jest – that would essentially amount to being "branded" with the iconic "Bayer cross" (Germans tend to have a way with vivid imagery). What was being implied? Several things. I was being groomed for a life-long career with the company. People joined Bayer antici-pating employment for life. It was to be a comfortable life. Bayer was intent on fulfilling its commitments to its employee stakeholders; excellent pay, benefits that included world class health care and on-site clinics, and perks such as low interest rate mortgages for home owners, a strong commitment to work–life balance and a strong corporate identity to cement company loyalty on the part of the employees. Bayer '04, its sponsored premier league football team, was only one of Bayer's many indulgences.

The model had worked well over the years. Loyalty to "the Bayer" was often expressed in terms of years and generations a family had worked for Bayer. Job mobility in the prevailing German context meant rotation within the Bayer Group. Part of the grooming involved an organizational cultural indoctrination; part was ongoing management development training since German companies at the time developed their own management resources (MBAs were then largely unknown in German industry). The company was prepared to invest five years of what was expected to be a 30 or more year career with the company. Bayer's "cultural branding" was not left to chance; it involved a rich blend of mandatory events including corporate initiation rituals and off-site cultural induction seminars. But it also included rigorous in-house managerial training in subject areas such as finan-cial management carried out in week-long seminars at Kaderschmieden such as the Universitätsseminar der Wirt-schaft at Schloss Gracht, a management training academy funded and shared by a consortium of German industry conglomerates housed in a medieval castle not far from Cologne.

Cultural integration, alignment of mindset, and the embedding of Bayer's legacy values and norms were at stake. Bayer's rich legacy: its stories – for example, Bayer chemist Felix Hoffmann's discovery of aspirin in 1897; its not entirely uncontested role in the Second World War IG Farben industrial complex; its post-war re-emergence as Bayer AG; and its phenomenal growth and success were all part of the rich corporate tapestry that formed the backdrop of the company's identity and culture. In short, in true loyalty to its stakeholders, Bayer provided all that was required for a fulfilling life-long career. In return, the company expected reciprocal loyalty from its employees.

Little wonder then that my decision to leave the company after five years triggered puzzlement among most colleagues; this was expressed in thinly veiled whispers: " . . . *how can you possibly leave 'the Bayer family' after only five years!*" From a few colleagues, however, I also heard: " *. . . it's good to leave while you still can; . . . wish I'd have left 10 years earlier; I could no longer now!*"

Insight Formation

Sense making leads to the formation of insight. Competitive differentiation gained by an organization begins with unique insight. Pietersen[40] argues that the battle for superior insight is really the starting point of competitiveness. Insight has been defined as the clear or deep perception of a situation; the often sudden understanding of a complex situation, or grasping the inner nature of things intuitively.[41] Insight is the outcome of the sense making process, which in turn is closely related to the organizational learning process. Prahalad and Bettis[42] suggest that organizational sense making leading to insight occurs via a process that draws on pre-existing knowledge systems and mental models – or schemas. The authors suggest that schemas are made up not only of legacy-related beliefs, theories, and values, but that they are also influenced by the organization's objectives since these in turn influence the sort of information the organization accumulates.

Mintzberg *et al.*[38] suggest that while the source of insight may remain mysterious, its presence is not. It is an ability to grasp the deeper meaning of an issue and how this issue fits into the bigger picture alongside other fragments of insight. Insight draws on skills other than pure analytical reasoning. In fact, much of what leads to insight cannot be verbalized and lends itself more to images and spatial abstraction, as we are reminded by Kekulé's experience (Box 3.1). Insight thereby is arguably much more an outcome of right hemisphere activity than a left brain exercise. Mintzberg[43] suggests as much in his reflection on what he refers to as the "soft underbelly of hard data" and the limited use of hard data for forming insight:

- Hard data is limited in scope and simply does not encompass the richness of non-quantifiable economic factors.
- Often hard information loses much of its strategic relevance through aggregation and simplification.
- Much hard information lacks immediacy; it is simply not available when needed most since it takes time to become available.
- A lot of *hard* information is surprisingly unreliable; it is subject to biases and distortion through processing.

STRATEGY IN PRACTICE: SENSE MAKING AND ITS LIMITATIONS IN ORGANIZATIONS

Clegg *et al.*[44] argue that many strategic errors originate with managers' false perceptions of the limitations of their sphere of influence in managing outcomes; they are indicative of deficiencies in understanding and utilizing the outcomes of sense making in the organization:

- Many managers still approach strategic decision making by relying on tools and planning procedures that assume the world represented by these is as controllable and as rational as these might suggest.
- Outcomes are much more determined by the success of sense making in the organization – and the degree to which sense making contributes to a shared and common understanding against a backdrop of diverse factors.
- Sense making seeks to bring into juxtaposition different interests, disciplines, knowledge backgrounds, and power relations – and ideally contributes to reconciliation of these within organizations.
- When strategies fail, it is often through the failure of managers to recognize the organizational context for what it really is: a highly politicized and contested setting prone to irrational behavior on the part of its members.

SUMMARIZING THE CHAPTER . . .

- Sense making seeks to create meaning and insight from both explicit and tacit knowledge and information.
- It draws as much on analytical reasoning as it does on intuition, heuristics, and other "soft" inputs that constitute integral elements of tacit knowledge.
- Often, the latter embody the more critical and relevant inputs to the sense making process.
- The collective set of inputs largely defies traditional mechanistic approaches to their analysis because of the intangible nature of important inputs.
- Sense making is intrinsically linked to organizational learning through various supporting mechanisms, many of which reside in the organization's tacit realm. Insight may be viewed as an outcome of organizational learning.

- The managerial challenge of sense making focuses on creating and nurturing an appropriate organizational context and culture – that is, an environment conducive to deep reflection, trust, collective sharing of insights, experiences and knowledge, and learning.

Notes

1. Green, J.I. (2003) *Carl von Clausewitz: The Essential Clausewitz – Selections from "On War"*, Mineola, NY: Dover Publications.
2. Greene, R. (2006) *The 33 Strategies of War*, London: Profile Books, p. 305.
3. Kay, J. (2010) Inquiry – You're Getting Warmer . . . , *Financial Times Magazine*, 352 (March 20 and 21, 2010).
4. Weick, K.E. (2001) *Making Sense of the Organisation*, Oxford: Blackwell Publishing.
5. Easterby-Smith, M., Thorpe, R. and Jackson, P.R. (2008) *Management Research*, 3rd ed., London: Sage.
6. Ibid.
7. Weick, K.E. (1979) *The Social Psychology of Organizations*, 2nd ed., New York: Random House.
8. Weick, K.E. (1995) *Sensemaking in Organizations*, Thousand Oaks, CA: Sage.
9. Mintzberg, H., Ahlstrand, B. and Lampel, J. (1998) *Strategy Safari*, New York: The Free Press.
10. Choo, C.W. (2002) Sensemaking, Knowledge Creation, and Decision Making, in Choo, C.W. and Bontis, N. (eds) *The Strategic Management of Intellectual Capital and Organizational Knowledge*, Oxford: Oxford University Press.
11. Nonaka, I. and Takeuchi, H. (1995) *The Knowledge-Creating Company*, Oxford: Oxford University Press.
12. Baumard, P. (1999) *Tacit Knowledge in Organizations*, London: Sage Publications.
13. Clegg, S., Kornberger, M. and Pitsis, T. (2008) *Managing & Organizations*, London: Sage.
14. Nonaka, I. and Takeuchi, H. (1995) (note 11 above).
15. Horvitz, L.A. (2002) *Eureka!: Scientific Breakthroughs that Changed the World*, Chichester: John Wiley & Sons Ltd.
16. *The Economist* (2009) Incognito (16 April – from the print edition).

17. Weick, K.E. (2001) (note 4 above).
18. The Economist Intelligence Unit (2014) Decisive Action, published jointly with Applied Predictive Technologies.
19. PWC Data Analytics (2014) Gut & Gigabytes, UK Country Report – Capitalising on the Art and Science in Decision Making (in conjunction with The Economist Intelligence Unit); source: www.pwc.co.uk/data-analytics.
20. Parikh, J., Neubauer, F. and Lank, A. (1994) *Intuition*, Oxford: Blackwell Business.
21. Eisenhardt, K.M. and Martin, J.A. (2000) Dynamic Capabilities: What are They?, *Strategic Management Journal*, Vol. 21, pp. 1105–1121.
22. Bromiley, P. and Rau, D. (2014) Towards a Practice-Based View of Strategy, *Strategic Management Journal*, Vol. 35, pp. 1249–1256.
23. Gigerenzer, G. (2007) *Gut Feelings*, London: Penguin Books.
24. Gigerenzer, G. (2008) *Rationality for Mortals*, Oxford: Oxford University Press.
25. Bingham, C.B. and Eisenhardt, K.M. (2011) Rational Heuristics: The "Simple Rules" that Strategists Learn from Process Experience, *Strategic Management Journal*, Vol. 32, pp. 1437–1464.
26. Weick, K.E. (2001) (note 4 above).
27. Taken from: Oldridge, D. (2007) *Strange Histories*, London: Routledge.
28. Baumard, P. (1999) (note 12 above).
29. Weick, K.E. (2001) (note 4 above).
30. Ibid.
31. DeFillippi, R. and Ornstein, S. (2003) Psychological Perspectives Underlying Theories of Organizational Learning, in Easterby-Smith, M. and Lyles, M.A. (eds) *Handbook of Organisational Learning and Knowledge Management*, Oxford: Blackwell Publishing.
32. Daft, R. and Weick, K.E. (1984) Toward a Model of Organizations as Interpretive Systems, *Academy of Management Review*, Vol. 9 (2), p. 284.
33. Ibid.
34. Baumard, P. (1999) (note 12 above).
35. Nonaka, I. and Takeuchi, H. (note 11 above).
36. Tovstiga, G., Odenthal, S. and Goerner, S. (2005) Sense Making and Learning in Complex Organisations: The String Quartet Revisited, *International Journal of Management Concepts and Philosophy*, Vol. 1 (3), pp. 215–231.

37. Crossan, M.M. and Berdrow, I. (2003) Organizational Learning and Strategic Renewal, *Strategic Management Journal*, Vol. 24, pp. 1087–1105.
38. Mintzberg, H., Ahlstrand, B. and Lampel, J. (1998) (note 9 above).
39. Weick, K.E. (2001) *Making Sense of the Organisation*, Oxford: Blackwell; [in this reference, the author makes further reference to Weick, K.E. (1995) *Sensemaking in Organisations*, Thousand Oaks, CA: Sage, for more details on the seven properties of sense making].
40. Pietersen, W. (2002) *Reinventing Strategy*, New York: John Wiley & Sons, Inc.
41. Webster's Online Dictionary [www.websters-online-dictionary .org/].
42. Prahalad, C.K. and Bettis, R.A. (1986) The Dominant Logic: A New Linkage between Diversity and Performance, *Strategic Management Journal*, Vol. 7, pp. 485–501.
43. Mintzberg, H. (1994) *The Rise and Fall of Strategic Planning*, New York: The Free Press.
44. Clegg, S., Kornberger, M. and Pitsis, T. (2008) (note 13 above).

CHAPTER 4

Insight-Driven Strategic Analysis

*All models and frameworks of analysis are inherently flawed;
some are nonetheless useful.*

—Anonymous

IN THIS CHAPTER, WE:

- critically reflect on the process underlying rational strategic analysis; its purpose, role, and limitations in sense making and the generation of insight;
- revisit the notions of value creation, capture and delivery, and stakeholder positions in view of their centrality in the strategic thinking process;
- introduce a typology consisting of a hierarchy of frameworks of rational strategic analysis based on high-level and supporting-level analysis;

- describe the roles of high-level and supporting-level frameworks of analysis;
- propose a simple step-by-step approach to conducting an insight-driven strategic analysis;
- review and discuss the limitations of strategic analysis.

Strategic analysis is about sense making. It is about making sense of all those elements in the firm's competitive environment that are relevant to its current and future competitive position. These elements might be external to the firm; they might relate to the emergence of new opportunities, but they might also relate to potential threats to the firm's current position of competitive advantage. Elements relevant to the firm's competitive position also include factors internal to the firm; specifically, these have to do with the firm's ability and disposition to respond appropriately to changes in its external competitive context. Hence, strategic analysis is about making sense of both external and internal contexts relevant to the firm's competitive position. Typically, combinations of changing external and internal factors trigger the need for sense making. To that end, strategic analysis is a core element of the strategic thinking process; a process the firm needs to engage in on a continual basis, regardless of whether it is seeking to protect or to establish a position of competitive advantage.

Clearly, however, in order for the analysis to be *competitively* relevant it needs to be purposeful. The purpose of sense making is to generate insights derived from external and internal factors that when suitably aggregated are relevant to the core purpose of the firm. As argued in earlier chapters, the strategic mandate of the firm relates to its ability to establish a position of competitive advantage on the basis of a differentiated value offering. Hence, the outcome of strategic analysis should enable the firm to make better decisions in response to events that challenge that mandate. Analysis thus seeks to come to terms with questions such as *where* to compete, *how* to compete, and *when* to do *what* in pursuing new opportunities or fending off threats from competitors. The question of *why* the firm would choose to compete at all in a given context is another important strategic question. In essence, strategic analysis through sense making should provide appropriate responses to the questions posited by the five building blocks of strategy discussed earlier in Chapters 1 and 2.

Strategic analysis draws on a multidisciplinary combination of rigorous scientific and informal processes that are used to derive correlations, and identify and evaluate trends, patterns, and performance gaps.

Strategic analysis as shown in Figure 4.1 delivers at least three important contributions to the strategic thinking process at the sense making stage. First, it contributes to making sense of the triggers that give rise to the strategic challenge in the first place. It

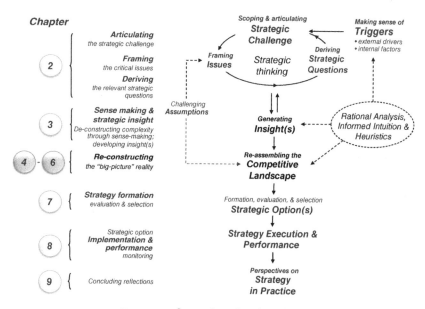

Figure 4.1 Strategic rational analysis

does so by guiding the framing of relevant strategic issues and the derivation of suitable strategic questions relevant to the strategic challenge at stake. In this way, strategic thinking contributes to the articulation of the strategic challenge and helps managers ascertain that the challenge is indeed of strategic relevance and importance to the firm.

Second, strategic analysis contributes to the generation of the insights elicited by the strategic questions derived – recognizing, however, that not all strategically important questions posed can necessarily be answered at a given point in time. As discussed in the previous chapter, this has to do with the complexity and ambiguity of real business environments.

Third, strategic analysis provides guidance in piecing together the individual bits and pieces of insight into an aggregated "bigger picture" relevant to the strategic challenge at stake. It is on the basis of this invariably incomplete picture, from which key attributes of the relevant strategic landscape are nonetheless discernible, that strategic options are subsequently derived. In this way, strategic analysis involves the deconstructing of complex, real contexts, the generation of insight, and the reconstruction of the reality relevant to the firm's strategic context. In this chapter we introduce and examine some basic notions related to strategic analysis. In particular, this chapter lays the foundation for the two levels of strategic analysis dealt with in this book: high-level, "big-picture" and supporting-level strategic analyses. These are subsequently examined in greater detail in Chapters 5 and 6, respectively.

Strategic Rational Analysis: How *Rational* is it Really?

Good analysis requires reliable data. Frameworks and models that we use in analysis are useful only when populated with meaningful data. This presents at least two fundamental dilemmas to the strategy practitioner:

1. Strategy is fundamentally about the future – and simply put, there is no data available about the future. Any data available to the strategist is by default historical. We may make extrapolations into the future on the basis of data currently available, but such projections hold only if circumstances reflecting today's reality more or less remain unchanged into the future. Under these circumstances, the future would be largely predictable and existing data can be used to generate insight about potential future outcomes. But this does not reflect current business reality. The current reality of real business environments, regardless of the industry or market context, suggests something very different: time horizons for decision making are shrinking and long established "rules of the competitive game" are no longer valid because the game itself is fundamentally changing. What we are experiencing increasingly are *high-velocity markets* as described by Eisenhardt and Martin[1]; in other words, rapidly evolving market environments in which competitive boundaries are blurred, successful business models have yet to be established, and market players are ambiguous and shifting.

2. Even if data is available and sufficiently reliable, strategic analysis is limited by the *irrationality* intrinsic to real organizations and business environments. *Rational* strategic analysis builds on the premise that organizations and their competitive environments act and perform rationally and therefore predictably. They don't always. Any endeavor involving humans is prone to irrationality. Within an organizational context irrationality may manifest itself as biased decision making, hidden agendas, or politically motivated power plays within the organization's informal networks. Irrationality may also be a factor in the firm's external competitive environment: competitors may resort to deliberately deceptive ploys or ruses to mask their true strategic intentions.

Further Limitations of Rational Strategic Analysis

Strategic analysis has fallen under considerable criticism in management circles in recent years. The management consulting industry is at least partially at fault for this. Strategy consultants have been particularly proficient at releasing a deluge of tools, methodologies, frameworks, and techniques of analysis onto the market. Literally hundreds of tools and techniques of analysis are currently in circulation. However, those tools and techniques are only as useful as the data available to populate them. Given that strategy is about the future, there is, in reality, relatively little reliable data available. Indeed, extrapolations of existing data into the future are increasingly limited by the growing uncertainty of competitive environments. So, no matter how sophisticated the analysis technique, the maxim "rubbish in, rubbish out" holds here as much as it does elsewhere.

In view of the competitive realities facing organizations today most approaches relying solely on rational strategic analysis are therefore inadequate. The paucity of reliable data available for analysis is only one reason for this. Another reason is that all frameworks of strategic analysis simplify reality. Frameworks and models reflect reality only partially. This necessitates the introduction of further simplifying assumptions. Assumptions, however, introduce a further potential source of distortion. For example, a typical assumption traditionally made in assessing the firm's external environment is that industry boundaries are constant and well defined, and that organizations know exactly who their competitors, suppliers, and customers are. In the past these assumption may have been valid to some extent in some industry sectors. Today, however, these assumptions are largely obsolete in view of highly dynamic environments in which in many industries industry boundaries are rapidly disappearing altogether. The smartphone sector provides an apt illustration. The smartphone industry emerged from a convergence of at least four formerly distinct sectors: telecommunications, traditional media, computing, and a newcomer – social media. Its trajectory had its origins in the conventional mobile telephone industry (where Nokia once had established a formidable position), but it rapidly encompassed media platforms (ecosystems) driven by new entrants such as Apple and its iTunes, and social media platforms such as Facebook, Twitter, Instagram, and Snapchat. In the new competitive landscape, former industry boundaries are largely irrelevant. Competition has migrated beyond the actual gadget (where Nokia nurtured world class competencies) to competition on the basis of new operating systems (such as Google and its Android operating system), and even more recently to the social media space, where relative newcomers (such as Facebook) are in the process of further redefining competition.

Even in cases in which frameworks demonstrate validity over a limited range of parameters, unreliable data – whether obsolete, incomplete, or simply irrelevant – renders these useless.

Data may also be deliberately misused. The practice of managing on the basis of performance ratios such as the "return on equity" or ROE ratio is a case in point. Many companies seek to achieve a better return on their equity. While there is nothing wrong with this objective *per se,* it does lead to problems when distorted in use. Managing for ROE was standard practice at Lehman Brothers. Ultimately it turned out to be the firm's undoing, however. Lehman Brothers is no more because managing for ROE encouraged its management to over-borrow, even when the first indicators of an economic recession appeared on the horizon. Debt in bad times does not earn returns as it does in good times. It isn't equity. Lehman ignored this fact. It practiced extreme leverage by shrinking the ratio's E in the denominator recklessly low. In doing so, Lehman tweaked its numbers and paid its executives according to that measure. Managing for the wrong ratio caught up with the company in a fatal way. Many other ratios such as gross margin and earnings per share are equally prone to misuse. It is relatively easy to make them look good while damaging the business's real business bottom line.

Box 4.1 Of Models and Men

The recent financial crisis that began in 2007 has dealt a devastating blow to the credibility of analytical models and theories used in the prediction of financial market performance. One in particular, the "efficient-markets hypothesis" or EMH, has come under sharp criticism. Its essence: the price of a financial asset reflects all available information that is relevant to its value. Wall Street came to draw powerful conclusions from this relatively straightforward assumption. What it implies is that if the EMH holds, then markets will price financial assets correctly, and deviations from equilibrium will not last long. Ideas such as the EMH coupled with the complex mathematics that describes them have given rise to the Wall Street profession of "financial engineering." A number of financial products emerged over the years from the ensuing effort: derivatives and securitizations, ever more intricate credit-fault swaps and collateralized debt obligations. It was thought at the time of their appearance that these inventions were making the financial markets safer and the economy healthier. Only gradually did skeptics begin questioning the validity of the models. Fact of the matter is that the vast majority of derivative contracts and securitizations have performed precisely as their models predicted they would. It has been argued that exceptions triggered the financial catastrophe.

So what went wrong? Myron Scholes, who won the 1997 Nobel Prize for his contributions to the Black-Scholes formula for pricing options, one of the most widely used models in the finance industry, has argued in defense of the EMH by pointing out that *"there are models, and there are those that use the models."* The problem in Scholes' view is not with the validity of the models, rather the way in which they were used by Wall Street and the City (London's financial community). Financial analysts fed the models with data that incorrectly suggested conditions that were much more benign than they were in reality. The models moreover inherently assume that markets behave rationally.

Behavioral economists, who apply the insights of psychology to finance, have been particularly skeptical of the markets' inherent rationality. Not only do humans behave irrationally, particularly in the face of losses, they have argued; people tend to be overly confident of their own abilities and tend to extrapolate recent trends into the future – thereby extending the applicability of the models used far beyond their intended range of validity.

The debate is far from over, though. To date, no new model has emerged to replace the efficient market hypothesis paradigm. And behavioral economics has yet to provide evidence for how it affects prices. What we do see once again is that it is not the models, rather the human factor that introduces the risk through irrational behavior and faulty judgment.

Perhaps new approaches that seek to integrate analysts' research findings – but that are void of the biases and emotions that can influence trading decisions – might be more suitable as forecasting algorithms for computer-driven stock-trading models. Whether or not these and other new advances that set out to reconcile both rational and behavioral inputs to analysis and decision making will prove to provide a better paradigm remains to be seen. Hopefully, we will not need another financial meltdown to answer that question.

Sources: The Economist (2009) Financial Economics: Efficiency and Beyond (July 18, 2009); *The Wall Street Journal* (2012) A Twist on "Quant" Trading: Weave in Analysts' Research (contributed by Jenny Strasburg, May 23, 2012).

Arguably, though, the criticism against strategic analysis has been misplaced. The fault really doesn't lie with analysis, but rather with its misguided application and the blind faith that many managers attach to it. Managers find comfort in numbers – anything "hard" to justify an important decision, even if the numbers are largely irrelevant. We need to remember that all frameworks are inherently flawed by virtue of their oversimplification of reality. Real environments are ambiguous and complex; as a rule, frameworks do not capture many attributes of real business environments. This realization does not render them useless, but it does have implications for how we use them. Moreover, not all frameworks are equally useful. A number of frameworks still in circulation are either long since obsolete, or else well on their way to obsolescence – though this doesn't appear to keep managers from still attempting to draw sense from them.

We argued earlier in this section that strategic analysis needs to be purposeful; by extension, the choice and application of frameworks of analysis need to serve the purpose of the analysis. Suitably selected and applied, frameworks of strategic analysis can shed light on a small part of the complex reality of the situation in question. When these perspectives are collectively integrated and appropriately aggregated, we begin to see a pattern emerging. This pattern, though incomplete, does provide an approximation of the bigger picture. This is the best we may achieve. However, when combined with informed intuition and skilled interpretation, even an approximation derived on this basis may be adequate for strategic decision making. The real skill in strategic analysis thus lies in (1) beginning with a clearly defined challenge and (2) deriving the "right" strategic questions, (3) in the choice and application of appropriate frameworks of analysis for sense making, and ultimately (4) in the integration and aggregation of the insights thereby generated towards reconstructing the firm's competitive reality in terms of a useful strategic landscape. The firm's competitors face the same challenge, of course. Hence, the real challenge in strategic analysis lies in the combined skill and speed with which the firm succeeds in "cutting to the chase" with regard to making sense of its competitive environment in a way that enables it to respond more quickly to change than its competitors.

Frameworks and models of strategic analysis can therefore help guide and support our thinking, but they will never replace it. Despite the abundance of frameworks in the management literature, relatively few suitably selected and properly applied can yield a lot of insight. This is not suggesting that we ignore the complexity of a business context. It is suggesting, however, that it is *how* we use frameworks and models that matters. And as argued earlier, most often the limitations are not even related to the frameworks *per se*, rather to the validity and reliability of the data on which assumptions derived from the analysis are based.

BOX 4.2 BEYOND THE "DIMON PRINCIPLE"

Not having access to validated and proven hard evidence is a reality often encountered in business. Insight-driven strategic analysis is challenging under these circumstances. Strategic decisions demand to be made nonetheless. Different industry sectors deal with this dilemma in different ways. Financial services appear to have been particularly prone to engaging in high risk ventures with a predilection that has been both naïve and surprisingly brash.

J.P. Morgan Chase, currently the US's largest bank by assets, emerged from the recent economic meltdown relatively unscathed. But it is now facing its own version of a corporate meltdown; it provides a prime example of the gullibility large established institutions can fall prey to. Initially waved off as a "tempest in a teapot" by its chief executive, James Dimon, its fiasco ended up as a $2 billion trading loss. In disclosing the news of the loss at a hastily organized news conference on May 10, 2012, Dimon furtively suggested that the trading that led to the fiasco had *"violated the Dimon principle."* He did not elaborate on the meaning of the "Dimon principle." Perhaps, just as well. If J.P. Morgan's dealings in the past are any indication, at stake may be its tendency to letting complex risk run unfettered, and not countering prevailing sector logic with arguments that might have challenged and disproved J.P. Morgan's own beliefs.

Richard Feynman, the Nobel Prize-winning physicist, formulated a simple alternative principle that Dimon would have been wise to heed: *"You must not fool yourself – and you are the easiest person to fool."* Closely associated with unchallenged assumptions is wishful thinking. In a commencement address delivered to a Caltech audience in 1974, Feynman made reference to the "cargo cult" of Pacific islanders, who believed that they could make airplanes bearing food and clothing land simply by lining up alongside makeshift airstrips as they had during the Second World War.

J.P. Morgan Chase and similar institutions deploying techniques such as the "value at risk," or VAR, technique that is used to estimate the potential vulnerabilities of their investment decision making are well advised to remember that *"the riskiest moment is when you are right,"* in the words of economist Peter Bernstein. British philosopher and social critic Bertrand Russell pointed out that *". . . the less evidence someone has that his ideas are right, the more vehemently he asserts that there is no doubt whatsoever that he is exactly right."* Fact of the matter is that we often do not have the evidence we require; but this demands all the more that we monitor ourselves for vehemence, possibly by applying a "pre-mortem" – a technique proposed by psychologist Gary Klein: (1) soliciting advice from people whose views you respect; (2) asking them to reflect critically by imagining looking back a year from now, on a disastrous investment you have made; (3) asking them to list all the possible causes leading to the failure. And finally, not forgetting "*. . . that the smarter you are, the more easily you can fool yourself.*"

Source: The Wall Street Journal (2012) Forget the Dimon Principle and Try the Feynman Rule (contributed by Jason Zweig, May 14, 2012).

The greatest benefit derived from using frameworks of analysis relates to the clarity they can contribute to the thinking process. Often it's not about the actual output of the analysis, rather the focus and structure the frameworks can bring to the debate on the topic at hand, for example around the boardroom table. Frameworks can help focus the discourse around the table. In such situations, even the simple act of bringing something to paper or the white board in a structured way can help immensely in channeling meaningful debate and moving the collective thinking forward in a unified direction.

Getting Started: Value and Stakeholders' Perspectives

In Chapter 1 we argued that the firm's reason for being revolves around its obligations for creating and capturing *value*; not just any value, but *unique* and *superior* value that sets it apart from its competitors. Hence, insight about the *value at stake* and its strategic relevance for the firm are critical and it therefore stands to reason that an exploration of the relevant value at stake in such an endeavor represents a logical point of departure for strategic sense making. Value manifests itself in many different configurations; some visible and measurable; other forms are largely perception based and more difficult to fathom. Moreover, firms do not create value simply for the sake of doing so; value created by firms has recipients – these are the firm's *stakeholders*. Any consideration of the value created by a firm therefore necessarily involves its stakeholders.

We begin by examining value offerings as bundles of value comprising individual value attributes. We then explore the competitive relevance of the values by introducing the notion of the *value premium* – which we define to be a measure of the competitive advantage achieved by a given value offering.

Value Creation

Value can take on a variety of configurations. Its expressions can range from highly tangible and measurable, to forms that are intangible and very difficult to measure. An example of tangible value might include visible ergonomic attributes of a product design feature such as the feel of a mobile phone in a user's hand, or a measurable quantity such as a dividend payout on a share. Intangible forms of value are perceived as such; they might include experiential attributes of a transaction such as a dining experience at a restaurant, or social benefits perceived by relevant (benefactor) stakeholders resulting from a charitable activity. Though not directly measurable, perceived value is no less important than quantifiable forms of value. Indeed, value delivered through services – regardless of sector – is a good example of intangible value.

Value offerings invariably present themselves as value bundles, whereby the bundle comprises individual value components comprising both tangible and intangible forms of value. For example, a value offering such as a smartphone represents a value bundle consisting of individual value components such as brand, technical functionality, price, user experience, design attributes (which might range from ergonomic to aesthetic), and so on, as indicated in the following equation format:

$$COMP_{VO} = aV_1 + bV_2 + cV_3 + dV_4 + \ldots$$

where $COMP_{VO}$ represents the composition of the value offering; V_i the individual value attributes such as brand (e.g. V_1), technical functionality (e.g. V_2), price (e.g. V_3), user experience (e.g. V_4), and so on; and coefficients a, b, c the weighting factors indicting the importance of the individual value attributes. Note that some of the value attributes represent tangible (and therefore measurable and quantifiable) forms of value (such as *technical functionality* and *price*) while others represent intangible and therefore subjective or perceived forms of value (such as *brand* and *user experience*).

The composition of the value offering, $COMP_{VO}$, is useful as a starting point. However, it doesn't say anything about the *competitiveness* of the value offering when compared to competitors' offerings. For this, we need to examine its competitive relevance, CR_{VO}, which we define to be a product of its uniqueness, U_{VO}, and superiority, S_{VO}:

$$CR_{VO} = U_{VO} \times S_{VO}$$

where CR_{VO} represents the competitive or strategic relevance of the value offering; U_{VO} it uniqueness (which might reflect the difficulty of its replication); and S_{VO} its superiority relative to alternative value offerings of competitors.

The value premium, VP_{VO}, achieved by any particular value offering is expressed by the product of its composition and competitive relevance:

$$VP_{VO} = CR_{VO} \times COMP_{VO}$$

This expression of the value premium reflects the degree of competitive differentiation achieved by an individual value offering. For example, one might think of the value premium Apple's iPhone has achieved in the smartphone market, measured, for example, by the global market share it has gained, or by the size of margins achieved relative to those of its competitors. This perspective is particularly relevant to one specific stakeholder segment – that of the potential customer looking to purchase an Apple iPhone.

However, Apple has other stakeholders as well, as much as it competes on a range of value offerings, of which its iPhone is only one. Apple's shareholders, its investors, constitute another group of Apple stakeholders. This stakeholder group would be primarily interested in $VP_{Portfolio}$, Apple's *corporate* value premium achieved across its *portfolio* of value offerings, which is represented by a summation of value premiums achieved by its individual, i.e. "*j*", *product families*:

$$VP_{Portfolio} = \sum_{j=1}^{n} [CR_{VO} \times COMP_{VO}]_j$$

This perspective reflects Apple's overall competitive performance and is comprised of a composite of the value premiums achieved in its various business areas.

Box 4.3 Microsoft – Unshackling the Shutters

Microsoft's Windows platform will no doubt go down in business history as an example of an extraordinarily shrewdly conceived value bundle. Microsoft's flagship operating system was the core of a tightly integrated bundle of programs with which the technology giant deliberately exerted its "velvet glove" dominance over desktop personal computer users for the better part of several decades. With its Office suite, Microsoft extended its domination into the business world with a bundle of software that included e-mail systems, databases, and other business applications. This formidable bundling propelled Microsoft to overtake IBM as most valuable technology company in the 1990s.

Microsoft was emphatically obsessed with strengthening its Windows platform. An incontestable law during the tenures of former CEOs Gates and Balmer, known internally as the "strategy tax," decreed that everything Microsoft did had to contribute to the strengthening of Windows' crushing dominance. Many of Microsoft's most brilliant innovations were culled because of its "strategy tax." For several decades, this approach appeared to work well for Microsoft – that is, if one disregards the slate of antitrust difficulties its drive for market domination got the company into.

Microsoft's stranglehold on the market has been steadily crumbling. To be sure, Microsoft Windows and Office are still generating a lot of cash, but their domination of the market is far from what it once was. Software is increasingly becoming a service delivered over the internet and open standards have spawned a multitude of competing vendors. Gone are the days when data resided solely in desktop computers. Data is now stored and number-crunched in the "cloud," and its users want to access it "on-the-go"; that is, via their mobile devices. Moreover, they don't want to pay for the software. "Freemium" business models based on open standards – the nemesis of Microsoft's proprietary Windows platform – introduced by rivals are luring away customers with dazzling new applications that better cater to the needs of people on the go.

Microsoft missed several pivotal opportunities along the way: ironically, the technology giant had early stakes in cloud computing, which it bungled. In the interest of protecting its existing product concept Microsoft chose to develop a cloud computing system (named Azure) that essentially replicated its bundle of proprietary programs. This left a gap for other cloud providers, foremost Amazon, to move in with cloud services offering raw computing power that could be run on a range of programs. Similarly, Microsoft was one of the first to recognize the potential of smartphones, but in this case it also chose to force users to use Windows on them rather than developing a more suitable operating system.

Notably, Microsoft's market share by operating systems in 2014 amounted to no more than 3%.

Microsoft's new boss, Nadella, has set a new course for the company; his key objective is to radically move the company from being a "Windows-only" company to one more closely resembling a global network of data centers that provide online services for individuals and businesses alike. As Microsoft celebrates its 40th anniversary this year, nagging questions remain about its future. In retrospective, one lesson it appears to have learned is that it was too protective, for too long, about a value bundle that gradually ceased to be one.

Sources: The Economist (2015) Microsoft at Middle Age: Opening Windows (April 4, 2015); Thomas, D. (2015) Smartphone Makers Battle for the Limelight, *Financial Times* (February 28, 2015).

Value Capture

In the previous section, we focused on value creation. The implicit presumption was that the firm enjoys the full benefit of the value it creates; in other words, a firm retains the full benefit of the value premium it succeeds in creating. That is not necessarily so. Firms do not necessarily appropriate all of the value they create. Therefore, a consideration of value created, alone, is not sufficient for ensuring a firm's competitiveness, no matter how competitively differentiated its value offering may be. Just as important as the amount of value created is the amount *retained* by the firm. The difference between value created and value captured has been referred to as *value slippage*.[2] Symbolically, the relationship between value captured, $V_{Captured}$, value created, $V_{Created}$, and value slippage, $V_{Slippage}$, can be expressed as:

$$V_{Captured} = V_{Created} - V_{Slippage}$$

Sources of value slippage typically lie in the firm's value chain and relate to the perceived bargaining relationship between the firm and its suppliers on the one hand, and its customers on the other.[3] Value capture, sometimes also referred to as *value appropriation*, allows for the fact that firms that create value in certain circumstances will either lose or be forced to share that value with other stakeholders' parties. These might include employees, competitors, or even society at large. Value slippage occurs if the firm creating value does not retain all of it. This typically occurs when *use value* (i.e. value perceived by recipient) is higher than the respective *exchange value* (what the recipient ends paying for that value). In other words, value slippage occurs when recipients extract greater value from the value offering than they end up paying for it.

Consider the following perhaps unconventional though nonetheless noteworthy case of value slippage that illustrates the point: Arthur Fry and Spencer Silver, the 3M chemists credited with the invention of the Post-it note, never did earn more than the obligatory non-monetary recognition customarily accorded inventors in US companies despite the approximately $1 billion their innovation still generates annually for 3M. This appears not to have been an issue with either inventor; the two innovators were simply complying with standard US patent convention and practice that generally limits any monetary gain to individuals contributing to an invention leading to commercial success. Notably, the situation is quite different in Europe, where under European patent law the right of a patent remains with its inventor.

The notion of value slippage, therefore, is by no means purely theoretical. Consider the current plight of many publishing companies. As more consumers than ever are accessing and demanding free content online, traditional revenue streams to its producers are dissipating. The so-called freemium model introduced by many online producers is an attempt to recapture at least some of the value created by the producers of online content.

The current tussle between Universal, the world's largest music company, and Spotify, a disruptor in the nascent music streaming sector, illustrates the challenge facing incumbents at a time of rapid change in the distribution of music. Spotify's freemium model, which caters to about 60 million users and 15 million paying subscribers, relies on attracting users to a free streaming service that offers a selection of music and some limited functionality. Its intent, however, is to convert these users to paying subscribers for future revenue streams. This has hurt traditional players such as Universal and Apple's iTunes, which have relied on revenues from digital downloads in the past. A reliable source of income for the past decade, digital downloads have since peaked and are in decline, while the explosive growth in music streaming driven by disruptors such as Spotify is irreversibly transforming the music industry landscape – and along with it, proven formulas for value capture.[4]

Even young, new-economy companies are not being spared. Facebook is clearly capable of creating value for its 1.3 billion users; yet as its highly volatile share price suggests, it is not at all clear that the company will succeed in capturing sufficient value to justify its colossal market capitalization and price-earnings ratio.[5]

Clearly, value slippage provides little incentive for a firm to continue creating value in the long run. Maximization of value capture is therefore a strategic imperative for firms. *Competition* and *isolation mechanisms* have been proposed as two key concepts for understanding the notion of value capture[2]:

- *Competition:* a consequence of increased competition is that the exchange value of the value offering will decrease to a point where supply equals demand. At this point, value created by the firm must be shared with its competitors, while end users (customers) benefit from the lower price resulting from increased competition. In effect, increased competition leads to a commoditization of the value offering, which is precisely the situation firms should seek to avoid.

- *Isolation mechanisms:* include any means by which the firm can endow its value offerings with uniqueness and superiority relative to alternative offerings by competitors. Uniqueness and superiority of the value offering, in turn, typically yield a situation of limited supply and high demand, which in turn results in increases in use value (as perceived by the end user) and exchange value (what the end user is prepared to pay). Increases in both use and exchange value therefore result in a higher value premium.

From a firm's perspective, therefore, value capture correlates with the value premium achieved by the firm. A firm that succeeds in maximizing appropriation of its value stands to achieve a proportionately high value premium. Conversely, a high degree of competition typically results in a high degree of value slippage. Customers are happy in this situation because increased competition typically leads to falling prices; however, the value appropriated by any individual player competing in that market is diminished accordingly.

There are notable exceptions to this generalization, however. The market success of Apple's iPhone 6 models is a case in point and exemplifies how an exceptional product offering in a maturing market can maintain a high level of value capture. The smartphone has long since evolved into a commodity offering; stiff competition from both established and new competitors and shrinking margins attest to that. Yet Apple, with its strategy of targeting customers willing to pay a premium for its products, achieved gross margins of 39.9% in its fiscal quarter ending in December 2014. This was thanks in large part to the success of its iPhone 6 and iPhone 6 Plus models, released in September 2014 and possibly set to become one of Apple's most popular smartphones. For comparison, Apple's close competitor, Samsung, achieved profit margins of only 7.5% in its last quarter of

2014.[6,7] Apple's current success notwithstanding, its notably low price-to-earnings ratio of about 15 reflects anxiety on the part of the investment community over how long the company will be able to sustain the anomaly.

Thus far our exploration of value created and captured has focused, at least implicitly, on value from an *economic* perspective, in which the outcome in terms of the value premium achieved is typically expressed in terms of profit margins. Although the strategic management literature tends to focus primarily on the economic and business perspective of value creation, it is a rather limiting view. Many organizations are not driven by the profit motive, yet are just as intent on, and successful at, creating value.

Organizations such as non-governmental organizations, so-called NGOs, charities, even governmental bodies, and agencies, have very clear mandates for creating value – which, in many instances, are arguably no less important than those of commercial enterprises. Quantifying and measuring that value, however, can be quite daunting. Some non-profit enterprises refer to their value outcomes in terms of *profit-equivalents*; expressions of value that may be as ethereal as a heightened sense of well-being, contentment, or security. To be sure, these may be very impactful value outcomes; any assessment of value appropriated by the enterprise responsible for their creation, however, is often highly elusive.

Stakeholders and their Positions

Stakeholders are recipients of the value offering created by the firm. We have also argued that the creation, capture, and delivery of value – ideally, uniquely superior – to its various stakeholders defines the core purpose of the firm. This can be a rather daunting challenge as various stakeholders' interests and expectations may clash; it demands deft handling of potentially conflicting interests on the part of the firm. In doing so, the firm's strategy needs to take account not only of the stakeholders' interests and needs, but also of their legitimacy and urgency of claim to value, and their power and influence. Influential stakeholder groups in the different sectors might include:

- *Business sector:* shareholders, employees, customers, suppliers, competitors, business analysts, local and national government, some pressure groups, and industry regulators;
- *Public sector:* political parties, civil service, local authorities, employees, the general public and constituents, business lobbies, pressure groups, and the media;
- *Not-for-profit sector:* members, patrons, donors, charities commissions, beneficiaries, employees and unpaid workers, pressure groups, the media, and others competing for funding;
- *Society at large:* citizens, special interest groups, and activist groups.

Particular stakeholder groups may remain passive and virtually ignored by an organization for substantial periods of time, only to start flexing their muscles in response to particular critical incidents such as changes in ownership, performance issues, strategy, terms and conditions of employment, location, or environmental policies, for example.

Stakeholders can be viewed from a variety of perspectives. A simple view takes stakeholders' needs, interests, and power to influence decision making into consideration. Key stakeholders are those with acute needs and who are prone to exert a high degree of power over decision making. This group needs to be carefully monitored and managed at all times.

BOX 4.4 ETSY'S PUBLIC OFFERING

The ongoing debate on the purpose of the enterprise was touched on earlier in this book (Chapter 1, Box 1.1). Etsy, the online craft bazaar born in a Brooklyn loft as a platform for peddling handmade wooden articles, recently rekindled the debate. Etsy's "going public" in April 2015 has given new impetus, in particular, to the discourse on corporations' value creation mandate. Etsy is an unusual corporation; it is a certified *Benefit Corporation* – a so-called B Corp – and one of a growing number of companies that has pledged to uphold social and environmental obligations set by a non-profit organization called B Lab. Etsy is only the second for-profit enterprise of more than 1000 B Corp companies to go public. Its move to go public is ultimately a test of Wall Street's willingness to adapt to changes in investor attitudes regarding the profit motive. A growing number of business leaders and investors are seeking ways of making money while making a difference – a difference that goes beyond the current shareholder model focused purely on profit maximization. Noble though its higher cause may appear, Etsy's challenge will be to balance multiple stakeholders' demands; it will face demands from those who think not enough social objectives are being fulfilled as well as from those who think too many are being accomplished.

Source: Tabuchi, H. (2015) As Etsy Goes Public, its Pledge to do Good will be Tested, *International New York Times* (April 18/19 2015).

Stakeholders' positions are not stagnant, they evolve. Stakeholders that at one time may not have been in a position of power despite a high level of interest and needs may migrate into positions of power. A case in point is the environmental lobby that has gained in importance in recent years. Hence, we are well advised to monitor all stakeholders relevant to our business.

Mitchell *et al.*[8] extend this simple two-dimensional perspective on stakeholders to three stakeholder dimensions: power to influence, urgency of claim, and legitimacy of claim. Their framework identifies those individuals or groups that share all three as the *definitive stakeholders*. However, a number of other combinations invoke only one or two of the three dimensions, so that a total of seven possible stakeholder positions emerge from these authors' proposed model. Firms are well advised to take all perspectives into account, and to continually monitor the various stakeholder groups as they evolve over time.

In recent years there has been increasing activism from certain shareholder groups such as environmentalists, equal opportunities groups, political activists, and religious and other pressure groups. All can at some point in time have a direct or indirect impact on the firm's strategy. It is important to remember that the firm's stakeholders, as recipients of the value created by the firm, are intrinsically linked to its *raison d'être*. Hence, one important output from strategic analysis is a better understanding of the implications of its stakeholders' needs and expectations for the firm's strategy.

High-Level and Supporting-Level Strategic Analysis

How does one most effectively approach setting up a strategic analysis? Where does one begin? How does one avoid "losing sight of the wood for the trees"? In this section we examine a typology for frameworks of strategic analysis that addresses these questions (Figure 4.2). The typology structures frameworks into two levels of analysis. The first, a *high-level* analysis, provides a view of the "bigger picture" that integrates both external and internal factors; importantly, it does so in the context of the specific value offering that is at the core of the strategic challenge that prompted the analysis at the outset. In doing so, the high-level perspective focuses the strategic analysis on the core strategic consideration at stake – that of creating and delivering a unique and superior value offering to its relevant stakeholders. Moreover, this level of analysis probes the strategic boundaries of the opportunity space representing the firm's competitive position and thereby offers a powerful means of structuring the thinking of the analysis around the core of the strategic challenge in question.

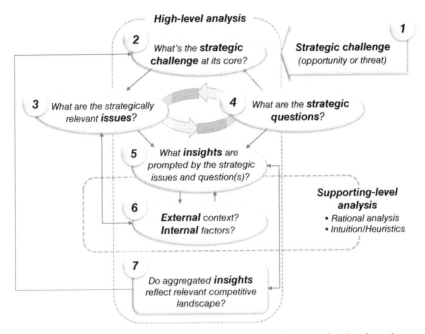

Figure 4.2 Insight-driven strategic analysis: high- and supporting-level analyses

We examine two high-level frameworks of analysis – the *value proposition* and the *unique competing space* frameworks in Chapter 5.

The supporting level of analysis draws on frameworks of analysis that selectively provide depth of analysis on either external or internal factors. Supporting-level frameworks of analysis can provide useful *contextual* insight – insight on either external competitive contexts or internal firm contexts that reflect the organization's basis of competitiveness. Examples include the *key success factor analysis, industry maturity analysis,* and the *strategic resources audit and analysis.*

The two levels of strategic analysis are not interchangeable. Both serve a specific purpose in the strategic thinking process that underpins the strategic analysis. Strategic analysis begins with a scoping of the strategic challenge on the basis of a high-level analysis. Strategic issues and questions derived from these lead to the derivation of relevant insights to be generated. It is only at this point that the supporting level of analysis is invoked – to support the generation of insights relevant to the strategic challenge.

Students and managers most often encounter difficulties when they attempt to delve straight into a supporting-level analysis rather than systematically approaching the analysis from a strategic thinking perspective.

Setting Up and Conducting a Strategic Analysis

It has been said that many roads lead to Rome. Nonetheless, not all are recommendable; some roads may, indeed, keep you from getting there at all. Similarly, there are numerous conceivable approaches to strategic analysis. Not all, however, lead to useful insight, and there are those that as often as not lead astray. On the other hand, there are also those approaches that "cut to the chase" and thereby leave less room for straying from the task at hand. The general approach shown in Figure 4.2 is congruent with the latter case; it identifies key steps and the questions that need to be addressed at the various stages of the analysis.

The first step (with reference to Figure 4.2) in conducting a strategic analysis consists of identifying and scrutinizing the problem (which might be an opportunity or challenge) for potential strategic impact and relevance. It is important at this point to ensure that the problem (or challenge) is indeed strategically relevant and that its resolution is worth pursuing; that it, indeed, justifies the effort that is to be spent on it.

The second step is an extension of the first step. Its purpose is to probe the strategic relevance of the challenge to be analyzed and to establish its link to the firm's competitive position; its relevance to the value offering at stake. The third and fourth steps are iterative; their purpose is to frame the issues and, ultimately, the strategic question (or questions) that are to be explored in the analysis. Both the articulation of strategic questions and the framing of issues analysis have been dealt with in Chapter 2. For the purpose of strategic analysis a broad clustering of issues, for example, in matters relating to the external competitive context and those relating to the firm's internal basis of competitiveness, can be helpful in achieving some degree of structure already at this stage of the analysis. Generally, strategic questions emerge from a convergence of associated issues. Step five builds the outcomes of the issues framing and articulation of the strategic questions: issues and questions prompt insights. Insight, we argued in Chapter 3, is a key input into sense making. The foregoing issues analysis throws open questions that prompt insight. Not all questions can be answered – and this for various possible reasons.

Competitive environments, we have argued in earlier chapters, are ambiguous and complex; potentially critical insights are often not available or accessible. Hence, an important part of this step is to determine which insights are required, which are available, and possible implications for the strategic analysis arising from those insights not available. Insights are generated through application of appropriate supporting-level frameworks of strategic analysis that focus on either the external or internal contexts (step 6). The nature of the insights required determines which frameworks are selected and where the emphasis of the analysis is to be – whether on external or internal factors. At an advanced level of analysis the objective is to achieve a high level of integration between the various frameworks used in the analysis. We will examine how this is done in Chapter 6. Finally, in the seventh and last step of the analysis process, insights are aggregated and integrated in a way that enables the reconstruction of the bigger picture relevant to the strategic challenge at hand. As we have argued in earlier chapters, real competitive contexts are ambiguous, fluid, and continually changing. Hence, we will never get the "complete" picture; however, if astutely conducted the strategic analysis can provide us with a sufficiently "realistic" assessment of the strategic context relevant to the challenge at stake to enable appropriate decision making.

Subsequent Chapters 5 and 6 elaborate on the high-level and supporting-level frameworks of analysis, respectively.

STRATEGY IN PRACTICE: SIMPLE STEPS IN SETTING UP AN INSIGHT-DRIVEN STRATEGIC ANALYSIS

1. Starting with a relevant strategic challenge . . .
   - What is the challenge – is it a problem to be resolved, an opportunity to be captured, a threat to be countered?
   - Why is it a problem – and for whom?
   - What would be the consequence of simply ignoring it; would this have a substantial bottom-line impact on the business?
   - How does it manifest itself?
   - Who are the stakeholders who stand to gain (or lose) by its resolution (or failure to achieve resolution)?
   - How will its resolution make any difference to the competitive position of the firm; what is the expected impact?
2. Scoping the strategic dimension of the challenge . . .
   - What is the strategic element at the core of the challenge?
   - What makes it "strategic," as opposed to "operational"?
   - How does it relate to the firm's competitive position; its ability to defend or create a uniquely superior value offering?
   - What is its potential strategic impact (temporal, spatial, etc.)?
3. Framing the strategic issues . . .
   - What are the strategic issues associated with the strategic challenge?

- What makes them "strategic"; how do they relate to the strategic challenge at stake?
- How are these linked?
- How might issues be clustered in a meaningful way (e.g. those related to the external; those related to internal factors)?

4. Articulating the strategic questions . . .
   - What are the (relatively few) questions that emerge from the issues; and how do these relate to the core of the strategic challenge at stake?
   - How (and why) will resolution of these make any difference to the challenge at hand?

5. Identifying the insights prompted by the strategic questions . . .
   - What insights are prompted by the strategic questions?
   - Does the issues analysis enable a broad clustering of insights – and how might this structuring of insights contribute to a better understanding of the issues related to the challenge at stake?
   - Which insights are potentially important but cannot be accessed or generated?

6. Extricating the insights: external and internal contexts . . .
   - What are the external and internal factors relevant to the strategic challenge – which insights can be extricated from these factors?
   - Which are the appropriate frameworks of analysis and what insights do these contribute to the analysis?
   - Which factors are linked; how might an integration of insights derived from appropriate frameworks of analysis contribute to a better understanding of the strategic challenge

7. Consolidating and aggregating the insights . . .
   - How valid and reliable is the competitive landscape that emerges from the analysis?
   - Is it relevant to the strategic challenge that prompted the analysis in the first place?
   - What parts are missing; how critical are the missing pieces?

- What potentially important insights are missing or simply not accessible?
- What are the implications and the potential impact of the missing insight(s) for strategic decision making?
- Do the aggregated insights reflect the competitive landscape of the relevant strategic challenge?

SUMMARIZING THE CHAPTER . . .

- Strategic analysis is an integral element of strategic thinking and supports the creation of insight.
- Given the centrality of value – its creation, delivery, and capture – to the firm's core purpose, strategic analysis necessarily begins with a good understanding of the value at stake and its potential recipients, the firm's stakeholders.
- Strategic analysis, supported by appropriate frameworks, models, and strategic thinking, then sets out to explore the greater context, external and internal, relevant to the firm's creation and capture of that differentiating value.
- The application of frameworks of strategic analysis needs to be purposeful; their use is prompted by the insights derived from strategic issues framing and the derivation of strategic questions.
- Frameworks of analysis are limited by their inherent oversimplification of reality, assumptions of rationality, and the validity and reliability of the data available.
- A few, relatively simple frameworks appropriately applied and integrated can generate a disproportionate amount of useful insight.
- Often the greatest value generated by the application of frameworks of strategic analysis lies not so much in their specific outputs, but rather in the focus and structure they can contribute to the thinking and dialogue around the boardroom table.

Notes

1. Eisenhardt, K.M. and Martin, J.A. (2000) Dynamic Capabilities: What are They? *Strategic Management Journal*, Vol. 21, pp. 1105–1121.
2. Lepak, D.P., Smith, K.G. and Taylor, M.S. (2007) Value Creation and Value Capture: A Multilevel Perspective, *Academy of Management Review*, Vol. 32, No. 1, pp. 180–194.
3. Bowman, C. and Ambrosini, V. (2000) Value Creation versus Value Capture: Towards a Coherent Definition of Value in Strategy, *British Journal of Management*, Vol. 11, pp. 1–15.
4. Garrahan, M., Ahmed, M. and Cookson, R. (2015) Universal Presses Spotify to Change Model, *The Financial Times* (March 21/22, 2015).
5. Michel, S. (2015) Innovation Isn't Worth Much if You Don't Get Paid for It, *Harvard Business Review*, October 2014, pp. 70–85.
6. Cheng, J. and Lee, M.-J. (2015) Apple Challenges Samsung's Lead, *The Wall Street Journal*, Vol. 32, No. 254 (January 30–February 1, 2015).
7. Stewart, J.B. (2015) How Apple Overtook a Behemoth, *International New York Times* (January 31–February 1, 2015).
8. Mitchell, R.K., Agle, B.R. and Wood, D.J. (1997) Toward a Theory of Stakeholder Identification and Salience: Defining the Principle of Who and What Really Counts, *Academy of Management Review*, Vol. 22, No. 4, pp. 853–886.

CHAPTER 5

High-Level, "Big-Picture" Strategic Analysis

If you can't explain it simply, you don't understand it well enough.

—Albert Einstein

IN THIS CHAPTER, WE:

- examine the purpose and role of high-level strategic analysis in strategic sense making;
- introduce two high-level frameworks of strategic analysis – the *value proposition* and *unique competing space* frameworks – and discuss their application toward generating strategically relevant insight;
- examine how these high-level frameworks can guide the overall strategic process through aggregation and integration of a number of individual approaches, models, and frameworks;

- close with a final analysis framework, the *opportunity–response* framework, which addresses the "when?" question related to strategic scheduling.

The purpose of high-level, big-picture strategic analysis is to probe and, ultimately, to provide a "big-picture" mapping of the firm's strategic position in its greater competitive context. Good strategic analysis is purpose driven; high-level analysis therefore necessarily aligns with the context of a specific strategic challenge. A "big-picture" analysis encompasses three fundamental elements and brings these into juxtaposition: (1) the strategic *value at stake* – i.e. the value consideration at the core of the strategic challenge in question; (2) the firm's external competitive context relevant to that challenge; and (3) the firm's internal competitive context relevant to the strategic challenge. Central to the firm's strategic position is its ability and disposition to create and deliver a uniquely superior *value offering* to its relevant stakeholders; high-level, "big-picture" analysis provides a mapping of the firm's relevant context within which that occurs.

In this chapter we introduce two high-level, "big-picture" concepts and their associated frameworks of strategic analysis – the *value proposition* framework and the *unique competing space* framework. The two frameworks are complementary; and, importantly, both high-level frameworks converge on an expression of the value offering that is at the core of a particular strategic challenge that has prompted their use. Moreover, as high-level analyses, the value proposition and unique competing space approaches are comprehensive; they ultimately collate and integrate a number of supporting frameworks of strategic analysis – and, importantly, they bring these into the context of the core strategic consideration at stake.

The power of high-level analysis derives from the structured guidance it contributes to the strategic thinking process. Appropriately applied high-level analysis helps guide the sense making process from its inception through to the piecing together of a reconstructed "big-picture" view of the company's competitive landscape. This level of analysis focuses attention on the essential elements of an organization's competitiveness. This might be its relative position to where opportunities for value creation and delivery exist, its current competitive position in delivering that value, or an indication of the strategic direction required to achieve that objective.

Toward that end, the high-level strategic analysis addresses the firm's salient strategic questions – the "where" do we want to compete; "how" do we want to compete; the "what" in terms of value offering at the core of the strategic differentiation; and the "why" do we want to compete at all.

We close the chapter with an examination of a third framework, the *opportunity–response* framework, which while not explicitly focusing the "what" does address the time dimension, that is, the "when" question.

The Strategic Value Imperative

Strategy we have argued earlier is about *winning*. Firms compete by differentiating themselves from their competitors in the way in which they create, deliver, and capture value from their value offering. The notion of value and the notion of value delivery to the firm's stakeholders were explored in Chapter 4. Firms "win" by creating and delivering a uniquely superior value offering to their stakeholders – and maximizing their appropriation of that value created. This is the firm's strategic value imperative. As we might imagine, the firm's stakeholders may represent a diverse group of people and constituents; their expectations of the value to be delivered may be equally diverse; these may range from highly tangible returns (such as a dividend on stock held by a shareholder) to highly intangible expectations (such as customer experience in a services transaction). The latter form, though difficult to quantify, is no less important than the former measurable form of value. The growth of the services sector, for example, has led to an increasing emphasis on intangible forms of value. Whatever its form, we argued in the previous chapter that it is the creation and delivery of a superior value offering to its stakeholders that comprises the core purpose of the firm – and that this confers on the notion of value a central position in strategy. It therefore follows logically that the notion of value is central to the two high-level, "big-picture" strategic analyses that are examined in this chapter.

Value Proposition Concept, Framework, and Analysis

The notion of the value proposition as a formal concept is a relatively recent development in the field of strategic management. This is not to suggest, however, that successful firms have not understood and put into practice its basic tenets in the past. Strategy thinkers such as Peter F. Drucker,[1] Gary Hamel, and C.K. Prahalad[2] laid the early groundwork for the formalized concept of the value proposition in their writings in the early 1990s. Drucker's classic *Harvard Business Review* article "The Theory of Business" is especially insightful. It derives the firm's theory of business in terms of three input elements. These take the form of basic assumptions regarding the firm's (1) *external competitive environment*, (2) *internal basis of competitiveness*, and (3) *core purpose* and *aspirations*. The role of managers is to continually challenge the firm's assumptions in these three areas. He argues further that together these assumptions form the basis of the firm's *strategic intent*. Drucker's *theory of business* correlates closely with what we now refer to as the value proposition. The value proposition finds its articulation in the strategic intent – which in its simplest form is an expression of the firm's unique and superior value offering.

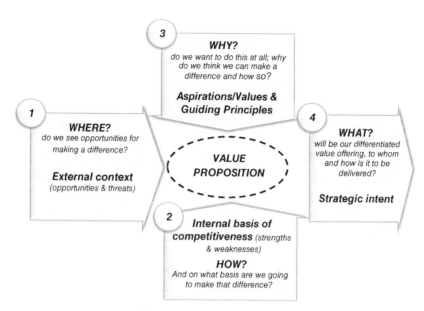

Figure 5.1 Value proposition concept and framework

The value proposition is insightful not only as a strategy concept. It also provides the basis for a powerful high-level framework of strategic analysis. The elements of the value proposition framework derived from the concept are presented schematically in Figure 5.1.

The value proposition framework presented schematically in Figure 5.1 indicates the three basic input elements in Drucker's theory of business; these are overlaid with the questions "where?," "how?," and "why?" in respect of a firm's engaging in business. These culminate in the "what?," which as an expression of the value proposition is an articulation of the firm's strategic intent.

1. Where (Are the Opportunities for Value Creation and Possible Threats to Our Ability to Do So)?

The first of the inputs to the value proposition focuses on assumptions regarding the "where?" question. These probe the external competitive environment of the firm. The "where?" element challenges the firm's assumptions regarding where in its external competitive environment it sees opportunities for creating and delivering a unique and differentiated value offering – and how these opportunities might be changing. External competitive environments represent not only opportunities, they can also harbor threats to the firm's competitive position; hence, this element also probes where and wherein these might lie, and possible implications for the firm. The external competitive environment of the firm can be structured in several levels. First, there is the *macro-economic* level that includes societal, political, and technological factors; sometimes these are referred to as the PEST factors (political, economic, societal, and technological). These global factors affect all industries and markets, though in different ways. Subordinate to the macro-level factors we can position the *industry* or *sector* level of analysis. This level of analysis focuses on attributes of the industry the firm in question competes in. Industries can be further segmented into markets (e.g. the automotive industry can be segmented into markets such as compact vehicles, mid-sized vehicles, and luxury vehicles). The *market* level of analysis focuses on making sense of the specific market attributes in which the firm competes. The "where?" element reflects two of the strategy building blocks introduced in Chapter 1 (see Box 1.1): the first building block representing the firm's external competitive environment and the third, which addresses the firm's stakeholders' needs.

2. How (Are We Going to Create and Deliver the Value Offering)?

The second input component of the value proposition, the "how?" question, focuses on the *internal basis of competitiveness*; it challenges the firm's assumptions regarding what it needs to excel at in order to create and deliver a uniquely superior value offering. Hence, it probes the firm's ability to create and deliver a superior value offering to its stakeholders. These assumptions address primarily the firm's resources and capabilities and the firm's *uniqueness* and *superiority* in the way it combines, reconfigures, and exploits these towards creating a uniquely differentiated value offering. By extension, the "how?" question also addresses the firm's organizational context; its structure, processes, practices, and ability to align these effectively. In the broadest sense, the "how?" question probes the firm's strengths and weaknesses; how these might be changing, and possible competitive implications for the firm. This element of the value proposition corresponds to the second building block of strategy (Box 1.1).

3. Why (Are We Doing this At All)?

The third and final constituent to the value proposition, the "why?" question, probes assumptions regarding the firm's *aspirations*, its *guiding principles*, and *values.* It challenges the firm's assumption regarding what it considers to be meaningful results, how it envisions making a difference through its value offering, and its motivations for doing so.

The "why?" element delivers the rationale that underpins the firm's "how?". It probes the organization's intrinsic disposition towards creating value. It captures the firm's passion, its aspirations as an organization, and collective sense of higher purpose related to the task at hand. Closely associated with the firm's "why?" is its sense of identity, which in turn reflects its collective mindset and paradigm. This element of the firm's value proposition is the most subtle one and, arguably, also the slowest to change. External contexts addressed by the "where?" question can change very rapidly; internal contexts captured by the "how?" also change, though generally less rapidly due to organizational inertia. However, organizations normally don't change their aspirations and guiding principles on a whim. They can change; however, the change typically occurs over a longer period – in some cases even years. Firms such as Intel (from memory chips to microprocessors), IBM (from mainframe computers to personal computers to services), and Nokia (from forest products to telecommunications) are examples of firms that have experienced fundamental transitions in their conception of why they are in business.

Together, the three inputs converge on the fourth element in the value proposition framework (element "4" in Figure 5.1) as an output; the firm's strategic intent.

4. What (Is Our Differentiated (Uniquely Superior) Value Offering)?

The "what?" question captures the firm's *strategic* aspirations and its fundamental competitive orientation. It says as much about where the firm will focus its efforts as it does about where it will *not* focus effort.[2] The "what?" question embodies the firm's articulation of its value proposition; it is the expression of its *strategic intent.* The strategic intent captures the essence of a firm's strategic aspirations by collating the firm's assumptions regarding the where, how, and why relevant to the firm's differentiated value offering. Moreover, the strategic intent introduces an element of *stretch* to the firm's value proposition by recognizing that there may be a gap between the firm's current reality (its current ability to fulfill its value proposition) and what it aspires to achieve. In doing so, the strategic intent continually challenges the organization's current reality with what it aspires to be and to achieve.

The strategic intent also addresses the mode and format in which the differentiated value the firm creates is delivered. The mode in which a firm creates its value offering and the format in which the firm delivers it relates to its *value disciplines.* Treacy and Wiersema[3] propose that value disciplines can take on one of three possible dimensions – *operational excellence, product leadership,* and *customer intimacy.* Although this is changing due to shifting industry boundaries, the value discipline a firm focuses on still largely depends on the industry and the nature of competition in that industry in which it chooses to compete. Operational excellence is typically associated with mature or commodities-based industries in which cost pressure demands focus on reduction of operating cost. Product leadership pertains mainly to industries focusing on high value-added markets such as luxury goods and bespoke product/service offerings, in which innovation, brand, and value attributes other than price provide potential for sizable margins. Customer intimacy is characteristically the focus of the value discipline in the service industries. In these, the value exchange takes place in a transaction involving a relational component. Management thinking on the notion of value disciplines has evolved since its introduction. Most managers today recognize that a value offering most probably does not necessarily fall neatly into any single value discipline. Despite increasingly blurring boundaries in many industries, firms for the most part are yet defined by their industry. A firm's industry assignation provides an initial orientation with respect to its primary value discipline; increasingly, however, competitive differentiation is derived from the firm's ability to pull together a differentiated value offering that spans all three value disciplines.

Box 5.1 Lego – Playing Seriously

Lego's growth trajectory over the past 10 years has been nothing short of spectacular. Over that period, its sales have quadrupled. In the course of last year alone, the Danish company edged aside Mattel to become the world's leading toy manufacturer and surpassed Ferrari as the world's most powerful brand in the rankings of Brand Finance.

Given that it makes what is essentially a commodity, Lego's success is all the more remarkable. A deconstruction of its value proposition offers some telling clues . . .

First, beginning with the easy part: Lego's basis of competitiveness is firmly supported by what is probably the world's most efficient operating model. The company's extraordinarily high 34% operating margin in 2014 attests to that. Its logistics are unmatched by competitors.

Second, and not quite so well known, is how the company approaches its markets through its serious study of play. The company's name Lego is an abbreviation of the Danish term *leg godt*, which means "play well"; understanding what that means has been the company's core obsession. Lego deploys cutting-edge ethnographic techniques that help build an understanding of how children play in their natural environment as it delves into the question of *why* children play. This includes observing children's brains under MRI while they play with various toys. However, Lego is not leaving it at that. The company has a far more ambitious goal: it aims to understand the greater social context of children's cultures. Lego's unparalleled focus and research have yielded unique insights on what is important to children and how to create meaningful experiences for them.

Third, Lego's ethos, in many ways, is aptly captured by its "joy of building, and the pride of creation," coupled with a view of the world in which imagination rules; a world in which one need not necessarily follow the instructions, build exactly to plan, and keep everything in its completed form.

Lego posted impressive results in 2014: a rise in total sales by 13%, and a surge in profits by 15% to a record $829 million. If nothing else, these results attest to Lego's ability to deliver on its own credo of "playing well."

Source: Rasmussen, M. (2015) Lego's Serious Play, *Strategy + Business* (March 26, 2015).

Unique Competing Space Framework and Analysis

One thing that sets industry leaders apart from less successful competitors is how they approach their strategy. They do not leave it to chance. Competitive advantage, when achieved, is invariably an outcome of deliberate effort. Firms that succeed in gaining competitive advantage continually strive to achieve clarity with regard to their competitive position, difficult as this might be in real business contexts. They seek to understand the determinants of their unique window of opportunity for creating value – their *unique competing space*, and they continually monitor the *boundaries* of their unique competing space as their competitive context evolves. This enables them to pre-emptively take appropriate strategic action when this is called for.

How might we better understand the firm's unique window of opportunity on creating and delivering value? What is the firm's unique competing space and what are its strategic boundaries? Why are they so critical? How can a better understanding of these help in identifying ways of achieving competitive advantage? These are the questions we address in this section.

The Firm's "Unique Competing Space"

A firm's competitive position can be viewed in various ways. It can be a competitive stance; for example, the firm's position in relation to competitors. Alternatively, it can be the firm's domain within which it is advantageously positioned to create and deliver a unique value offering. Recent management thinking is focusing on this latter perspective. Collis and Montgomery[4] refer to the firm's opportunity space for creating a uniquely differentiated value offering as a "strategic sweet spot"; the competitive domain in which the company succeeds in meeting customer needs in a way that rivals can't. The domain in question, however, is clearly not one dimensional. Rather, it displays spatial character;

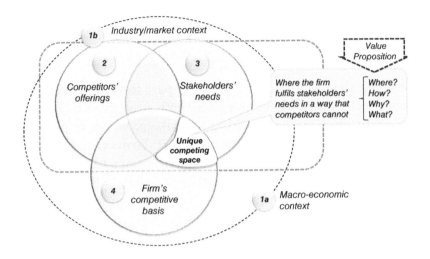

Figure 5.2 The firm's unique competing space

therefore, this domain is more correctly viewed as a space. We refer to it as the firm's "unique competing space" in this book. The spatial character of the domain in question, shown in Figure 5.2 as a shield-like space straddling the spheres labeled "3" and "4," has very important strategic implications; it is bounded by three interfaces representing the competitive boundaries of the firm, each of which will be explored in greater detail further on in this section.

Semantics aside, the conceptual notion underpinning the domain in question is powerful. The firm's unique competing space indicates where the firm creates and delivers a value offering in response to customers' needs in a way that competitors cannot. The unique competing space thus portrays the firm's competitive domain; whereby the value proposition substantiates the essence of the unique and superior value offering suggested by that domain. It is the strategic mandate of the firm to *establish*, *defend*, and *grow* this domain. Strategic challenges, when they arise, inevitably relate to the firm's ability and disposition to do so. Threat-driven strategic challenges invoke defensive responses whereas opportunity-driven challenges invoke response targeting expansion of the unique competing space. "Strategic" challenges facing the firm are indeed strategic if their anticipated potential impact on the firm's unique competing space is substantial.

The conceptual rationale underpinning the firm's unique competing space rests on multiple clusters. Three of the clusters (*competitors' offerings, stakeholders' needs,* and *firm's competitive basis*), shown by spheres labeled "2," "3," and "4" in Figure 5.2, respectively, are interlocked in a relationship depicted by a Venn diagram. These three clusters are enclosed by perimeters representing the firm's macro-economic ("1a") and industry/market environment ("1b"), respectively.

The firm's unique competing space provides a lens on the component elements of its strategy relevant to the particular value at stake. It brings into alignment, for example, what sets the firm's value offering apart from what competitors have on offer; the needs of its stakeholders, and how the firm mobilizes its resources to create the value offering at stake.

Box 5.2 Novo Nordisk's Unique Competing Space

Novo Nordisk is unique among pharmaceutical manufacturers today. While bigger rivals have sought to restructure through mergers and acquisitions Novo Nordisk has largely stayed its course. The Danish company is in the business of producing drugs that treat diabetes; it is already the world's biggest maker of insulin.

The potential competing space is lucrative. Few diseases hold greater promise for returns in the coming years. Diabetes, a chronic condition requiring lifetime treatment, currently afflicts some 180 million people worldwide. The World Health Organization estimates that number to double by the year 2030. A number of factors are contributing to this: an aging population and a rising incidence of obesity in the rich top the list. Novo Nordisk has been investing effort in finding new treatments for type 2 diabetes, a condition that develops in adulthood when overweight people become desensitized to the insulin the body produces naturally. This is also the most prevalent form of the disease. Insulin, being a natural product, is not patented. However, drugs that stimulate its natural production in the body can be patented. This, and in the area of more effective insulin formulations, is where Novo Nordisk sees its unique competing space. The company is currently well on track to getting its insulin Tresiba approved by US regulators, well ahead of schedule. This development would underpin Novo Nordisk's medium-term target of 15% growth in operating profit.

Evidence of the Danish insulin producer's unique competing position is borne out by its 70% plus premium to the European large-cap pharmaceuticals sector on a price-earnings basis over the past five years. As diabetes becomes more common, its diagnosis and treatment progress, Novo Nordisk unique competing space is firmly established.

Sources: The Financial Times (2009) *The Lex Column* (Friday, October 30, 2009); Thomas, H. (2015) Novo Nordisk's Insulin Move Is Right Medicine, *The Wall Street Journal* (March 27, 2015).

The Firm's Macro-Economic and Industry/Market Environment

The *macro-economic environment* indicated by the ellipse encircling the three interlocked circles (indicated as "1a" in Figure 5.2) comprises all those factors in the firm's macro-environment that are of relevance to its competitive position. These include the firm's political, economic, societal, technological, regulatory, and environmental factors; they correspond to the macro-level factors discussed in the context of the value proposition in the previous section. A secondary external environment represented by the rectangular boxed region ("1b") narrows the focus of the external perspective to the firm's industry and market level. It is important to remember that factors representing the firm's external competitive context, on whatever level, cannot be influenced by any individual firm.

Competitors and Their Competing Offering

The cluster in Figure 5.2 representing the *competitors' offerings* ("2") narrows the focus of the analysis to the firm's competitors. In this cluster we find all those industry and market players who, alongside the firm, are vying to fulfill the value needs of customers in the relevant market. The constitution of the group representing the firm's competitors may be diverse; invariably, we may find established players as well as new entrants and emerging competitors. In the central domain formed by the overlapping of all three circles we find all competitors who find themselves in a position to fulfill customers' current needs to some degree. Needless to point out, this is a hotly contested space. Analyses that provide insight on competitors' abilities and activities, and the nature of competition provided, are of relevance in this space. As in the case of the macro-economic analysis, snap-shot analyses are useful; trend analyses provide more powerful insights.

Stakeholders and Their Needs

Stakeholders' needs are represented by the sphere labeled "3" in Figure 5.2. This sphere represents the greater community of stakeholders. Stakeholders might include the firm's customers, suppliers, investors, and relevant regulatory authorities. In a public sector context stakeholders typically include beneficiaries and constituents. Generally, whether customers or stakeholders in the broader sense, this group represents the recipients and consumers of the value created and delivered by the firm and potentially its competitors. Critical insights for the firm include: Who are the stakeholders? What are their needs? How are these changing? The identity of stakeholders is not always clear; their needs often not entirely clear. Stakeholders – customers being a case in point – at times don't really understand their own needs and how these are changing. Hence, it is important for the firm to be close to its stakeholders, to anticipate their needs when these emerge and to be agile in responding to these.

The Firm and its Basis of Competitiveness

The lower sphere ("4") in the Venn diagram shown in Figure 5.2 representing the firm's *competitive basis* encompasses not only its resources (physical and financial) and capabilities (representing its intellectual capital), but also the greater organizational context embodying the firm's structure, processes, practices, culture, and leadership. Therefore, this circle represents the basis on which the firm competes, its competitive *wherewithal*. The perspective prompted by this representation of the firm's competitive position prompts a critical premise: the fact that the firm possesses resources and capabilities does not necessarily mean that it is successful in exploiting these in a way that makes them relevant to its unique competing space, that is, in a way that enables the firm to derive competitive advantage from them. In order for this to be the case the firm must ensure that it succeeds in transferring its resources, capabilities, and practices across the interface representing the unique competing space. We will explore this very important implication in greater detail further on in this chapter.

Box 5.3 SIMPLICITY AND THE BEAST

Management scholars have long pondered over the trade-off between simplification of complex contexts and the consequences associated with the potential loss of contextual specificity. The increasing complexity of business environments has added urgency to the question. More often, businesses deal with complex competitive contexts by introducing ever more complexity to their internal business routines. This introduces ever more inertia to the organization's ability to react swiftly to external change. The business rationale behind simplifying internal complexity therefore is compelling. Businesses have a natural tendency to become more complex, not less. "Simplifying and repeating" is a basic tenet argued by management thinkers Zook and Allen in their recent book *Repeatability*. Complexity, they argue, is the silent killer of modern business. Successful companies, the authors argue, share the following three virtues: (1) they focus on a highly distinctive core business; (2) they keep their business model as simple as possible; and finally (3) they relentlessly pursue new opportunities to replicate this model.

Companies cited by the authors adhering to these virtues include IKEA, McDonald's, Lego, and Apple. One might argue that the virtues proposed by Zook and Allen, indeed, encompass key enhancing factors for building and expanding the unique competing spaces these companies have succeeded in securing for themselves. These and other companies have made a cult of simplicity. Apple CEO Tim Cook has been quoted to say: *"We believe in the simple, not the complex; we believe in saying no to thousands of projects so that we can really focus on the few."* Indeed, the success of these companies would appear to corroborate their obsession with simplicity and their ability to replicate.

However, if the foregoing appears to be just a little too formulaic, it might well be just that. *The Economist's* "Schumpeter" throws a countering thought into the ring: just how do simplicity and repeatability help deal with disruptive innovation? The counterargument continues by pointing out that many once successful companies like Kodak, Nokia, and Blockbuster did not succumb to complexity or an inability to "repeat." Nokia, indeed, *championed* repeatability with clear business models, a distinctive business model, and a commitment to global rollout of its products. Nonetheless, in April 2012 this company had its credit rating cut to "junk" status. So, what is the lesson to be learned?

Formulaic approaches are to be enjoyed with caution. They often isolate individual elements that don't capture the entire story. Nokia's failure to anticipate the market impact of a new entrant (Apple and its iPhone) had primarily little to do with a lack of ability to simplify and repeat. Nokia's dilemma can be illustrated with the help of a unique competing space perspective: its difficulties stem from an inability to counter multiple change on all of its strategic boundaries; changes in the competitors' offerings, changes in the customers' needs, and, not least, inability to counter these effectively on the basis of its competitive wherewithal. Most companies can handle serious issues arising at any single strategic boundary without difficulty; issues arising simultaneously at two boundaries are a significantly greater challenge for most firms. Nokia's current problems arise from significant simultaneous change at all three strategic boundaries. No amount of simplification and replication can placate this beast.

Sources: Zook, C. and Allen, J. (2012) *Repeatability: Build Enduring Businesses for a World of Constant Change*, Boston: Harvard Business School Press; "Simplify and Repeat", Schumpeter, *The Economist* (April 28, 2012).

The Unique Competing Space, Value Proposition, and Competitive Positioning

The firm's unique competing space is intrinsically linked to its value proposition. The firm's value proposition articulates the strategic rationale of the firm's competitive advantage, which in turn is what gives rise to the firm's unique competing space. Schematically, the unique competing space represents a geometric mapping of the firm's competitive position; conceptually, it represents the opportunity space underpinning its competitive position. Both notions, the unique competing space and the value proposition, are intrinsically linked to strategic growth. There are several good reasons for this: the existence of a unique competing space substantiated by a uniquely superior value proposition signifies that a firm has the potential for growth. "Growth companies," firms perceived to have substantial growth potential, are viewed and valued differently by stakeholders, whether Wall Street, potential investors and customers, even current and potential employees. A growth company commands a premium that might be expressed in terms of price–earnings multiples based on future profitability potential. Alternatively, it might simply be the immense psychological boost to employees and other key stakeholders derived from being associated with a "hot" company, and the excitement of being part of that momentum. Facebook and Twitter, it is said, has attracted a lot of engineering talent from formerly "hot" technology companies such as Google and Microsoft. Companies that continually challenge their value proposition and nurture their unique competing space never acquire the staleness that befalls companies who lose their competitive position in the market place.

We have argued that the firm's value proposition provides the substantiation of its unique competing space. An important implication of this is that we would expect to find viable strategic options exclusively within the domain of the firm's unique competing space. The relevance of the firm's unique competing space in the context of strategic options is examined more closely in Chapter 7.

Most importantly, however, the firm's unique competing space is not a stagnant domain. It represents a dynamic domain that is continually subjected to perturbations at its boundaries as competitive circumstances change. Changes thus occurring might

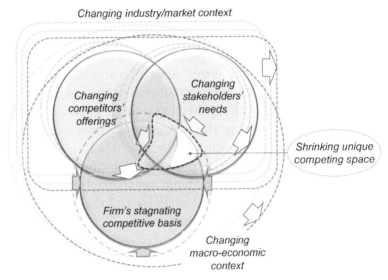

Changing industry/market context

Changing competitors' offerings

Changing stakeholders' needs

Shrinking unique competing space

Firm's stagnating competitive basis

Changing macro-economic context

Figure 5.3 Losing competitive ground: shrinking unique competing space

relate to threats to the firm's existing competitive position as much as they might represent new opportunities for competitive expansion. Changing competitive conditions can be readily visualized with the help of the unique competing space framework. Imagine the scenario mapped in Figure 5.3 depicting a declining competitive position:

1. *Changes occurring in the external macro-environment;* these might be driven by changes in the firm's macro-economic, regulatory, technological, and/or socio-economic environment. Changes in the macro-economic environment have a trickle-down effect that lead to changes in the firm's industry context, and, ultimately, in the markets in which it is competing.

2. *Customers' changing needs;* reflecting changes in the firm's market space; possibly entirely new market opportunities that might be emerging. Changes in the "customer" domain may also include changing stakeholder positions.

3. *Competitors threatening the firm's unique competitive position;* in fact, threats that are encroaching on the firm's competitive space. Competitor pressure may reflect increasing

strength of existing competitors, the emergence of new entrants to the market, or substitutions to the extant market offering.

4. *Critically, the firm's loss of competitive ground;* indicated by lack of appropriate response to changes in its competitive environment and failure to successfully fend off competitors' encroachment of its unique competing space leads to an ever-shrinking unique competing space.

Loss of competitive ground is shown by the shrinking unique competitive space. The firm's position of competitive advantage is thereby seriously compromised and as a consequence its unique competing space is shrinking. What has happened? The spatial perspective of the unique competing space enables a powerful means of examining this question by an exploration of the firm's strategic boundaries – the boundaries that form the periphery of its unique competing space. In the next section we will examine the firm's strategic boundaries, the impact of

---

Box 5.4 BlackBerry Crumbled

Not that long ago BlackBerry was the premier mobile gadget and a genuine tech status symbol. As recently as 2009 BlackBerry was named by *FORTUNE* to be one of the fastest growing companies in the world, with earnings growing by 84% a year.

BlackBerry's demise came abruptly. Multiple missteps have seen its market share of smartphones plummet from 50% in 2007 to near insignificance in 2015 as customers have dropped the once ubiquitous smartphone for Apple iPhones and Google Android devices.

Numerous reasons led to BlackBerry's failing. Insights on what went wrong and where, based on sources close to the embattled smartphone maker, can be broadly grouped into the three main clusters representing BlackBerry's unique competing space boundaries:

1. *Third boundary – embattled internal turf:* BlackBerry's problems, arguably, began with growing *internal* dysfunctionality. One of the disabling factors often cited in explaining BlackBerry's difficulties was the split personality in the executive suite that led to dysfunctional decision making at several key points in time. While one of the CEOs, company founder Mike Lazaridis, was pushing for a make-or-break launch of a next-generation BlackBerry with a new operating system, his co-CEO Jim Balsillie was intensifying efforts on a separate strategy focused on licensing some of the company's proprietary technology. Compounding this problem was a (shared) blinding confidence in the basic BlackBerry that led to fatal miscalculation of the market's acceptance of a touch screen.

2. *Second boundary – ineptness in sensing changing market needs.* Related to the internal conflict but with implications for BlackBerry's market orientation was a prolonged debate over its core customer. This not only added to the internal tensions, but led to launches of attempted catch-up products that failed to generate the intended market impact. BlackBerry ultimately failed to anticipate that private consumers and not business customers were driving the evolution of the smartphone market. In trying to fulfill the smartphone market's needs, BlackBerry remained obsessed with e-mail functionality (which, notably, experienced several widespread blackouts in 2011) even when customers had long since moved on.

3. *First boundary – formidable competitors' offerings.* More fundamentally, however, BlackBerry failed to respond to the emerging applications (apps) economy, which endowed its competitors with devastating advantage.

While it was preoccupied with e-mail functionality, BlackBerry's competitors envisioned entirely new modes of connected communication consisting of powerful mobile computers that provided not only e-mail services but also enabled Web-browsing "on the go." Competitors also introduced "next-wave" mechanisms that supported mass adoption of their products and services, such as platforms for developers to create applications that sought to embed the user experience.

BlackBerry's struggles continue despite attempts to find new sources of income to counter ever-dwindling sales of its handsets. At the height of its success in 2011 the company reported more than $5 billion in quarterly revenues; in the final three months of its most recent fiscal year (2015) BlackBerry reported revenues of $660 million, its lowest quarterly revenues in eight years.

Sources: Connors, W. (2012) Multiple Missteps Caused Research in Motion's Fall, *Wall Street Journal* (July 2, 2012); Gustin, S. (2012) BlackBerry Crushed, *TIME* (July 16, 2012); BlackBerry sales at eight-year low, *Financial Times* (March 28/29, 2015).

changes to the conditions prevailing at the boundaries and strategic implications of these for the firm's competitive position.

STRATEGY IN PRACTICE: SHRINKING COMPETITION POSITIONS

Companies typically find themselves in situations in which their unique competing space is shrinking when:

- . . . they fail to detect and interpret correctly shifts in their external competitive environment; when they continue to compete in ways that in the past may have led to competitive differentiation but now no longer provide the basis for competitive advantage.

- . . . they fail to protect their unique competing space against encroaching competitors. This may happen when companies fail to recognize new competition; when they fail to protect their assets – or, simply when they fail to sustain their competitive edge through neglect of their strategically relevant resources and capabilities.
- . . . they lose touch with their stakeholders and fail to understand their stakeholders' changing needs.

Unique Competing Space and the Firm's Strategic Boundaries

Firm boundaries have long been a central theme in strategic management. Multiple perspectives have been developed over the years to help create a better understanding of the significance of the firm's boundaries and the implications of these for the firm's competitiveness and strategic position. Much of the research agenda focusing on the firm's boundaries, however, has been shaped and driven mainly by the rather limiting perspectives of either transaction cost economics or exchange efficiency. To a great extent, this has led to a discourse on firms' boundaries that has focused on boundary decisions as make-or-buy choices, the rationale of which is provided by governance efficiency considerations.

Even with recent extensions to thinking on the firm's boundaries that go beyond efficiency considerations, however, the focus of the extant firm boundary research has nonetheless remained primarily theoretically focused. Little of the theory related to the firm's boundaries readily translates to guidance for strategic sense making, and ultimately strategic decision making.

The unique competing space perspective provides the conceptual basis for a simple heuristic approach that seeks to address that deficit. The heuristic builds on the basic premise that issues of strategic importance and relevance to the firm invariably make their appearance at the firm's strategic boundaries when they arise. The unique competing space thereby provides a pragmatic explication of the role of the firm's strategic boundaries in establishing a position of competitive advantage.

Key elements of that premise are:

1. The firm's strategic boundaries comprise three interfaces representing (a) an interface to the firm's competition, (b) an interface to the cluster representing the needs of the firm's stakeholders, and (c) a firm-internal boundary representing a threshold separating the firm's potential basis of competitiveness (e.g. its resources, assets, and capabilities) and its actual exploitation of that basis for competitive advantage.
2. Issues of strategic relevance to the firm, when they emerge, invariably crop up at one or more of its strategic boundaries. Continual monitoring of the firm's strategic boundaries therefore provides a means of keeping tabs on those really critical issues of strategic importance without "losing sight of the wood for the trees."
3. The three boundaries are inextricably linked; changes at any one boundary invariably result in changes at one or both of the other boundaries.

In the following section we explore each of the three elements in turn.

1. The Firm's Strategic Boundaries

The firm's unique competing space is a domain bounded by three interfaces. The three interfaces form the boundaries of the firm's unique competing space. Each boundary carries different strategic implications for the firm's competitive position. Viewed collectively, the three boundaries provide a powerful perspective on the firm's competitive position. The first boundary (indicated by boundary "1" in Figure 5.4) represents the interface to the firm's competitors.

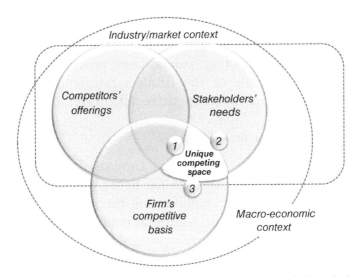

Figure 5.4 Unique competing space and the firm's strategic boundaries

The boundary labeled "2" represents the interface of the firm to its stakeholders. The third strategic boundary, labeled "3" in Figure 5.4 represents a firm-internal interface or threshold across which the firm must transfer capabilities and resources relevant to the unique opportunity presented by the customers' needs.

Let's examine each of the three strategic boundaries and their implications in turn.

"The Line of Demarcation": Strategic Boundary "1"
The strategic boundary designated as "1" (Figure 5.4) represents a line of demarcation; the competitive front to the firm's competitors and their offerings. Notably, competitors along this front are also in a position to deliver a value offering that addresses the needs of the customers in the market segment in question to a limited extent. This common ground domain is represented by the triangular space formed by the intersection of all three circles; it is a hotly contested field of competition in which the firm and all its competitors are in a position to deliver a value offering that *partially* fulfills the market's needs. The firm's unique competing

space, on the other hand, represents that opportunity space in which the firm (ideally) alone is in a position to create and deliver value in a way that its competitors cannot. Note that in reality, the firm may actually share its "unique" competing space with one or few other competitors; the salient point, however, is that the firm's unique competing space represents an opportunity that is *strategically attractive*, even if shared with one or a very few other competitors. By *strategically relevant* we mean that competition in this space presents opportunities for reaping returns on effort invested that exceed comparable market returns of the firm's competitors. What are the strategic implications of this strategic boundary for the firm? First and foremost the firm must understand the nature of the "demarcation," the nature and extent of the differentiation between its own value offering and that of the competitors'. Second, the firm must protect its competitive turf against any attempts of its competitors to encroach on its unique competing space. The firm can do this via both defensive and preemptive approaches. It can defend its competitive front to the competition by suitable protection of its intellectual property inherent to its unique value offering; this might include patents, copyright, and trademarks. Furthermore, it can invest in preemptive measures that strengthen and consolidate the advantage represented by its unique competing space; this might include strategic investments in building its brand. Another powerful, likewise preemptive, measure would be to invest effort in building and nurturing the firm's innovation capabilities. Innovating faster than the competition is a most effective mechanism for protecting the firm's unique competing space from competitors' threatening advances.

Box 5.5 Newcomers on the Block

The small but growing market for niche, boutique ski makers in the USA is an example of how a number of small companies are drawing new lines of demarcation in a relatively mature market space. Currently, some 80 niche ski makers, mostly in snowy states like Maine and Wyoming, are going face to face with big-name ski manufacturers, including Fischer, K2, Dynastar, and Völkl – who still control 90% of the US$533 million ski market, but who are relying increasingly on manufacturing of their skis in overseas locations, with about 35% of their skis currently made in China.

Chinese-manufactured skis no longer cut it for a growing segment of older, diehard, and affluent skiers who tend to have time and money to ski often. Increasingly, these skiers are gravitating to hand-crafted, high-tech, and high-end skis that satisfy specific experiences like deep-powder skiing in a way that Chinese-made skis cannot. The boutique ski makers who specialize in making hand-crafted skis, often out of a living room, garage, and local machine shop rather than a foreign factory, are meeting the demands of the emerging ski segment. They have been described as "small companies that bring a huge amount of passion and innovation to the industry . . . they're going up against the Goliaths, but they have very specific target markets and are selling to very specific customers . . . ." The competitive prospects of the boutique ski makers are promising; they generated between US$20 million and 30 million per year through the economic downturn and are set to capture another 3–5% of the ski markets in the next 5–10 years according to industry experts. At prices up to US$2,300 for a custom-milled pair of skis and yearly sales growth as high as 80%, the newcomers on the block are indeed a group to be watched.

Source: Diddlebock, B. (2012) Sweet Spot. Niche Skimakers are Making a Run for Diehard Skiers, *TIME Europe Edition* (April 9, 2012).

"The Customer Interface": Strategic Boundary "2"

The importance of nurturing an intimate relationship with one's stakeholders is undisputed. The unique competing space framework provides a graphical perspective of what this implies in the firm's greater competitive context. The boundary designated "2" in Figure 5.4 represents the firm's interface to its stakeholders. In a commercial sense, these represent its stakeholders, which might include its customers, suppliers, investors, and relevant regulatory agencies. This boundary is strategically relevant because it represents the interface across which the firm ultimately seeks to deliver its unique value offering to its stakeholders. The better the firm understands and "manages" this interface, the better it is positioned to ensure delivery of its value offering across this boundary. Strategic management of this interface requires an understanding of the customers' needs that in cases may exceed the market's own understanding of its needs. Firms might use various techniques such as ethnography and advanced customer relationship management approaches to build and nurture this understanding. Needless to point out, understanding and insights developed at the customer interface provide important impulses for appropriate measures directed at boundaries "1" and "3." These might include unique insights that might trigger new, innovative forms of the value offering to address emerging needs in the market.

Successful firms deal with their customer interface in different ways. Amazon.com CEO and founder Jeff Bezos' quirky habit of using an empty chair to symbolize the customer at Amazon's strategy meetings is exemplary.[5]

"The Internal Threshold": Strategic Boundary "3"

Of the three boundaries, the internal threshold is the least obvious and, arguably, the most critical to the firm's ability to build and sustain its competitiveness. From a *resource-based* perspective, the lower circle depicting the firm's competitive basis might be thought of as representative of its repository of resources and capabilities. However, mere possession of resources and capabilities does not endow the firm with any competitive advantage. The firm's resources and capabilities must be configured in a way that they are relevant to the firm's unique competing space – and figuratively transferred across the boundary "3" to be of any strategic relevance. The firm's stock of resources and capabilities, encompassing both tangible and intangible forms, are embedded in an organizational context that consists of the organization's processes, structure, culture, practices, mechanisms – and ultimately leadership. Strategic utilization of the firm's resources requires astute and skillful orchestration of the entire organizational context. In terms of the five building blocks of strategy introduced in Chapter 1 (Box 1.1), interface "3" addresses the fifth building block, which is about "getting the organizational act together."

Not all of the firm's resources are equally relevant or appropriate for creating the value offering that underpins its unique competing space. Some of the firm's resources may, in fact, be outdated and no longer of strategic relevance for any of the firm's value offerings. Moreover, a firm's organizational context might be averse to creating value; its culture, process, and practices may not be optimally aligned for exploiting its resources and capabilities in accordance with the value that is to be created. In this sense strategic boundary "3" represents an internal organizational *threshold* across which relevant resources and capabilities need to be configured and mobilized in order for that value on the basis of which the firm aspires to stake its competitive claim to be created. Boundary "3" lies clearly within the perimeter of the circle representing the firm's basis of competitiveness. This carries important implications: mobilization of the firm's resources and capabilities across this threshold boundary are entirely within the firm's sphere of control.

Resources that are relevant to the firm's unique competing space must be appropriately bundled, configured, and mobilized across the internal threshold (boundary "3") in order to be competitively relevant to the firm. Many firms fail to achieve this. Despite claiming ownership of resources that are potentially relevant to their unique competing space, they do not succeed in mobilizing them across the internal threshold.

Why does this happen? There are many possible reasons. Firms sometimes are not fully aware of what they possess in terms of potentially strategic resources and capabilities. Firms often "don't know what they know" and consequently fail to exploit their own strategic resources. Or, firms simply don't succeed in "getting their act together"; aligning their resources, processes, practices, and culture in a way that allows them to fully exploit their strategic potential competitive position. Cases of lost opportunity of this type abound.

Box 5.6 Amazonian Disruptor

Once merely an online bookseller, Amazon today is a $182 billion empire that has diversified its portfolio of value offerings to other merchandise, devices, and even web services. Along the way, the internet giant has disruptively upended many of the incumbent players in those markets. Although Amazon has regularly frustrated Wall Street with its erratic earnings, the investment community has richly rewarded Amazon's performance with a 30% increase in its stock price in the first quarter of 2015 alone.

Much of Amazon's success, arguably, can be traced to what Bezos frequently refers to as the "the three big ideas at Amazon": (1) long-term thinking, (2) customer obsession, and (3) a willingness to invent. Collectively these three credos distinguish and define Amazon's unique competing space. Individually, each of the "ideas" can be readily mapped to one of the three boundaries encompassing its unique competing space.

Amazon's long-term thinking credo manifests itself in several ways: at its core is an astute understanding of the competition – and its differentiated position relative to these. The internet giant has always taken the long-term view – and has habitually ignored Wall Street's pleas for consistent earnings growth. On the other hand, it has clearly set itself apart from its Silicon Valley counterparts, including Apple, who pride themselves on their ability to sell high-profit devices that generate premium margins. Amazon has always sold low- or no-profit devices at the bare minimum required to break even – in favor of ever more volume. One of Bezos' favorite sayings is: "Your margin is my opportunity."

Even as Amazon's portfolio of market offerings has expanded, it has zealously maintained focus on delivering a good customer experience across its multiple market interfaces. Amazon's customer experience credo is closely coupled to its obsession with the last of its three credos: its organizational capability in innovation. Both are deeply embedded in the company's culture. Bezos on how the two are linked: *"We innovate by starting with the customer and working backwards. That becomes the touchstone for how we invent."* Moreover, this forms the basis of Amazon's differentiated strategic stance; as Bezos explains: *"When they're [the competition] in the shower in the morning, they're thinking about how they're going to get ahead of one of their top competitors. Here in the shower, we're thinking about how we are going to invent something on behalf of a customer."*

High margin-focused competitors are well advised to heed Amazon's understated disruptive threat, succinctly articulated by Bezos: *"Other companies have more of a conqueror mentality; we think of ourselves as explorers."*

Source: http://finance.yahoo.com/q?s=AMZN (accessed on April 23, 2015); Lashinsky, A. (2012) Jeff Bezos: The Ultimate Disruptor, *FORTUNE Europe Edition* (December 3, 2012).

2. Strategic Boundaries: Strategic Issues

Changing conditions at the firm's strategic boundaries compels the firm to engage in sense making. Perturbations at the firm's strategic boundaries give rise to critical issues that prompt the need for sense making in the first place. The notion of a strategic *boundary condition* is borrowed from the physical sciences where boundary conditions define the nature of a domain at its periphery. From the physical sciences analogy we also understand that changes to the domain are typically initiated through perturbations at its boundaries. Perturbations at its periphery characteristically provide first indications of an impending change to the prevailing situation within the domain. Weather fronts are a case in point; minor disturbances that develop into major changes to the prevailing weather system are discernible initially at the system's periphery.

And so it is with competitive business environments. These are also complex, riddled with ambiguity and continually changing. Complexity in business environments stems from the fact that multiple factors are at play at any point in time. This leads to changing conditions in the firm's competitive environment, which firms characteristically experience initially as disturbances to conditions at the boundaries of their competing space. Because these often act on more than one boundary, the sum effect may be complex. Adding to the complexity, boundaries are often not clearly discernible, particularly in emerging contexts – such as shifts in factors relating to the competition, or emerging markets. Firms often recognize and understand the implications of changes at the boundaries of their unique competing space only too late.

Changing conditions at competitor boundary "1" may result when existing or new competitors appear on the scene with an improved value offering that appeals to customers' needs. Expiring intellectual property protection may represent another change at the line of demarcation to the firm's competitors.

Changes to conditions at stakeholder/market boundary "2" may reflect changing customer tastes and preferences – triggered possibly by new offerings introduced to the market by competitors. Alternatively, they might reflect changing stakeholder needs and positions of power to influence decision making. Finally, change to the firm's internal threshold (boundary "3") may result when firms excessively cut investment in their R&D, become complacent in nurturing new capabilities, and fall prey to organizational inertia.

The strategic boundary perspective provides a profoundly useful means of "cutting to the chase" when framing strategic issues. Strategic issues, when they arise, invariably do so when the firm experiences perturbations at one or more of its strategic boundaries. Even changes seemingly far removed from the immediate firm context, such as changes in the firm's macro-economic environment, can trigger trickle-down effects resulting in changes in the industry and market environments that are of immediate relevance to the firm. The impact of these changes, if strategically relevant to the firm's competitive position, will have an impact on one or more of the boundaries of its unique competing space. The focus on the firm's strategic boundaries when seeking to make sense of strategic challenges – regardless of whether prompted by threats or opportunities – enables a considerable narrowing of the strategic analysis on issues that are, indeed, strategically relevant from the outset. This has important implications for the quality of the sense making. First, it enables firms to focus and concentrate relatively quickly on the essence of the relevant strategic challenge. Time can be a critical factor when firms need to make sense of factors underlying emerging strategic challenges. The ability to "cut to the chase" on strategic issues quickly can be an immense competitive advantage. Second, the ability to focus on the essence of a strategic matter from the outset helps firms from getting distracted by issues that are irrelevant to the challenge at hand. Again, the ability not to get side-tracked on issues irrelevant to the task at hand can be immensely important to the firm's competitiveness. Finally, an analysis that converges on the core of the strategic problem at stake enables precision and rigor in the articulation of the strategic questions to be addressed and resolved.

Invariably, changing conditions seldom affect only one of the boundaries. This increases the complexity of the analysis in that a purely rational approach is seldom adequate. Sense making must draw on a combination of inputs; insights based on informed intuition, a continual challenging of assumptions, and realistic interpretation of multiple signals through rational analysis.

When engaging in strategic sense making many managers often find themselves randomly searching for the proverbial "needle in the haystack" when it comes to framing issues and articulating strategically relevant questions. Too often, this approach amounts to little more than "shooting at clay pigeons with a shotgun in the dark." Probability would have it that one might occasionally actually hit one; more often than not, however, this effort remains futile. The unique competing space – in particular, a focused analysis of its boundary conditions – provides a profoundly more powerful approach to the task.

3. Strategic Boundaries: Interdependencies of Boundaries

Two important strategic perspectives on the firm's boundaries present themselves on examination of the unique competing space framework. The first relates to the strategic relevance of each of the three boundaries individually, each of which introduces a unique strategic perspective on the firm's unique competing space. Of particular interest are the implications for the firm's competitive position introduced through changing conditions at the boundary in question. The second perspective relates to the impact of change at any one boundary on one or two of the other boundaries. Change at one boundary is often inextricably linked to change at one or two of the other boundaries. For example, a competitor's preemptive new offering may be in response to changing consumer needs and preferences in the market; this, in turn, may prompt the firm to examine, reconfigure, and mobilize its portfolio of capabilities in response.

BOX 5.7 STRATEGIC BOUNDARIES: EMPIRICAL RESEARCH

Empirical research carried out at Henley Business School examined the source and nature of strategic issues in business practice. The research approach drew on the strategic boundaries perspective associated with the unique competing space concept. A survey of senior executives in 75 UK-based firms representing a cross-sampling of industries and firm sizes queried perceptions regarding:

- which of the three boundaries predominantly gives rise to strategic issues;
- the nature of the issues arising at the firm's strategic boundaries; and
- interrelationships between issues linked to each of the firm's three strategic boundaries.

The research findings confirm that, in many ways, the firm's boundaries define the essence of the organization; issues at the firm's boundaries collectively reflect strategic challenges relevant to the firm's competitive position at a given point in time. The findings suggest that strategic issues most frequently arise as a result of changing conditions at two of the firm's interfaces – the interface to its competition (boundary "1") and the interface to its stakeholders (boundary "2"). Changes at these (external) interfaces give rise to strategic issues that relate to the firm's ability to respond suitably. A principal component analysis suggests issues related to changes in competition explain the greatest amount of variance (16.5% of variance explained). This is closely followed by issues associated with boundary "3" (15.7% of variance explained), which relate to the firm's ability to respond appropriately. Issues related to changes at the interface to the stakeholder cluster (boundary "2") account for 14.7% of the variance explained. Correlation analysis provides insight into the nature and intensity of interdependencies between the firm's boundaries. Figure 5.5 shows a mapping of the correlations between issues linked to the three firm boundaries. Individual linkages are indicated by arrows connecting the boundaries; these indicate the nature and frequency of the interrelationships. The significance of the linkages, on the other hand, is indicated by the "p" values that emerge from the statistical analysis. The more significant the interrelationship, the higher the "p" value; highly significant linkages are indicated with bold arrows in Figure 5.5. The research findings point to the pivotal significance of the firm's third boundary in orchestrating, aligning, and ultimately mobilizing its resources in response to challenges brought by changes in the firm's competition and markets.

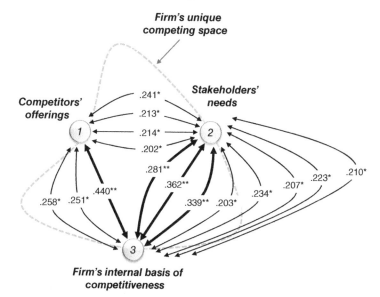

Figure 5.5 Correlation analysis; empirical evidence of nature and intensity of interrelationships between firms' strategic boundaries (Kendall's tau (2-tailed); sample size of 75; $*p < 0.05$; $**p < 0.01$)

The research findings do not surprise; they are consistent with our intuitive understanding of where firms typically face the greatest challenge in strategy practice: the greatest

> challenges facing firms are typically not new competition or changing market conditions, rather their inability to get their own act together in responding to changes in their external competitive environment.

The interdependency of the firm's strategic boundaries introduces complexity to the challenge of managing changing conditions at the firm's boundaries. Most firms can cope with change at one of its boundaries. The situation becomes more critical when firms experience significant change at two of its boundaries simultaneously. Significant changes at all three boundaries present the most daunting challenge. Significant and pervasive change simultaneously at all three strategic boundaries very often throws the firm into a tailspin from which it is often difficult to recover.

Unique Competing Space: Portfolio Perspective

A firm's competitive position is more often than not based on a *portfolio* of individual value offerings, which collectively comprise the firm's unique competing space; although, of course, each of the individual value offerings can also be thought of in terms of a unique competing space.

A unique competing space (and its associated value proposition) can be defined for any value offering for which it is possible to define: (1) a specific customer/stakeholder need to be fulfilled; (2) a disposition, ability, and capacity on the part of the firm to fulfill that need – ideally, in a uniquely superior way; and (3) potential competitors. Hence, one can envisage the firm consisting of a portfolio of unique competing spaces comprising its individual value bundle offerings. Individual value bundles may exhibit a value premium; these, in turn, may contribute to a cumulative value premium representing a summation of all

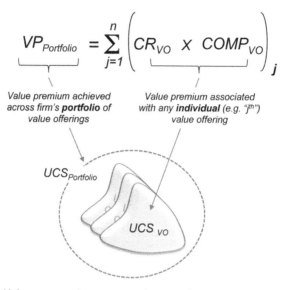

$$VP_{Portfolio} = \sum_{j=1}^{n} \left(CR_{VO} \times COMP_{VO} \right)_{j}$$

Value premium achieved across firm's **portfolio** of value offerings

Value premium associated with any **individual** (e.g. "j^{th}") value offering

$UCS_{Portfolio}$

UCS_{VO}

Figure 5.6 Unique competing space, value premium, and portfolio perspective

value bundles – associated value premiums that comprise the firm's portfolio (Figure 5.6). Individual unique competing spaces in that portfolio invariably exhibit differing degrees of competitive impact; this is reflected by their size. Some might be relatively small – such as in emerging or maturing markets – while relatively few might contribute a disproportionate share of the impact. One can think of this in terms of the Pareto principle, whereby, for example, 80% of the firm's competitive impact is derived from 20% of the firm's value offerings. It is the collective competitive impact of the firm's portfolio of unique competing spaces that is at stake when taking an investor/stakeholder perspective. This determines the firm's overall position of competitiveness. The firm's strategic objective is, therefore, to optimize the strategic impact of its portfolio of unique competing spaces over all of its value offerings. This can be a daunting task when considering that the average Global 1000 company competes in approximately 50 markets.

In practice, not all of the firm's value offerings may be associated with a value premium. For some of its value offerings, the firm

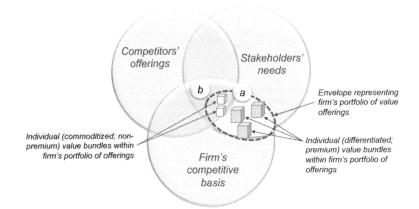

Figure 5.7 Portfolio perspective: premium and non-premium contributions to overall portfolio of value offerings

might be competing in mature, commoditized markets, in which case the value offerings would be positioned in the space labeled "b" in Figure 5.7. There might be a sound strategic rationale for why the firm chooses to do this: while value offerings in commoditized markets might in themselves not achieve a value premium, they might constitute important complements to the firm's other value offerings that do achieve significant value premiums. A firm may also be keen not to offer its current customers any excuse for going to the firm's competitors for commoditized value offerings. As argued earlier in this section, the firm's overall strategic objective is to maximize its strategic impact across its entire portfolio (indicated by "a" in Figure 5.7). In doing so, it might well accept marginal losses on some value offerings in return for disproportionately high returns from other value offerings in its portfolio of value offerings. In practice, this is a complex and multidimensional challenge.

Box 5.8 Big Blue's "Big Iron"

IBM recently unveiled a new version of its 51-year-old mainframe computer. The product for which IBM is still best known is now to help bring about a stabilization in the technology giant's hardware business in the company's current effort to get back on track. Sometimes referred to as IBM's "Big Iron," the mainframe is to help curb IBM's 16% revenue decline in its hardware business in the first nine months of 2014, which has seen customers shift parts of their IT to cloud services offered by competitors.

Even after more than half a century, IBM's mainframe business continues to be an integral and important portfolio component of its corporate unique competing space. Analysts estimate that mainframes contribute between a quarter and a third of the company's profits, mainly on account of the software and services sold alongside them. IBM's mainframes are used by companies such as banks, telecom operators, and retailers who regularly need to process massive volumes of data. Latest models are particularly suitable for handling high volumes of transactions triggered by the recent explosion of mobile applications. Notably, and reassuringly for IBM, mainframes remain largely immune from emerging cloud computing systems that are challenging its other businesses.

Source: Waters, R. (2015) IBM puts Faith in "Big Iron" Mainframe to Revive Sales, *Financial Times* (January 14, 2015).

Summary and Limitations

The power of the unique competing space framework derives from its comprehensiveness and the incisiveness it contributes to the strategic analysis on a high level. Similar to the value proposition framework in that it assembles and integrates factors related to firm's external and internal competitive positions in the context of its strategic mandate, the unique competing space presents a graphical depiction of the firm's competitive window of opportunity. As such, the unique competing space represents a mapping of the firm's strategic landscape.

As with all abstractions of reality, there are caveats worth noting in regard to the application of the unique competing space framework. The Venn diagram depiction of the firm's competitive position is deceptively simple; it is a simplification of reality. In reality, the boundaries demarcating competitors might be far from obvious; markets might be emerging and difficult to identify on the radar screen. Figure 5.2 portrays the spheres representing competitors, customers/markets, and the firm to be of equal diameter. This is unlikely to be the case in reality; the exact size and borders of the three elements might be difficult to discern; this might be further compounded by perturbations at the peripheries of the unique competing space, which blur actual happenings at the individual boundaries. The two-dimensional depiction of the unique competing space in Figure 5.2 is, of course, another abstraction; firms' competitive environments are typically multidimensional with windows of competitive opportunities existing in adjacent markets and contiguous competitors. This is difficult to depict in two dimensions.

Limitations aside, the unique competing space can be profoundly useful in guiding our strategic thinking in a way that enables us to focus on the essence of the strategic matter at hand without losing sight of the greater competitive context.

STRATEGY IN PRACTICE: CRITICAL REFLECTION ON YOUR FIRM'S UNIQUE COMPETING SPACE . . .

- What's the unique value at its core?
- What makes it unique and superior?
- What makes it most vulnerable – and why?
- How clearly discernible are the boundaries of your firm's competing space?
- If not clearly discernible, why might this be the case?
- Which of the boundaries is most critical to your firm's position of competitive advantage – and why?

- What are the critical issues at the critical boundaries – and why?
- What issues might be the result of compounded effects of simultaneous perturbations at several boundaries?

Opportunity–Response Analysis Framework

The *opportunity–response* framework, which is examined in the final section of this chapter, probes both external and internal perspectives. This framework contributes insights that link relevant external and internal contexts, but it does not explicitly relate these to the strategic value issue at stake. This is the key difference between high-level frameworks discussed earlier in this chapter and the opportunity–response framework of analysis. This framework does, however, probe the final important strategic question – the "when?" question, which is addressed by neither the value proposition nor the unique competing space frameworks. The opportunity–response framework brings both external and internal perspectives into juxtaposition; subsequent sections then introduce a selection of external and internal frameworks and examine their applicability.

The opportunity–response analysis framework brings together a number of elements of strategic analysis that collectively yield potentially useful insights. The framework presented in Figure 5.8 consists of two axes – a horizontal axis representing a time horizon and a vertical axis representing an appropriate performance measure (for example, market share growth, or a return on investment) – and two intersecting curves. The upper curve (labeled "1"), depicted by a decreasing function, represents a particular market *opportunity* as it evolves in the company's external competitive environment. The lower curve (labeled "2"), depicted by an increasing function, represents the firm's *response* to that market opportunity. More precisely, curve "2" reflects the firm's competitive position relative to the market opportunity at

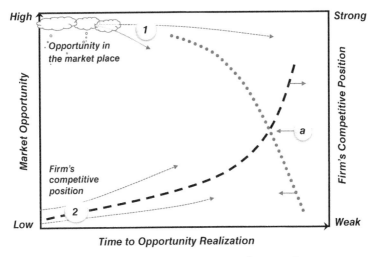

Figure 5.8 Opportunity–response framework

any point along the time horizon. The firm's competitive position is an indication of ability to deliver on the market opportunity represented by the upper curve (labeled "1").

As such, the lower curve ("2") in Figure 5.8 captures the firm's internal basis of competitiveness; its knowledge, capabilities, resources, and organizational wherewithal relative to the market opportunity at any point in time. The lower curve is therefore sometimes referred as the company's *knowledge* or *experience* curve. At some point in time, the firm's ability to respond matches the respective demands of the market opportunity. This point is depicted by the intersection of the two curves at the point labeled "a." The opportunity–response framework addresses a final question in addition to the where, how, why, and what questions posed in conjunction with the value proposition framework. It introduces the "when?" question to the strategic equation to be resolved. The opportunity–response analysis suggests that the timing of a firm's response is not arbitrary; that it is dependent on the firm's ability to position itself appropriately to the market opportunity in order to successfully exploit that opportunity.

The graphical form of the approach represented by the opportunity–response framework appears to have been first proposed by DeGenaro.[6] We will see further on, however, that the framework's underpinning rationale has its strategy roots in a framework proposed by Andrews[7] already in 1971. The schematic is essentially a graphical representation of the simple *SWOT* (*strengths, weaknesses, opportunities, threats*) framework. The upper curve, shown in Figure 5.8 as "1," represents opportunities and/or threats in the firm's external competitive context. The lower curve ("2") represents the firm's strengths and/or weaknesses that relate to its internal basis of competitiveness.

STRATEGY IN PRACTICE: THE SWOT ANALYSIS

The origins of the SWOT analysis are not entirely clear; it is known to have been used by Harvard Business School academics in the late 1960s. Despite its popularity with managers, the analysis does not have any basis in theory as such; indeed, it has even been suggested that its origins may be tied to an idea – sketched out by a professor on the back of an envelope – that just caught on. The attractiveness of the SWOT may lie in its beguiling simplicity; its simplicity, however, is also the primary reason for its limitations. There are several critical limitations:

- First, the SWOT is outdated. Our understanding of real business contexts has evolved since the SWOT emerged on the scene. We now appreciate that strategy in real business contexts rarely allows the black and white approach to sense making suggested by the SWOT. In practice, strategy often demands trade-offs; a SWOT analysis does not deal well with these.
- Second, the SWOT is intrinsically imprecise and lacks purpose. The SWOT does not pin the components of its analysis to any core strategic objective, such as value differentiation. Moreover, it does not discriminate between

the firm's *strategic* resources and those of an *enabling* or *supporting* type; neither does it support the strategic analysis of emerging assets, such as new, emerging technologies.

- Most critically, however, SWOT is inherently ambiguous. Consider a case in point: Take, for example, the combination of a highly skilled labor force coupled with the very stable labor relations typically found in German companies. Does this represent a *strength* or a *weakness* for German companies? We might be initially inclined to identify this factor as a strength. However, when faced with the need to react quickly to changing market conditions, this apparent strength can quickly become a debilitating *liability* in view of Germany's rigid labor laws that critically restrict headcount flexibility. So, the best insight a SWOT can muster on this potentially critical issue is an enigmatic "it depends."

- As with other inherently "scattergun" approaches, the SWOT analysis provides little guidance to managers on suitable next steps.

Notably, while there is nothing inherently *wrong* with the SWOT analysis, managers have significantly better approaches to fall back on. Profoundly more insightful approaches to strategic sense making are available; frameworks such as the value proposition and unique competing space frameworks. These frameworks integrate elements of the SWOT while retaining the focus of the analysis on the essence of the strategic challenge at stake.

Opportunity–Response: Competing Trajectories

Clearly, the depiction of a firm's competitive position relative to opportunities in its competitive environment in Figure 5.8 is a simplification of reality. In reality, we would expect to find multiple trajectories emerging from a "cloud" of potential opportunities on the market opportunity side. Some of these opportunities dissipate and disappear rather quickly. Other trajectories, of course, materialize as viable market opportunity, although often this is apparent only in the retrospective since trajectories representing market opportunity are often difficult to discern when they first appear.

Market opportunities are triggered by environments that are in flux, driven by multiple drivers such as changing consumer needs, emerging technologies, and/or competitor activity. Opportunities emerging as a result of disruptive innovation might initially exist in competing forms that ultimately give way to a dominant form of the technology in question. New market opportunities emerge and exist for both incumbents and new entrants, though the inherent risk is often greater for the incumbent.[8,9] Inevitably, what represents an opportunity for a new entrant or challenger poses a threat to the incumbent.

Some apparent opportunities are delayed in their realization and ultimately don't materialize in the way originally anticipated. An example is the UMTS (Universal Mobile Telecommunications Systems) third generation (3G) telecommunications licensing drive in 2000. UMTS, the third generation mobile cellular technology for networks based on the GSM standard, was viewed by telecommunications players as the coming network platform. The auctioning of the licenses unleashed a bidding frenzy between telecommunications providers at the height of the dotcom boom. Mobile operators around the world, though mainly in Europe, ended up paying a total of $125 billion for licenses to build and operate 3G networks that ultimately failed to materialize in the way originally anticipated.

On the firm response side, we would similarly expect to find multiple competing trajectories representing competing firms vying to capture the same opportunity. Not all of the competitors will necessarily be starting from the same competitive position due to the unique legacies and path dependencies of the competing firms. Differences in starting points reflect asymmetries in the competitive positions of the competitors eyeing the same market opportunities. The rate of acceleration of individual competitors along their respective learning trajectory is determined by the competitive agility of the firms. Some competitors invariably drop out along the way.

Opportunity-Side Perspective

Market-side thinking in the late 1960s and 1970s was largely influenced by attempts to make sense of markets through analyses of the external competitive context. Porter's[10] *structure–conduct–performance* paradigm with roots in industrial–organizational economics represented a breakthrough in *opportunity-side* thinking when it was introduced in the late 1970s. It was to dominate strategic thinking in the 1970s and much of the 1980s. The structure–conduct–performance paradigm confined the firm's strategic role to scrutinizing and scanning the external competitive environment for opportunities and threats – and to orienting the firm's strategic course on this basis accordingly. The premise of the structure–conduct–performance paradigm was that while the external context cannot be influenced by any individual firm, firms must nonetheless understand their competitive environment and "adjust" their internal basis of competitiveness accordingly. However, little if any guidance on what this "adjusting" might entail, or how firms were to go about it was available at the time.

Response-Side Perspective

Response-side thinking emerged in the 1990s with the development of the *resource-based view* of the firm.[11,12,13] The premise of the resource-based view is that a firm's basis of competitive advantage derives from its ability and capacity to configure and exploit its resources and capabilities in a uniquely superior way.

Strategic competences, capabilities, and the embedded knowledge and learning, and the organization's ability to configure these in ways that enable the firm to create uniquely differentiated value offerings, are at the core of the organization's competitiveness. Notably, these activities are entirely within the firm's own sphere of control and disposition. The resource-based view thereby shifted the strategic emphasis from the external environment to the company's internal context; its ability to respond appropriately to opportunity in the external environment. An important point to be noted: the curve depicting the organization's learning trajectory with a smooth curve is a substantial simplification of what we might expect to find in reality. A firm's learning (or experience) trajectory may exhibit critical discontinuities and even disruptive setbacks. Another factor not necessarily apparent by the smooth curves representing competitors' trajectories is that there might be interactions between the curves, such as collusion, possibly even cooperation related to some form of strategic partnering between some of the competitors.

Opportunity–Response: A Dynamic Capabilities Perspective

The opportunity–response framework aligns the external competitive environment and the organization's internal basis of competitiveness and presents these in a dynamic context that is continually in flux. External contexts in which opportunities originate are more often than not complex, ambiguous, and defy any attempts at rational sense making. The firm's response under these circumstances necessitates a dynamic predisposition and ability on the part of the firm. Recent thinking in the management literature focused on the notion of *dynamic capabilities* has contributed new thinking on how firms might approach the task. While there is yet little consensus among strategy scholars on the exact nature of dynamics, there is nonetheless general agreement that dynamic capabilities encompass the disposition, capacity, and ability of a firm to respond appropriately to a need or opportunity for change.[14–16]

In positioning the role of dynamic capabilities in this context, Teece[8] has argued that it is not so much the positions companies occupy in an industry landscape as it is what they *do*; how they take cues from opportunities arising in their environment, how they reconfigure their own ideas and capabilities to develop new innovative value offerings, and how they then deliver these to the market. However, resources and capabilities do not effortlessly combine and reconfigure to form new capabilities. Dynamic capabilities are thought to play a key role in this activity that leads to the renewal and strategic repositioning of the firm. Dynamic capabilities are defined as *"the ability to sense and then seize new opportunities, and to reconfigure and protect knowledge assets, competencies and complementary assets so as to achieve sustained competitive advantage."*[8]

Figure 5.9 positions the three activities suggested by Teece's notion of shaping factors contributing to the firm's dynamic

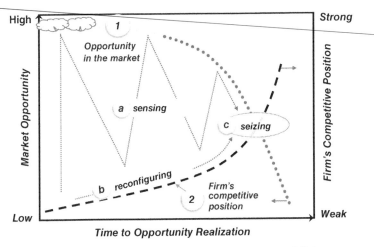

Figure 5.9   Opportunity–response and dynamic capabilities

capabilities schematically in the context of the opportunity–response framework.

Each of the three activities leading up to and including the seizing of the respective market opportunity can be considered to represent a class of dynamic capability. The first activity, *sensing* (denoted by "a") is essentially a detecting and sense making activity that focuses on identifying and correctly assessing opportunity trajectories as they emerge in the external environment of the firm. On the basis of the market intelligence that emerges from this activity, resources and capabilities within are *reconfigured* (denoted "b") in alignment with the interpretation of the market opportunity. The sensing and reconfiguring activities occur progressively over numerous cycles as the competitive position of the firm evolves to match the market opportunity. Finally, when resources and capabilities have been appropriately reconfigured to match the opportunity, the company exploits and captures the opportunity through *seizing* (denoted by "c").

Despite the lack of agreement on the exact role of dynamic capabilities in the reconfiguration of resources, one can nonetheless conclude that this critical strategic task cannot be left to chance; that it demands deliberate, purposeful, and entrepreneurial management effort.

Matching Opportunity with Response

The opportunity–response framework prompts us to think about the match between what an organization *might* do given opportunities and threats that present themselves in the firm's competitive environment and what it *can* do at any point in time given its organizational strengths and vulnerabilities. The underlying concept has actually been around for some time. Kenneth R. Andrews, in his classic book *The Concept of Corporate Strategy*,[7] defined strategy as the match between what the firm *might* do given the opportunities in its competitive environment and what

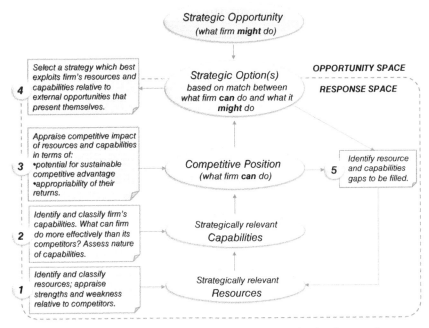

Figure 5.10 Opportunity–response analysis on the basis of strategic opportunity assessment

the firm *can* do on the basis of its internal basis of competitiveness as early as 1971.

The manner in which firms approach competitive repositioning in view of emerging market opportunities is critical to their competitiveness. While there is no standard approach, the schematic in Figure 5.10 does suggest a generic algorithm that draws on the thinking of both Andrews and Grant. It shows how the activity focused on matching resources and capabilities to opportunities in the environment might be carried out in practice. The schematic suggests another important point; it underscores a key conceptual difference between the structure–conduct–performance approach to strategy of the 1970s and 1980s and the resource-based view introduced in the 1990s. The scheme suggests how a firm might proceed in deriving a deliberate and purposefully crafted response on the basis of an assessment of its resources and capabilities.[17] Capabilities as a manifestation of organizational knowledge are dependent on learning for their development. However one defines resources and capabilities, the objective of the assessment is to match what the company *might* do on the basis of the opportunities in the environment, and what it currently *can* do as a result of its resource and capability position.

STRATEGY IN PRACTICE: QUESTIONS PROMPTED BY THE OPPORTUNITY–RESPONSE ANALYSIS

- What are the underlying drivers and trends that are shaping the trajectories representing market opportunities in our competitive environment?
- At what rate are these evolving; which ones should we be tracking?
- How do we go about sensing – and making sense of – trajectories that we are tracking?
- How do we transfer insight gained from our sense making back into the organization?
- How do we go about reconfiguring our resources and organization on the basis of insight gained in the market?
- Who are the competitors vying for the same market opportunity; what unique attributes do our competitors exhibit?
- What will be the next big breakthrough in the market – and who will ride that wave – will it be us or our competitors? And why?
- What would it take for us to break from the competitive pack?
- What would need to change in our basis of competitiveness in order to achieve this clear distancing from our competitors?
- How do we best approach and execute the necessary acceleration of our learning trajectory?

SUMMARIZING THE CHAPTER . . .

- High-level strategic analysis probes and ultimately seeks to provide a "big-picture" mapping of the firm's competitive context.
- The high-level perspective provides a comprehensive view that includes the strategic value at stake in the context of the firm's external competitive context and its internal basis of competitiveness.
- The two high-level analyses examined in this chapter are the value proposition and unique competing space concepts and frameworks.
- The unique competing space offers an insightful perspective on the firm's strategic boundaries.
- The firm's three strategic boundaries form the perimeter of its competitive domain; each is uniquely significant.
- Finally, the opportunity–response framework positions the firm's competitive position relative to market opportunity; it thereby addresses the "when?" question.

Notes

1. Drucker, P.F. (1994) The theory of the Business, *Harvard Business Review*, September–October 1994 Issue, pp. 95–104.
2. See Hamel, G. and Prahalad, C.K. (1989) Strategic Intent, *Harvard Business Review*, May–June; Prahalad, C.K. and Hamel, G. (1990) The Core Competence of the Corporation, *Harvard Business Review*, May–June.
3. Treacy, M. and Wiersema, F. (1995) *The Discipline of Market Leaders*, New York: Perseus Books.
4. Collis, D.J. and Montgomery, C.A. (2008) Competing on Resources, *Harvard Business Review*, July–August 2008, pp. 140–150.
5. See *FORBES* (May 7, 2012) Bezos is Best (*FORBES.com Views*).
6. Miller, W.L. and Morris, L. (1999) *Fourth Generation R&D*, New York: John Wiley & Sons, Inc., pp. xv–xvi.

7. Andrews, K.R. (1971) *The Concept of Corporate Strategy*, New York: Richard D. Irwin.
8. Teece, D.J. (2009) *Dynamic Capabilities & Strategic Management*, Oxford: Oxford University Press.
9. Teece, D.J., Pisano, G. and Shuen, A. (1997) Dynamic Capabilities and Strategic Management, *Strategic Management Journal*, Vol. 18(7), pp. 509–533.
10. Porter, M.E. (1980) *Competitive Strategy: Techniques for Analyzing Industries and Competitors*, New York: The Free Press.
11. Barney, J.B. and Clark, D.N. (2007) *Resource-Based Theory*, Oxford: Oxford University Press, pp. 69–71.
12. Grant, R.M. (1991) The Resource-Based Theory of Competitive Advantage: Implications for Strategy Formulation, *California Business Review*, Spring, pp. 114–135.
13. Peteraf, M.A. (1993) The Cornerstones of Competitive Advantage: A Resource-Based View. *Strategic Management Journal*, Vol. 14, pp. 179–192.
14. Helfat, C.E., Finkelstein, S., Mitchell, W., Peteraf, M.A., Singh, H., Teece, D.J. and Winter, S.G. (2007) *Dynamic Capabilities*, Oxford: Blackwell Publishing.
15. Helfat, C.E. and Peteraf, M.A. (2003) The Dynamic Resources-Based View: Capability Life-Cycles, *Strategic Management Journal*, Vol. 24, pp. 997–1010.
16. Helfat, C.E. and Peteraf, M.A. (2009) Understanding Dynamic Capabilities: Progress Along a Developmental Path, *Strategic Organization*, Vol. 7, p. 91.
17. Whereas Grant (1991) draws a distinction between resources and capabilities, Birchall and Tovstiga (2005) view capabilities as a subset of the firm's (intellectual capital) resource base. Capabilities are viewed as a manifestation of (strategic and actionable) organizational knowledge and, as such, one possible expression of the firm's resources (Birchall, D.W. and Tovstiga, G. (2005) *Capabilities for Strategic Advantage – Leading through Technological Leadership*, Basingstoke: Palgrave Macmillan).

CHAPTER 6

Supporting-Level Strategic Analysis

Reason does not work instinctively, but requires trial, practice, and instruction in order to gradually progress from one level of insight to another.

—Immanuel Kant

IN THIS CHAPTER, WE:

- elaborate on the nature, role, and application of supporting-level frameworks of strategic analysis in the context of sense making;
- differentiate between supporting frameworks of analysis that probe and seek to provide insight into the firm's external competitive environment and those that focus on the firm-internal context;

- introduce some key supporting-level frameworks of strategic analysis for making sense of external and internal contexts;
- review and discuss the limitations of supporting-level strategic analysis.

Strategic analysis is about sense making; it seeks to make sense of changes in the firm's external and internal competitive environments that might require responsive action on the part of the firm. Good strategic analysis, we have argued earlier, begins with the framing of issues that are strategically relevant. These, in turn, give rise to strategic questions that prompt insights relevant to the particular strategic challenge at hand. It was further argued that it is always advisable to begin with a *high-level* positioning of the greater strategic context in question in order "not to lose sight of the wood for the trees." Two high-level conceptual approaches suitable for that task, the *value proposition* and *unique competing space* frameworks, were examined in Chapter 5. The outcome of the high-level analysis is a mapping of the firm's greater strategic context; it positions the external competitive environment and the firm's internal competitive position in the context of the strategic value at stake. The high-level analysis therefore establishes the greater strategic context that consists of the firm's external competitive environment on macro-, industry, and market levels, and the internal context of the firm in question, while the supporting level of strategic analysis provides the details pertaining to the specific contexts.

Supporting-Level Analysis: External and Internal Analysis Frameworks

Strategic analysis is about generating insights prompted by the "right" strategic questions derived from rigorous strategic thinking. Individual analyses of the firm's external and internal basis of competitive context need to be purposeful. The analysis of these contexts is not an end unto itself; it is a means to an end. That "end" is ultimately a reconstructed composite comprised of integrated insights reflecting the firm's competitive landscape. The application of individual frameworks of strategic analysis, whether externally or internally focused, therefore needs to be purposefully insight driven. This demands astute selection and application of those frameworks most suitable for generating the insights sought. Ultimately, though, the objective is to achieve an *integration* of insights generated through the application of individual frameworks of analysis that enables a better understanding of the firm's competitive context.

In this chapter we examine supporting frameworks of analysis that focus on the external context and those that can be used to make sense of the firm's internal context. There are many such frameworks of strategic analysis in circulation today. Entire Internet sites are devoted to management frameworks and models of analysis.[1] A number of these can be useful if appropriately applied, while some are clearly dated if not altogether obsolete. All models and frameworks of strategic analysis are limited by their simplification of reality, and by the quality of the input data available for use in the analysis. Some strategy frameworks tend to reflect the historical evolution of the strategy discipline. Early frameworks such as the *Ansoff product/market growth* and the *BCG growth share* matrices that originated in the late 1950s and 60s were no doubt useful at the time, and to some limited degree still applicable yet today. However, our understanding of competitive environments has evolved. Competitive environments increasingly defy precise definition as they become ever more dynamic; assumptions that may have had some degree of validity several decades ago often no longer hold. On the other hand, the strategic management field has experienced notable advances; more powerful approaches to strategic analysis have emerged. In subsequent sections of this chapter we examine and reflect on some of these. Numerous approaches to strategic analysis exist. Many have been presented, debated and discussed at length in the management literature. It is not the objective of this book to replicate material that is readily accessible in any of the excellent recent textbooks on strategic management.[2] The objective is much more to:

- Narrow the focus to a select few supporting frameworks of strategic analysis that might be effectively used to make sense of the firm's relevant external and internal competitive contexts;
- Examine how these analysis approaches align with, and support, strategic thinking; how supporting-level analysis might be applied to generate the insight prompted by strategic issues and questions articulated;
- Examine how insights generated might be integrated to create highly perceptive perspectives on a firm's competitive landscape.

In the following sections of this chapter a select few frameworks of strategic analysis are introduced and critically reviewed; in doing so we adhere to the basic premises that:

1. A few frameworks, suitably selected and appropriately applied, can generate disproportionately valuable insight;
2. It is not necessarily the variety of the selection of frameworks; rather, the right choice of analysis approach and the way in which insights derived from these are integrated and consolidated to re-create a "big-picture" perspective of the firm's competitive situation in a way that most closely portrays the firm's competitive reality;
3. Supporting-level strategic analysis is limited by an intrinsic assumption of rationality on the part of relevant actors; real business environments do not necessarily substantiate this resumption.

Externally Focused Supporting Frameworks of Strategic Analysis

In this section we:

- Introduce a selection of key frameworks of strategic analysis focused on making sense of the firm's external competitive environment; in particular, these are frameworks that examine the firm's macro-economic, industry, and market contexts relevant to its competitive position;

- Examine how these frameworks can be applied to support the high-level analysis frameworks introduced in the previous section;
- Discuss limitations of the frameworks within the greater context of strategic sense making.

In Chapter 1 we reflected on the purpose of an organization and what it seeks to achieve in order to meet the value expectations of its various stakeholder groups. Understanding what the organization is trying to achieve provides us with a frame of reference for assessing the external environmental factors from a perspective that helps us identify insights that are critical for making sense of the external context.

This section begins with a consideration of the external environment from a broader *macro-level* perspective. We then explore the *industry level* of analysis. Industries are comprised of markets; hence, in the final part of this section we examine frameworks of analysis relevant to the firm's *market level* of analysis. A key tenet of the firm's external competitive context is that it is *beyond* the direct control of any single firm. This notwithstanding, market-leading firms may very well wield some degree of influence in certain markets by virtue of their unique position in those markets. Apple's influence on the smartphone market through the launch of its iPhone is a case in point. Governmental regulatory bodies, of course, are always wary of firms that are in a position to exert power in their markets. For all intents and purposes, it may be assumed that firms have very little if any means of influencing their external competitive environments.

Macro-Economic Environment

Firms and organizations operate in business environments that are changing rapidly. Global forces today are driving large-scale change in virtually all industry sectors. These changes have a major, long-lasting, and invariably irreversible impact on business and society. Macro-level effects ultimately cascade down to sectors, and, within these, to markets. To understand their impact and implications for market segments we need to develop an understanding of *what* is happening in the wider macro-economic environment, (where feasible) *why* it is happening, and (importantly) *how* it will affect the firm's sector, industry, and markets. The better we understand the cause and effect associations between the forces shaping our business and its markets, the better positioned firms are to respond appropriately if called for.

PwC, a management consultancy, recently reported research into trends in the global economy and their implications for business and governments; their findings suggest five key megatrends and patterns that are having a profound impact on the global economy and society[3]:

1. *Demographic and social change* – primarily influenced by combinations of greater life expectancy, declining birth rates, and unprecedented human migration;
2. *Shifts in global economic power* – leading to profound changes in consumption patterns and a rebalancing of international relations;
3. *Rapid urbanization* – massive expansion of cities through combinations of migration and childbirth and having major implications for infrastructure, employment, quality of life, and wealth creation;
4. *Climate change and resource scarcity* – accompanying demographic and social change, rapidly increasing demand for food, energy, and water – in a finite world with limited resources and capacity for carbon dioxide and other waste;
5. *Technological breakthroughs* – new advances in technology leading to fundamental changes in how business is conducted, transforming everyday life through digitally enabled innovation

in increasingly cross-disciplinary fields, including nanotechnology, biotechnology, and telecommunications.

Examination of this list indicates significant interdependencies between the individual trends and patterns. They not only coincide, rather they also tend to interact and simultaneously reinforce each other, leading to further disruptive change.

The PESTLE Framework

A number of the trends identified in the previous section are rooted in combinations of the following macro-level factors, known collectively by their acronym; these are the so-called *PESTLE* factors.

A PESTLE (acronym for Political, Economic, Societal, Technological, Legal, Environmental) analysis is a suitable point of departure for making sense of the macro-level environment of the firm. The factors that comprise this analysis are those that are thought to be strategically most relevant in assessing the macro-level environment relevant to the firm. In assessing which of the PESTLE factors are relevant to a given analysis, it is important to focus on those for which (1) the probability of change is significant, and (2) the anticipated impact on the business is also significant. The second of the two criteria is the most important. Even if the probability of something happening is low, if it is anticipated to have a major impact on the firm's competitive position then it should feature prominently in our strategic thinking and analysis. Developing a clear understanding of the cause and effect relationships between the factors in the PESTLE model is more challenging.

PESTLE factors represent broad *categories* of factors. Any environmental analysis includes a large number of variables, many of which will be subject to constant change. It is therefore a complex activity that can involve qualitative or quantitative analysis of data gathered. Firms often track key factors with the help of a dashboard template. The key constraint in a macro-factor analysis, invariably, is the validity and reliability of the data available for analysis. The dilemma facing many firms today – particularly in quickly changing, evolving markets – is that there is simply no reliable data available.

> **STRATEGY IN PRACTICE: WHEN CARRYING OUT AN ANALYSIS OF THE PESTLE FACTORS IT IS IMPORTANT TO KEEP THE FOLLOWING IN MIND:**
>
> - Not all of the PESTLE factors are equally relevant or important in respect to the specific analysis task at hand; it is important to narrow the primary focus on those that are. However, since competitive circumstances change, it is important not to neglect any of the factors.
> - Of those factors relevant and important to the analysis, not all are changing at the same rate; some are evolving more quickly than others. It is important to track those that are changing most rapidly. *Snapshot* analyses offer a static perspective whereas *trend* analyses of the relevant factors offers a more powerful view that suggests not only magnitude of change but also the direction of that change.
> - Most often, macro-level factors are interlinked; factors are interdependent and influence each other. It is important to assess the impact of other factors on a particular factor for a more integrated perspective on change in the macro-economic environment.

Sector and Industry-Level Analysis

Forces in the broader macro-level environment of business inevitably have an impact on the sector or industry environment in which a firm chooses to compete. While global, macro-economic factors affect all industries, individual industries are affected in different ways by macro-level factors. But how important are industry and business segment-level factors in the greater context of a firm's competitive performance; how much do they really matter? This question has been debated for some time. McGahan and Porter[4] explored this question using a sampling of data available from Compusat Business Segment Reports covering business activity in all sectors of the American economy except for the financial sector. Their findings suggest that industry-level and business-specific effects collectively contribute as much as 51% of variability in firms' relative competitive performance. More recent studies challenge these findings as we shall see further on in this chapter. The data used in the McGahan and Porter study originated from data compiled in the 1980s and into the early 1990s. Moreover, strategic thinking has moved on from the *industry-organization* paradigm of the 1980s to where we now attribute a much greater contribution of the firm's competitiveness to its utilization of its resources; this latter view having been shaped in particular by the resource-based theory of the firm introduced in the 1990s. These developments notwithstanding, the importance of a *good understanding* of the firm's external competitive context in strategic thinking and sense making has not been diminished in any way.

In this section we look at some dimensions relevant to the industry level of analysis. Two supporting frameworks of analysis are introduced: the *industry life-cycle (or maturity)* and the *industry value-chain analysis* frameworks. We examine how we might use these frameworks to gain a better understanding of the competitive dynamics of an industry and how these are affected by changes in that industry.

Industry Maturity, S-Curve, or Life-Cycle Analysis

The classic industry life-cycle model (sometimes referred to as the *industry S-curve model*) shows demand or performance (such as market share or return on investment) as a function of time.

The life-cycle is typically segmented into four stages: *emergent, growth, mature,* and *decline* phases. In the emergent phase of a life-cycle, performance is most often linked to a value offering related to functionality and growth is likely to be nascent. Customers are typically confined to "early adopters" of new ideas and products. Once, however, a value offering achieves a breakthrough point and a basis of competitiveness is established, growth can be dramatic. In the growth phase, players seek to meet the increase in demand while competing for a dominant position in the market. Eventually an industry moves into the mature phase of the life-cycle, which is characterized by a flattening of the growth curve and a gradual commoditizing of the value offering. Competition reduces to pricing, and an increase in sales is possible only at the expense of other players' market share. A maturing of the industry typically triggers a shakeout of competitors leading to a consolidation of the playing field. At this point the industry structure may resemble an oligopoly, dominated by a few large players. Finally, the industry moves into the decline phase as extant value offerings are replaced by disruptive new ones.

The overall span of life-cycles and the duration of individual stages within them can vary considerably from industry to industry. The rate of evolution is tied to the factors unique to the industry sector. Industry sectors such as power generation may evolve over decades while the telecommunications sector might exhibit life-cycles of less than a year. Generally, high-tech technology-related industries tend to have short life-cycles. While the growth phase of an industry life-cycle tends to be viewed as a favorable period, it may not be that for all players. Smaller players, unable to compete with the economies of scale or marketing budgets of the main players, may find themselves being squeezed out of a particular market. The mature phase, on the other hand, is not necessarily detrimental for everyone. First, this stage may last for years; second, market leaders with favorable cost positions are often well placed to exploit and reap benefit from "cash cow" offerings in their product portfolio.

Different phases of the life-cycle offer variable opportunities for value creation and delivery. While the emergent and growth phases offer opportunity for competitive differentiation on value attributes other than price, competition in the mature phase is typically characterized by falling margins and competition primarily on price. This latter stage is generally not attractive. Firms that compete successfully in maturing markets focus on operational excellence. Firms that don't achieve cost efficiency in this phase either exit or flounder.

STRATEGY IN PRACTICE: INDUSTRY LIFE-CYCLE ANALYSIS – LIMITATIONS

Life-cycle analysis enables us to make some projections on how an industry is likely to develop, and, based on this, appropriate strategic approaches in each phase. But, there are limitations:

- The relative length of each of the lifecycle phases varies significantly from industry to industry. Some, such as the building and hotel industries, have been in maturity for decades without showing signs of decline.
- Not all industries go through exactly the same process; maturing trends can be reversed by new social and/or technological trends. Industries can reinvent themselves producing resurgence in demand, as evidenced by Nespresso premium single-serve coffee capsules, Häagen-Dazs luxury ice cream, or easyJet with low cost flights.
- Some industries (such as fashion and media) can exert a powerful impact on demand and are relatively immune to economic cycling. Others may exhibit a cyclical pattern of rapid growth followed by equally rapid decline in response to change in the socio-economic environment.

Industry Value Chain Analysis

Industries are comprised of series of value-adding sectors. These are sometimes thought of as *primary* (e.g. raw materials extraction), *secondary* (e.g. processing and manufacturing), *tertiary* (e.g. provision of services), and *quaternary* (e.g. provision of scientific and engineering research). An industry value chain analysis provides insight into where value is created in a particular sector or across an entire industry; as such, it represents an ordering of the spheres of economic activity in an industry. Different spheres of activity contribute different elements to the creation of the value offering generated in an industry at any given point in time. Value is created along the entire length of the value chain. However, the distribution of where value is created along the value chain may vary considerably along its length; moreover, it is a function of time. This gives rise to value creation "hot spots" along the value chain – sections along the value chain in which value creation is disproportionately concentrated at a given point in time. Value hot spots are not static; they tend to migrate as the industry matures. Typically, potential for value creation is concentrated on upstream segments of the value chain in the early stages of an industry. As an industry matures its value hot spots tend to migrate downstream along the value chain.

An analysis of the firm's industry value chain can deliver a number of important insights and these can be used in a number of ways. For example, it can be used to identify where the value hot spots exist along the firm's industry value chain at a set point in time. Once located, this insight enables the firm to appraise where it is positioned relative to where the value creation opportunities are highest. Once this has been established, the firm might use this insight (alongside other insights) to derive suitable options that might include, for example, a repositioning of the firm along the value chain. Migration of the value creation hot spot that accompanies the maturing of an industry often forces consolidation and integration within a particular value chain segment (*horizontal* integration), or along the value chain (*vertical* integration).

STRATEGY IN PRACTICE: INDUSTRY VALUE CHAIN HOT SPOTS

Potential for value creation, we asserted earlier in this section, is not equally distributed along the industries' value chain. This gives rise to value creation hot spots, prompting the following important questions as firms reflect on their industry value chain, and, more importantly, their position in the industry value chain:

- Where in your industry's value chain are the value creation hot spots?
- How are these linked to the industry's key success factors; that is, what are the key success factors that define the segments of the value chain featuring the value hot spots?
- Where in the value chain is the firm positioned relative to the industry's value hot spots; what are the implications of the maturity stage of the industry for competition in that industry?
- How quickly, and where to, are the value hot spots migrating?
- Does the migration of the value hot spots represent an opportunity or a threat for the firm?
- What are the implications of the firm's position in the industry value chain for its unique competing space?

Market-Level Analysis

Industries typically encompass a number of markets. The automotive industry, for example, is comprised of markets ranging from low cost, compact vehicles to exclusive luxury limousines. The focus of the analysis of the following three frameworks is at the market level. It is at the *market* level, not at the *industry sector* level, that the firms face their competitors – much as manufacturers of luxury automobiles do not compete with firms manufacturing low cost, compact cars, although both are in the automotive sector.

Key Success Factor Analysis

Key success factors (KSFs) are the competing factors that most closely capture the competitive essence of a market place and offer a potentially powerful perspective on the market in question. Key success factors encompass the "rules of the market place" and are those factors that carry the greatest implications for success and performance of the firm in its respective market. Key success factors capture the "market place logic" – the underlying rationale for what constitutes successful competition in a particular market. Factors might include unique product attributes, or unique capabilities demanded of players in those markets alongside other intangible assets such as strong brand. In mature markets, the ability of players to operate at a low cost basis may be a key success factor. Often, combinations of factors form clusters of key success factors.

Importantly, key success factors are attributes of the market place. No individual player "owns" the key success factors of a given market. However, individual players may profoundly influence their evolution. A case in point is the influence Apple's iPhone exerted in the smartphone market when it was introduced in 2007. Once introduced, however, the iPhone set the standard for all competitors in the smartphone market – including Apple with any of its future smartphone offerings.

Key success factors represent the market needs and expectations on which the firm must deliver if it is to be successful. Stated slightly differently, firms succeed by virtue of their ability to deliver on the key success factors that characterize the markets they compete in. Firms that have been successful over long periods of time in stable markets often fall prey to losing their competitive position when market conditions evolve and change over time. Even the most successful companies find it challenging to sustain competitive advantage indefinitely. This is because as markets evolve, their underlying key success factors change as well. Key success factors can therefore be thought of as having a finite "shelf life." Firm's often fail to recognize this and fall into the trap of *legacy thinking*. They fail to keep their understanding of the market's evolving key success factors updated, even as they continue competing on the basis of obsolete key success factors.

Key success factors are sometimes confused with *key performance indicators*. The latter lie clearly within the domain of an individual firm, whereas key success factors are attributes of the market place. Key performance indicators might be thought of as a measure of the firm's ability to respond to the key success factors of the firm's market place.

Key success factors capture the essence of relevant stakeholders' needs; these might be obvious, but, in some cases, stakeholders (often this is the case with customers) may not yet fully understand their needs. Firms and organizations that are in a position to preemptively fulfill these needs stand to achieve competitive advantage. A notable example of this is the late Steve Jobs, former CEO of Apple, who used to claim that rather than asking he preferred to *tell* the markets what they wanted. Was Jobs' attitude in this matter an affirmation of his hubris – or was it, in fact, founded on deep insight? Possibly it was a bit of both. In reality, not many firms are in a position to preempt their markets in the way Apple was able to do in the past.

There is another perspective to key success factors that establishes a link to the firm's overall competitive position: key success factors of a given market can be assumed to encompass the *criteria* that delineate the firm's unique competing space for that particular market. Firms that succeed in delivering on these criteria better than their competitors thereby establish their unique competing space. By extension, key success factors intrinsically corroborate the uniqueness and superiority of a firm's differentiated value proposition.

Key success factors can be categorized into *qualifiers* and *order winners*. Qualifiers might be thought of as "license to play" factors that a player in the market must deliver in order to compete in that market at all. They do, however, ensure success for that player. *Order-winning* key success factors, on the other hand, are of the "license to win" type. The ability to deliver on order-winning key success factors enables the firm to establish a competitive edge in the market. Firms generally compete on the basis of their delivery on both qualifying and order-winning key success factors. As markets evolve and the competition encroaches on a firm's unique competitive position, the firm's order-winning key success factors gradually degrade to qualifying factors.

Key success factors are critical elements of the market level of analysis. They reflect and resonate with those unique market demands that comprise the firm's unique competing space. Key success factors offer firms a powerful means of gauging and calibrating the competitiveness of their strategic response in changing markets.

BOX 6.1 ORIGINS OF KEY SUCCESS FACTORS

How do key success factors come into being? Key success factors reflect rules of the market place; customers' preferences and perceptions of value. Order-winning key success factors reflect determinants linked to the creation of value premiums. It stands to reason that the emergence of key success factors is closely linked to the emergence of respective market places. Apple's newly launched iWatch provides an insightful case in point. Apple's iWatch has been touted as "the most advanced timepiece ever created" by Apple CEO Tim Cook. Not only does it tell the time, it can also respond to voice commands, monitor its wearer's heart rate, and be used as a credit card at payment points. Moreover, it is compatible with apps that tap into its user's social networks without the bother of having to use a phone.

But will the market want it – and, if so, *which* market will it be? Although the precise identity of the market in question is not yet entirely evident, it appears to be roughly in the space best described as the market related to "wearable technology." Wearable technology spans wearable, mobile devices that gather and display information, and technology that is embedded in a diverse wardrobe of products. *The Economist* reports that some 21 million wearable devices were sold last year. Wrist-worn devices, which include watches, formed the majority of these.

If the market can be broadly categorized as "wearables," a number of factors are shaping the nature of the value offering – and, in effect, the key success factors that (will) define the relevant market. Some of these factors are evident already: the availability of appropriate applications (apps); or, possibly, the absence of "killer apps" that provide more than conventional smartphones already now do. Another battle is shaping up around which operating system will ultimately dominate; Apple and Google are currently locking horns in this arena.

Other potential key success factors are emerging from market research. Morgan Stanley, an American financial services company, recently released findings from a study that polled potential users of wearable devices regarding which features they would prefer to see in these. The findings are based on a survey of 10,500 people in Brazil, Britain, China, France, Germany, Japan, and the United States. Factors deemed important include number of sensors on the device, wearing comfort, computing power, accuracy and reliability of data, overall design, and the (preferably discrete) appearance of the device.

It is thought that wearable devices hold the potential to radically transform certain industries such as health care. However, opportunities are also overshadowed by potential dilemmas. Loss of personal data, particularly medical data, through loss or theft of a wearable device poses threats that have yet to be resolved. Perhaps it is fears such as these that will need to be appropriately assuaged before the market for wearables ultimately takes off.

Source: The Economist (2015) Wearable Technology: The Wear, Why and How (March 14, 2015).

STRATEGY IN PRACTICE: A KEY SUCCESS FACTORS ASSESSMENT

The following questions probe the key success factors in your firm's markets:

- What are the market's order-winning key success factors and how do these relate to the value offering at the core of the market's expectation? How are these changing?
- What are the qualifying key success factors?
- What are the key assumptions made in your industry about its order-winning and qualifying key success factors?
- How quickly are the key success factors in your firm's markets changing; what is driving the change?
- How is your firm identifying and monitoring the key success factors in its markets; how are evolving and emerging key success factors being detected and tracked?

Competitor Analysis and Competitive Intelligence

Alongside efforts to gain a better understanding of their customer base and buyers' needs, firms need to continually monitor and make sense of their competitors' positions and activities. In highly competitive markets the gathering and analysis of competitor intelligence is of major strategic importance. One way of prioritizing competitor intelligence analysis is to focus on time horizons. Shorter business cycles usually require focus on current and existing competitors, whereas longer business cycles call for the analysis of potential new entrants and substitute products or services.

Competitor analysis can be applied to predict how competitors might behave and how they might react to a firm's own future strategy. Competitors can be assessed on the basis of the following dimensions[5]:

- *Strategy*: On what basis are competitors competing; what key success factors are they focusing on; what is it that sets them apart?
- *Objectives*: In what direction do competitors appear to be moving – and with what objectives? To what extent is their performance meeting these objectives? How are competitors' objectives likely to evolve?
- *Assumptions*: What assumptions do competitors hold about the industry and themselves? What "industry logic" are competitors adhering to?
- *Resources and capabilities*: What are the competitors' key strengths and weakness; what are their vulnerabilities?

Competitors' reactions to the firm's strategy are prompted by the following questions:

- What strategic changes will competitors initiate?
- How will competitors respond to our strategic initiatives?

The key success factor analysis introduced in the previous section provides a potentially insightful platform for a comparative competitor analysis.[6] In a first step, key success factors are identified, prioritized, and ranked (columns "1a" and "1b" in Figure 6.1). In a second step, the relative performance (columns "2a," "3a," and "4a") of the firm and its competitors "A" and "B" on each of the

		COMPARATIVE COMPETITOR PERFORMANCE					
		OWN FIRM		COMPETITOR "A"		COMPETITOR "B"	
KSFs (ranked)	IMPORTANCE[1] (a)	Performance[2] (b)	Score (a x b)	Performance (b)	Score (a x b)	Performance (b)	Score (a x b)
1.							
2.	1a	1b	2a	2b	3a	3b	4a	4b
3.							
etc.							

Comparative Scores: | Own Firm S [a x b] | Firm "A" S [a x b] | Firm "B" S [a x b]

Notes:
[1]Importance ranking (weighting) on a scale of 1 to 5 (5=most important; 1=least important)
[2]Performance estimation (how well the firm in question performs on this KSF) on a scale of 1 to 5 (5=excellent performance; 1=poor performance)

Figure 6.1   Comparative competitor analysis on the basis of a key success factor analysis.

key success factors is appraised. Scores are then formed for each of the competitors by multiplying the *importance* (common to all competitors for each key success factor) by the individual competitors' *performance* for each of the key success factors (columns "a" × "b"; for example, for the firm: "2a" × "2b"). Summed scores are then formed by adding up individual scores of the firm and its competitors (columns "2b," "3b," and "4b," respectively). The summed scores of each of the competitors are then compared. The higher the final summed score, the better the competitive performance of the competitor in question.

The comparative competitor analysis based on key success factors can be a useful tool in a number of ways. First, it forces managers to reflect critically on the precise definition of the market in question. Only once this is clear does it make sense to identify the market's attributes such as its key success factors. Second, regardless of the numerical outcome generated, the analysis focuses managers' attention and debate on the essential strategic elements pertaining to market in questions – its attributes, evolution, competitors, and the firm's own competitive position relative to all of these. Even if all this leads to is an agreement on what the disagreement is about, the analysis will at least have succeeded in ensuring that managers are on the same page – which often is a significant achievement in its own right.

There are challenges presented by the analysis. More often than not, the relevant key success factors are not numerically quantifiable. The appraisal of subjective measures relies on the reliability and validity of extracted perceptions. Reliable insights demand that the "right" questions are asked. Finally, it goes without saying that, ultimately, validation of the key success factors must be established in the market place.

STRATEGY IN PRACTICE: COMPETITOR INTELLIGENCE: CLUSTER ANALYSIS

Strategic cluster analysis compares and provides a visual picture of the strategies of companies in a similar industry. It is useful in a number of respects:

- In highly competitive industries with many competitors it may be difficult to track the activity of individual players. A clustering of competitors can help firms not to lose sight of trends that activities of individual competitors might not suggest.
- Clustering competitors into groups with comparable strategies can help build an understanding of how a particular industry operates, and why some companies appear to share common strategies, and why certain strategies appear unsustainable.
- A clustering approach enables a projection into the future by providing clues about what the emerging competitive landscape might look like.

The Porter "Five Forces" Framework

The origins of Porter's[7,8] "five forces" framework go back to the late 1970s. It reflects the *structure–conduct–performance* paradigm of industrial organization economics prevalent in that era. This paradigm views the structure of an industry or market as a key determinant of the state of competition in that context. Firms' conduct – that is, their strategy – is determined by the nature of competition in their respective competitive contexts. The "five forces" represent structural forces that determine the attractiveness (e.g. profitability potential) of a market place. The corresponding analysis places the emphasis on identifying the "right industry" and within that the attractive positions. It provides an external perspective that is most suitable for a market-level analysis. It is less suitable for an industry group or sector level analysis, unless that industry features similar or comparable value offerings. The "five forces" analysis can provide valuable insights into the nature of competition in a market and, by extension, the attractiveness of that market from the firm's perspective.

In essence, the "five forces" analysis framework is comprised of an industry value chain that features the possibility of additional inputs that account for the threat of new entrants and/or the threat of substitution of the value offering in question altogether.

The framework has limitations. First, it is based on assumptions that for the most part are no longer considered tenable. Our understanding of the determinants of industry rivalry, market dynamics, and competitive behavior of firms has progressed significantly since the framework made its appearance. Industry boundaries – a fundamental element of the Porter framework – are increasingly defying precise definition. Value chains are becoming ever more complex, with organizations simultaneously engaging in competition *and* selective collaboration; situations referred to as "co-opetition." There is also an increase in the number of complementary relationships, such as that between Microsoft and Intel, that the limited framework is incapable of taking into consideration. Many industries can be viewed as complex networks of mutually dependent players in which niche players assume important roles in complementing the market leaders. Adobe is a case in point: the software company was able to develop a niche market because its products were differentiated and did not challenge industry standards, such as Microsoft Word.

Hence, Porter's "five forces" framework has been criticized mainly for its assumption, including unrealistic conjectures, that:

- Players in the value chain – suppliers, competitors and buyers – are unrelated and that they do not interact;
- The source of advantage underpinning the value offering at stake is related to the industry or market structure; and
- The level of complexity and ambiguity in the market is low, so that players can readily stage and respond to competitors' moves.

Also limiting is the framework's neglect of the individual firms' resource base; the internal competitive basis of the individual firm and the implications of these factors for the nature of competition. Finally, the Porter "five forces" framework has been shown to be of limited application in the context of third and public sector organizations that do not "compete" in the conventional sense.

Internally Focused Supporting Frameworks of Strategic Analysis

The firm's external environment is undoubtedly an important determinant of the firm's strategic position. Arguably, however, the firm's internal factors are even more important. Empirical studies reported by Rothaermel and Hill[9] suggest that external industry effects explain about 20% of a firm's superior performance (recall the McGahan/Porter findings reported earlier in this chapter suggesting this number to be approximately 51%), while factors reflecting the firm's basis of competitiveness account for between 30 and 35% of its performance.

The firm's internal basis of competitiveness reflects its ability to establish a position of competitive advantage, and hence constitutes a critical element of strategic analysis. The supporting-level frameworks of strategic analysis examined in this section focus on generating insight into those factors that determine the firm's (ideally, uniquely differentiated) internal context. The firm's internal context is comprised of its assets, its formal and informal structure, infrastructure, processes and culture, and, ultimately, its leadership and management capability. The frameworks examined in this section seek to provide insight into these factors.

The resource-based theory of the firm provides the key perspective on the firm's internal analysis. Hence, the essential internally focused supporting frameworks of analysis address various aspects of the firm's resource base, which in the broadest sense includes the firm's organization. The internal analysis probes the disposition, ability, and capacity of the firm to establish a position of competitive advantage on the basis of how it exploits its unique bundles of strategic resources, and how it mobilizes these in a way that renders them competitively relevant. This final element of analysis thereby represents the final missing element of the big-picture analysis prompted by the high-level value proposition and unique competing space analyses dealt with in the previous chapter.

Strategic Resources and the Resource-Based View of the Firm

It is on the basis of its unique resource position and the way in which the firm uniquely configures and exploits its resources that determine its ability to differentiate itself in the way in which it creates and delivers a superior value offering. The resulting superior value thus generated by the firm, in turn, is what endows substance and validity to the firm's value proposition, and provides scope and breadth of the firm's unique competing space. Both the firm's value proposition and its unique competing space are thereby critically coupled to the firm's strategic resource base, and its ability to configure and exploit this resource base competitively.

The *resource-based view*, sometimes also referred to as the *resource-based theory of the firm*, can be critically linked to the firm's value proposition and unique competing space; it asserts that " . . . *all organizations can build and maintain long-term strategic advantage as a result of exploiting bundles of valued resources that other organizations cannot readily imitate.*" The works of a number of strategy scholars, including Barney and Clark,[10] Barney and Hesterly,[11] Peteraf,[12] Barney,[13] Wernerfelt,[14] and Grant[15,16], have made significant contributions in this area. The firm's strategic resources are those that enable it to differentiate itself competitively; they enable the firm to deliver on the order-winning key success factor.

The resources of the firm include a range of assets; these may include traditional physical or financial assets as well as intangible, intellectual capital-type assets. Increasingly, it is the latter category, in particular the firm's *capabilities* that enable it to differentiate itself. Capabilities may be of the *enabling* or *supporting* type. Although capabilities of the enabling and supporting type enable the firm to address the *qualifying* key success factors of its market place, they are not sufficient for achieving any significant degree of competitive advantage. The firm's *strategic* capabilities enable it to deliver on the order-winning key success factors established in a given market.

This point is important; phrased slightly differently: The resource-based view argues that where a firm is in a leading competitive position, or is building market share, there is a rationale for its ability to do so. That rationale is to be found in the way in which the firm deploys its unique, rare, valuable, and difficult-to-imitate resources; key resources of which are its strategic capabilities.

Capabilities as Strategic Resources

From a resource-based perspective, the firm's capabilities are assets of the intangible type. Embedded in the firm's intellectual capital, capabilities can be thought of as manifestations of organizational knowledge. They are of strategic relevance to the firm if they contribute to the creation of a differentiated value offering; strategic capabilities invariably draw on the firm's stock of strategically relevant knowledge. Strategic capabilities enable the firm to establish, exploit, and expand its unique competing space.

Capabilities are complex; they comprise messy bundles of distinctive skills, skill sets, and experiential knowledge – rather than single discrete skills or technologies. These help create disproportionate value for the customer, differentiate its owner from competitors, and allow entrance to new markets.[17] Moreover, capabilities represent an accumulation of learning over time; this implies that they are *path dependent*. Path dependency relates to the way in which capabilities evolve and develop. Capabilities do not emerge over night; it takes deliberate effort and time to develop, shape, and nurture them. Clearly, the organizational context in which they evolve – the existing resource and capabilities base, the culture of the organization, its leadership – all contribute to the shaping of the firm's capabilities.

A well-managed portfolio of knowledge-based capabilities is a prerequisite for building a strong and sustainable competitive advantage. Key competitive knowledge – primarily tacit knowledge embedded in complex organizational routines and evolving from experience over time – tends to be unique and difficult to replicate, imitate, and transfer. These features of a capability carry a number of important implications for competitive differentiation. One of these has to do with the ease with which a capability can be replicated, transferred, or lost to a competitor. For example, a high degree of *tacitness* can be an effective barrier to the diffusion of knowledge. From an external perspective, this represents a protective mechanism. However, for internal operations, high degrees of tacitness may hinder knowledge transfer and sharing, thus representing a challenge to be overcome. Firms must nurture mechanisms for purposely managing their stock of tacit knowledge.

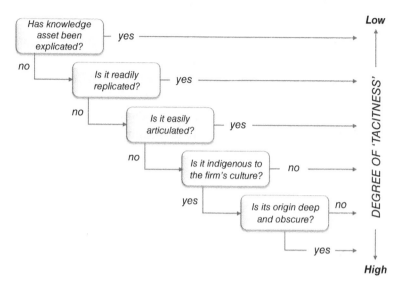

Figure 6.2 Algorithm for estimating degree of tacitness of a knowledge asset (Birchall and Tovstiga[18,19])

The tacit nature of the firms' capabilities raises formidable challenges for managers. How can something that is neither tangible nor explicit be "managed" for deliberate advantage? The management literature offers relatively little in response to this question. Some attempts have been made to scope the challenge. For example, Birchall and Tovstiga[18,19] propose an algorithm for appraising the *degree of tacitness* of a knowledge asset such as a capability (Figure 6.2).

The premise of the algorithm is that the greater the degree of tacitness of a knowledge asset, the greater its embededness in the organization's subconsciousness, and hence the lesser the extent of the organization's potential to "control" that asset.

Leonard-Barton's[20] proposed four interdependent dimensions describing the composition of capabilities provide another insightful perspective on the nature and constitution of a capability. Leonard-Barton argues that two of the dimensions are knowledge-competence repositories consisting of (1) people-embodied knowledge and skills, and (2) physical technical systems. The remaining two dimensions are organizational knowledge-control and -channeling mechanisms. These comprised (3) managerial systems, and (4) organizational culture, values, and norms.

Managing capabilities strategically extends beyond management of the individual capability. The firm's stock of capabilities consists of clusters of capabilities; capabilities are invariably intrinsically linked. Hence, it is useful to think of the firm's capabilities in terms of its *portfolio* of capabilities. Constituent capabilities may be of varying maturity and strategic impact. Various views on the portfolio perspective on capabilities have been proposed in the past. A mapping approach by Birchall and Tovstiga[18] proposes an algorithm for determining the strategic positioning of the firm's portfolio of capabilities in terms of its competitive impact (which may range from *emerging* to *obsolete*) and competitive position (reflecting the firm's degree of control over its portfolio of capabilities and its ability to exploit its current portfolio).

STRATEGY IN PRACTICE: YOUR FIRM'S STRATEGIC CAPABILITIES

You may wish to reflect on the capabilities in your own organization, or one that you know well:

- What is your business unit particularly good at doing?
- What is it that your customers value, and what makes them come back?
- What skills and other assets underpin this success?
- How rare are these strategic capabilities?
- How easily are your competitors able to imitate them and how can you make it more difficult for competitors to imitate what your firm does uniquely well?
- What issues and challenges emerge as you seek to embed and reinforce strategically critical skills and knowledge throughout the firm?

Dynamic Capabilities

Competitive environments change and so too must the firm's portfolio of strategic capabilities. The firm's strategic capabilities must be flexible and responsive to changing customer demands, and new and emerging market opportunities. Helfat *et al.* [21,22] and Teece[23,24] define dynamic capabilities as the capacity of organizations to shape, reshape, configure, and reconfigure their strategic resources and capabilities in response to changes in their competitive environment. Teece's conceptualization of three key activities associated with dynamic capabilities involving *sensing, reconfiguring*, and *seizing* was introduced in the previous chapter in the context of the *opportunity–response* analysis framework. Dynamic capabilities are arguably a class of capabilities in their own right; they are instrumental for the renewal and upgrading of the firm's primary capabilities, which enable and support its key business processes.

Identification and Appraisal of the Firm's Strategic Resources

The firm's strategic resources can be divided into two main categories. In the first we find the traditional *tangible* resources such as physical and financial resources; they are the "land, labor, capital" traditional, primary factors of production. These resources for the most part can be characterized as "having" resources; resources that can be readily accounted for on a balance sheet. In the second category we find the firm's *intangible* assets; these are sometimes characterized as the firm's "doing" assets. Strictly speaking, these are not assets in the traditional accounting sense. In practice, these assets express themselves as the firm's ability to "do" things (in a competitive sense, differently); they are either knowledge-based or manifestations of knowledge in the form of a capability or competence. They may also appear in the form of intellectual capital – bound assets such as *brand*. Capabilities and competencies are embedded in the firm's intellectual capital, which comprises the firm's human, structural, and relational capital.

Key to the notion of the firm's strategic resources, whether based on "having" or "doing" type, is the *strategic relevance* of these to the firm's capacity and ability to establish a position of competitive advantage. *Physical* and *financial* assets (recall the traditional "factors of production": *land*, *labor*, and *capital*) have been the means by which firms have traditionally established their competitive position. In many physical asset-intensive industries, this is still the case. Industries such as mining, oil exploration and production, and automotive manufacturing are highly dependent on physical and financial assets. Even in the services sector, where the value offering is essentially intangible and relationship based, physical factors such as location and facilities can be important factors on the basis of which firms competing in these markets seek to differentiate themselves.

Increasingly, however, the "doing" category of resources is being recognized for its ever greater and critical contribution to the firm's sustainable competitiveness. There are numerous indications of this. If one examines the relationship between the *book-to-market* value ratio (sometime referred to as "Tobin's q") of firms traded on any of the world's stock exchanges, one sees that the proportion of the intangible part of a typical firm's market capitalization has grown disproportionately since the early 1980s. The intangible portion of a firm's market valuation can be as high as 80% or more.[25] This introduces a high degree of volatility to the firm's traded market value. In recent times this has led to several stock market crashes – or "rupturing of the bubble" – as in the early 2000s and in the more recent economic crisis. Despite the vulnerabilities of high intellectual asset valuations, knowledge and its manifestations as capabilities and competencies are increasingly viewed to be at the root of wealth creation.

The firm's strategic resources and capabilities, as argued earlier, are those with significant impact on the firm's ability to create

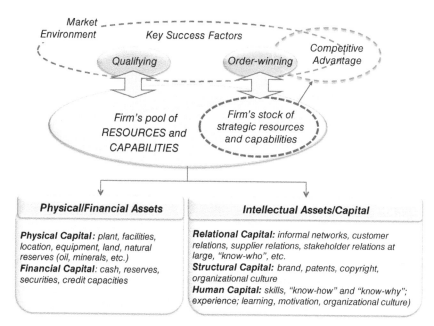

Figure 6.3 Firm's resources and capabilities; tangible and intangible assets[2]

and sustain a position of competitive advantage. As suggested in Figure 6.3, the firm's strategic resources and capabilities resonate with its markets' order-winning key success factors and contribute to the achievement of competitive advantage.

Building on the broad categorization indicated in Figure 6.3 we can proceed to identify the firm's stock of resources and capabilities in a semi-structured way with the help of the framework shown in Figure 6.4. The firm's resources with significant presence in the firm are broadly categorized according to their type – tangible and intangible – and subsequently in terms of their more specific designation. In a first step, all resources with significant presence in the firm are thus listed in column "a." In a next step, all resources and capabilities listed in column "a" are appraised as to their strategic relevance; the estimated values on a scale of "1" to "10" ("1" representing absolutely no impact; "10" representing a significant impact) are entered in column "b." Strategic relevance relates to the degree to which the resource of capability in

Illustrative Example		Resource with	Strategic	Firm's relative
	Resource	significant	relevance[1]	strength in this
	category	presence in firm		resource[2]
		(a)	(b)	(c)
Tangibles	Physical Capital	P1	7	8
		P2	6	6
	Financial Capital	F1	5	7
Intangibles	Human Capital	H1	3	4
		H2	6	4
	Relational Capital	R1	8	9
		R2	7	7
	Structural Capital	S1	8	4
		S2	7	6

Notes:
1) Strategic relevance: 1 = irrelevant; 10 = highly relevant
2) Relative strength: 1 = very weak; 10 = very strong

Figure 6.4 Semi-structured approach to identifying and appraising the firm's strategic resources and capabilities

question has an impact on the firm's competitive advantage. Finally, the same resources and capabilities are appraised as to their relative strength in the firm in column "c"; again on a scale of 1 to 10.

The summary of the appraisal of the firm's resources and capabilities are subsequently plotted on a simple matrix chart such as in Figure 6.5. The axes represent the dimensions "strategic relevance" (x-axis) and "relative strength" (y-axis). Individual resources and capabilities are represented by bubbles; the size of the individual bubbles might represent some further dimension, such as invest effort in that resource or capability. Ideally, the appraisal should indicate a clustering of the firm's resources in the upper right quadrant. This is where the resources identified are not only appraised to be strategically relevant, but the firm is also in a strong position relative to its competitors in respect of these resources and capabilities.

In the illustrative case shown graphically in Figure 6.5, most of the resources and capabilities are positioned in the upper right-

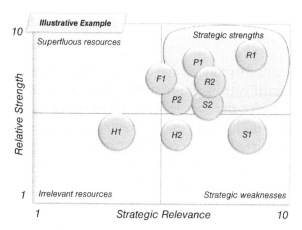

Figure 6.5 Graphical appraisal of firm's strategic resources; identification of strategic relevance and strength of firm in respect of resources and capabilities. (Note: the figure is based on the illustrative performance ratings of resources and capabilities in Figure 6.4)

hand quadrant, which is where they are not only of strategic relevance, but the firm is also in a strong position in respect of each of the resources in question. However, resources "H1," "H2," and "S1" are shown to be in the lower left and lower right quadrants, respectively. The firm would be advised to invest effort in moving resources "H2" and "S1" into the upper right quadrant as these are strategically relevant. "H1," on the other hand, is largely irrelevant, hence the firm would be advised to either phase out this resource, or to invest significantly with the intent of moving it diagonally upwards towards the upper right quadrant.

As with all mappings of this kind, one can gain further insight by tracking the evolution of individual resources and capabilities over time; one can also indicate interrelationships (dependencies) between individual resources. Finally, one can add even more detail by plotting comparable resources of key competitors for comparative purposes.

Appraising the Firm's Strategic Resources and Capabilities

The frameworks introduced and discussed in the previous section enable an identification and first appraisal of the firm's strategic resources. Despite the fact that many resources are difficult to appraise due to their intangible character, resources and capabilities can be subjected to a more precise appraisal. Two approaches to a more precise appraisal of the firm's resources and capabilities are introduced and discussed in this section; these are Grant's "profit-earning potential" of a resource of capability,[5] and Barney and Clark's "VRIO" (valuable, rare, imitable, organization)[10] framework.

Grant's[5] Profit-Earning Potential of a Resource or Capability

Grant's approach to appraising the strategic importance of an individual resource or capability relates the strategic relevance and importance of a resource or capability to its "profit-earning potential." An asset's "profit-earning potential" is a measure of its strategic relevance. Three criteria clusters probe this condition on the basis of:

1. The extent to which the resource or capability contributes to establishment of competitive advantage in the firm;
2. The degree to which it does so sustainably; and
3. The appropriability of that resource and capability.

The three criteria are further segmented into eight further sub-criteria as shown in Figure 6.6:

How does one apply this framework? Individual resources are individually appraised on the basis of a scoring of the eight factors representing the subcriteria, whereby these are broadly defined in the following way:

- *Scarcity*: A measure of the resource's abundance and availability.

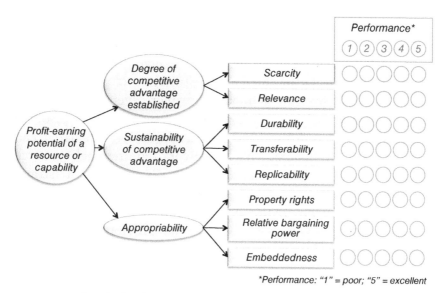

Figure 6.6   Grant's "profit-earning potential" framework for appraising strategic importance of a resource or capability

- *Relevance*: A reflection of the degree to which the resource can be linked to one or more of the current key success factors.
- *Durability*: A measure of the resource's sustainability and resilience over time.
- *Transferability*: A measure of the resource's mobility; primarily within the firm, but also its diffusion potential across the firm's boundaries.
- *Replicability*: A measure of the ease with which a resource can be copied or imitated.
- *Property rights*: Addresses the ownership profile of the resource, intellectual property rights, and extent to which the firm owns these.
- *Relative bargaining power*: Reflects the degree to which the firm is in a position to exercise control over the asset's exploitation.
- *Embeddedness*: A measure of accessibility of the resource; sometimes linked to a related concept of *stickiness* of a particular resource; for example, sticky knowledge is often an integral part of a regime such that it cannot be extracted in a meaningful way.

A scoring column for noting estimated performance of the individual resource or capability on each of the criteria is indicated in Figure 6.6. Clearly, most if not all of the eight criteria indicated are subjective in nature; hence, an estimation of performance is often the best we can achieve. However, even an estimated performance score on any of the criteria for a particular resource or capability, if carefully reflected and appropriately debated, can contribute useful insight. This framework requires each resource or capability to be appraised individually. Estimations of "strategic relevance" of resources or capabilities identified and subjected to a first appraisal on the basis of the semi-structured two-dimensional approach described in the previous section can now be verified and reported with greater confidence.

The VRIO Framework

The VRIO framework proposed by Barney and Clark[10] presents an alternative means of appraising the competitive impact of a resource or capability. The framework is shown in Figure 6.7 and can be used much in the same way as the previously discussed framework; individual resources and capabilities are systematically scrutinized for their competitive impact.

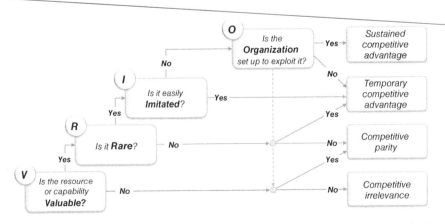

Figure 6.7 VRIO framework for systematic appraisal of strategic relevance of individual resources and capabilities

Individual resources or capabilities are probed for how *valuable*, *rare*, and *imitable* they are; a final step of the algorithm queries the extent to which the organization is enabled to *exploit* the resource or capability. The final "O" step resonates with the fifth building of strategy introduced in Chapter 1 of this book. The implication is important: a firm may be in possession of resources or capabilities that are indeed valuable, rare, and not easily imitated; yet if it is incapable of exploiting a particular resource or capability, possession of the same may endow temporary advantage at best.

Analysis of the Firm's (Internal) Value Chain

In a previous section we introduced the industry-level value chain and saw how its analysis provides insight on where value creation is concentrated along the industry value chain. Firms also have an internal value chain. The internal value chain provides insight into how the firm is utilizing its processes, resources, and capabilities to create the value it delivers to the market. A generic framework of the firm's internal value chain attributed to Porter[8] provides a visual mapping of the alignment of the firm's value creating activities and processes.

Ideally, the firm's internal value chain aligns strategically with the value chain in its industry. This is the case when (1) the firm is positioned at a point along the industry value chain where the potential to create value is high (i.e. at or near an "industry value hot spot"), and (2) the firm's own value-creation processes are optimally configured for creating and delivering that value. In reality, we rarely find this idealized constellation – but it is what firms seeking competitive advantage continually strive to achieve.

The value chain mapping distinguishes between primary activities and supporting activities. Moreover, among the primary activities we would expect to find variable contributions from individual process stages to the total value created across the firm's value chain. It should be the strategic objective of the firm to align and focus its effort on those of its activities that contribute most significantly to where the potential for creating value is greatest in the industry value chain. In some cases this might lead to a migration of the firm's activities downstream along its industry value chain – or possibly relocating the firm in an entirely new industry.

STRATEGY IN PRACTICE: YOUR FIRM'S INTERNAL VALUE CHAIN

Here is an exercise you may wish to do to help you understand your organization's value chain and its competitive implications:

- Map your organization's internal value chain with the help of the Porter internal value chain framework; next, map the relevant segments of the industry value chain in which your firm is competing.
- Identify value creation hot spots in your firm's internal and external value chains and the parts of the chain, or linkages, where significant value is being created and delivered.
- Identify the nature of value creation at these value hot spots. What are the possible strategic implications of their location for your firm?
- What are your organization's value creating capabilities in relation to where the value hot spots are situated – both externally and internally?
- How are the value hot spots evolving and shifting? What are the potential vulnerabilities induced by these changes?

The Formal and Informal Organization: "Getting the Organizational Act Together"

In this final section we examine the organizational context within which the firm seeks to exploit its resources and capabilities for the

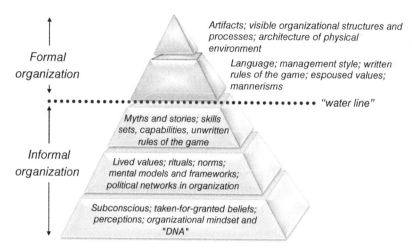

Figure 6.8 "Iceberg" model of the organization: formal and informal organization

purpose of securing and potentially expanding its unique competing space. The organizational context is arguably the least accessible domain of analysis; much of what really matters strategically
remains hidden to the eye; many of the relevant factors contributing to a firm's internal basis of competitiveness are situated below
the organization's "waterline" as suggested in Figure 6.8, which is
sometimes referred to as the organizational "iceberg" model.[26]
These factors go beyond the firm's resources and capabilities to
include both formal and informal structure, processes, practices,
routines, culture, and, ultimately, leadership and management
styles.

Critically, these need to be in alignment in order for the firm to
achieve any degree of competitiveness. Needless to point out, the
most strategically relevant resources and capabilities are of little
use to an organization that fails to "get its act together." A
military analogy is useful here: sophisticated weaponry in the
hands of those incapable of using it is essentially useless. So it is
with organizations seeking to establish their competitive position – the firm's resources and capabilities can unfold their full
competitive potential only if and when the organizational context
is optimally aligned with this purpose.

The iceberg model suggests different levels of the organization, only a fraction of which is apparent to the visible eye. The essence of the organization – embodying its culture – is embedded in its "submerged" informal part. This is where we find the organization's stock of strategically relevant knowledge, its intellectual assets embodying human, structural, and relational capital – inextricably entwined with its culture. The informal organizational levels are essentially impossible to "manage" in the traditional sense of the word; the best we can do is to create and nurture *enabling conditions* that allow the organization to unfold its full competitive potential. In practice, this is much easier said than done.

STRATEGY IN PRACTICE: ON THE USE OF FRAMEWORKS OF STRATEGIC ANALYSIS

- *Pieces of the bigger picture.* First, all frameworks, models, and techniques are simplifications of reality; hence, we need to challenge their applicability for a given analysis as much as we need to challenge the reliability and validity of the inputs once we decide to use them. Appropriately used, individual frameworks deliver insights that contribute pieces to the "big-picture" puzzle ultimately to be assembled. However, insights are only as valid and reliable as the quality of the data that goes into the analysis. It is the cumulative picture assembled from the various bits of insights that we are ultimately seeking; inevitably, however, pieces of the bigger picture will be missing.
- *Trends, not snapshots.* Second, many frameworks such as the *PESTLE* analysis, key success factor analysis and value chain analyses (both industry and internal) are most often used simply to develop a snapshot analysis at any point in time. More powerful insights can be gained by extending these analyses to trend analyses. Trend analyses tell stories in a way that snapshots cannot. When mapping out a simple PESTLE analysis graphically, indicating trends by simple vectors (e.g. direction of arrow indicating general

direction of change; length of arrow indicating magnitude of change) adds significantly to the transparency and expressiveness of the analysis.

- *Singing from the same hymn sheet.* Finally, the real value in carrying out an analysis does not necessarily lie in the absolute correctness of the analysis outcome. In many situations, such as in the case of emerging markets, no amount of analysis will produce an absolutely "right" answer. The real value of the analysis then lies in the focus and discipline it brings to the thinking and debate around the boardroom table, even if the outcome is "agreement on what the disagreement is about." To that end, appropriate analysis frameworks – particularly when brought to flipchart or whiteboard – can help to channel thinking, and help senior managers to align their thinking and to effectively "sing off the same hymn sheet."

Limitations

The purpose and usefulness of supporting-level frameworks of analysis lie first and foremost in the insight they might contribute to our sense making – if appropriately used. Frameworks and models necessarily provide simplified and therefore distorted pictures of reality. This we need to keep in mind at all times. External environments invariably present themselves in highly complex patterns; internal contexts are no different. Both can only be unraveled with appropriate tools of analysis – at best.

Pieces of insight derived from the application of individual tools and techniques of analysis may introduce error. As a rule, all insights generated by individual frameworks need to be challenged for their underlying assumptions; outcomes must be verified and validated to the extent possible. This is particularly critical in the case of rapidly changing and evolving environments, where insights developed have a very limited shelf life. Ultimately, however, the usefulness of any application of frameworks is limited by our skill and ability to piece together and integrate individual contributing elements of the analysis to construct a realistic representation of the "bigger picture" – one that enables better and improved strategic decision making.

SUMMARIZING THE CHAPTER . . .

- Supporting-level strategic analysis contributes an integral element to strategic thinking; it adds granularity to the overall analysis by supporting the creation of specific insights.
- Given the centrality of value – its creation, delivery, and capture – supporting-level strategic analysis has the purpose of exploring the greater context relevant to the firm's creation and capture of a differentiated value offering.
- The application of frameworks of strategic analysis needs to be purposeful; their use is prompted by the insights derived from strategic issues framing and the derivation of strategic questions.
- Frameworks of analysis are limited by their inherent over-simplification of reality, assumptions of rationality, and the validity and reliability of the data available.
- A few, relatively simple frameworks appropriately applied and integrated can generate a disproportionate amount of useful insight.
- Often the greatest value generated by the application of frameworks of strategic analysis is derived not so much by their specific outputs, but in the focus and structure they can contribute to the thinking and dialogue around the boardroom table.

Notes

1. For example, www.valuebasedmanagement.net presents an exhaustive listing of management models with hyperlinks to brief descriptions of the model or framework in question.
2. See, for example: Grant, R.M. and Jordan, J. (2012) *Foundations of Strategy*, Chichester: John Wiley & Sons.

3. Lancefield, D., Vaughan, R. and Boxshall, R. (2015) How to Seize the Opportunities When Megatrends Collide, *Strategy + Business*, Spring 2015 Issue (February 2015).
4. McGahan, A.M. and Porter, M.E. (1997) How Much Does Industry Matter, Really? *Strategic Management Journal*, Vol. 18 (Summer Special Issue), pp. 15–30.
5. Grant, R.M. (2010) *Contemporary Strategy Analysis*, Seventh Edition, Chichester: John Wiley & Sons.
6. Wheelen, T.L. and Hunger, J.D. (2012) *Concepts in Strategic Management and Business Policy*, 13th (International) Edition, Upper Saddle River, NJ: Pearson.
7. Porter, M.E. (1980) *Competitive Strategy: Techniques for Analyzing Industries and Competitors*, New York: The Free Press.
8. Porter, M.E. (1985) *Competitive Advantage: Creating and Sustaining Superior Performance*, New York: The Free Press.
9. Rothaermel, F.T. and Hill, C.W.L. (2005) Technological Discontinuities and Complementary Assets: A Longitudinal Study of Industry and Firm Performance, *Organization Science* Vol. 16, pp. 52–70.
10. Barney, J.B. and Clark, D.N. (2007) *Resource-Based Theory*, Oxford: Oxford University Press, pp. 69–71.
11. Barney, J.B. and Hesterley, W.S. (2006) *Strategic Management and Competitive Advantage*, Upper Saddle River, NJ: Pearson–Prentice Hall.
12. Peteraf, M.A. (1993) The Cornerstones of Competitive Advantage: A Resource-Based View, *Strategic Management Journal*, Vol. 14, pp. 179–192.
13. Barney, J.B. (1991) Firms' Resources and Sustained Competitive Advantage, *Journal of Management*, Vol. 17, pp. 99–120.
14. Wernerfelt, B. (1984) The Resource-Based View of the Firm, *Strategic Management Journal*, Vol. 5 (2), pp. 171–180.
15. Grant, R.M. (1991) The Resource-Based Theory of Competitive Advantage: Implications for Strategy Formulation, *California Business Review*, Spring, pp. 114–135.
16. Grant, R.M. (2010) (note 5 above).
17. Hamel, G. and Prahalad, C.K. (1989) Strategic Intent, *Harvard Business Review*, May–June Issue, pp. 63–76.
18. Birchall, D.W. and Tovstiga, G. (2004) The Strategic Potential of a Firm's Knowledge Portfolio, in Crainer, S. and Dearlove, D. (eds) *Financial Times Handbook of Management*, 3rd edition, Harlow: FT–Prentice Hall/Pearson Education.
19. Birchall, D.W. and Tovstiga, G. (2005) *Capabilities for Strategic Advantage – Leading through Technological Leadership*, Basingstoke: Palgrave Macmillan.

20. Leonard-Barton, D. (1995) *Wellsprings of Knowledge*, Boston: Harvard Business School Press.

21. Helfat, C.E, Finkelstein, S., Mitchell, W., Peteraf, M.A., Singh, H., Teece, D.J. and Winter, S.G. (2007) *Dynamic Capabilities*, Oxford: Blackwell Publishing.

22. Helfat, C.E. and Peteraf, M.A. (2009) Understanding Dynamic Capabilities: Progress along a Developmental Path, *Strategic Organization*, Vol. 7, pp. 91.

23. Teece, D.J. (2009) *Dynamic Capabilities & Strategic Management*, Oxford: Oxford University Press.

24. Teece, D.J., Pisano, G. and Shuen, A. (1997) Dynamic Capabilities and Strategic Management, *Strategic Management Journal*, Vol. 18 (7), pp. 509–533.

25. For example, Apple Inc.'s market value on April 24, 2015 was US $758 billion; its price/book (Tobin's "q") value on this day was reported to be 6.13. Hence, the proportion of Apple Inc.'s market value attributable to intangible assets was 84%. (Source of data: https://uk.finance.yahoo.com/q/ks?s=AAPL; accessed on April 24, 2015.)

26. The "iceberg" model is often attributed to Edgar H. Schein (1992) *Organizational Culture and Leadership*, 2nd edition, San Francisco: Jossey-Bass Publishers; Schein proposes three levels of the organization: (1) the visible part consisting of artifacts; (2) a lower level consisting of espoused values; and (3) an even lower, subconscious level comprised of basic underlying assumptions.

CHAPTER 7

Strategy Formation and Evaluation of Strategic Options

The real challenge in crafting strategy lies in detecting the subtle discontinuities that may undermine a business in the future. And for that there is no technique, no program, just a sharp mind in touch with the situation.

—Henry Mintzberg

IN THIS CHAPTER, WE:

- examine how strategic options are generated from the reconstructed "big-picture" that emerges from preceding steps of the strategic thinking process;
- explore simple mechanisms for strategy formation that are based on high-level concepts such as the unique competing space introduced in earlier chapters;

- examine the formation of strategic options in various organizational contexts;
- reflect on an *opportunity–response* perspective of strategic formation;
- examine appropriate approaches to the evaluation of strategic option based on principles, such as the building blocks of strategy, introduced in earlier chapters; and
- derive suitable criteria for the evaluation of strategic responses and reflect on their limitations.

There is no scientific approach to strategy formation. Strategic options emerge and take shape through astute sense making, continual challenging of assumptions, and careful crafting of suitable alternatives in response to a strategic challenge that presents itself. Just as importantly, there is no such thing as a single "right" response to a strategic challenge. All strategic responses feature potential liabilities. Hence, the final choice of a strategic option comes down to selecting a *preferred* option over potentially suitable alternatives through careful weighing and consideration of relevant evaluation criteria.

Earlier chapters of this book examined sense making and its role in the strategic thinking process. Purposeful sense making, it was shown, begins with (1) the articulation of the relevant strategic challenge, the framing of relevant issues, and the derivation of strategic questions to be explored through the generation of insight relevant to the strategic challenge, (2) the deconstruction of the organization's complex reality to narrow the focus of the analysis on those factors relevant to the strategic challenge in question, followed by (3) the reconstruction of reality through piecing together of the "bigger picture" on the basis of insights generated through sense making.

In following through with the strategic thinking process to this point, where does this leave us? The "bigger picture" relevant to the strategic challenge in question is now in place. The firm's bigger picture reflects the current and relevant competitive landscape prompted by the strategic questions that were articulated at the outset of the strategic thinking process. Although inevitably incomplete, it nonetheless provides a basis for strategic decision making. We are now in a position to explore strategic options that present themselves in that reconstructed strategic landscape. If the analysis has been done appropriately, the choice of options will have been narrowed down to a relatively few; these few options encompass potentially suitable strategic responses to the strategic challenge that prompted the analysis in the first place. From the relatively few options identified, we then seek to single out the one that *most suitably* addresses the strategic challenge.

In this chapter (see Figure 7.1) we explore that process by which strategic options are formulated, evaluated, and ultimately narrowed to the choice of a single appropriate strategic response.

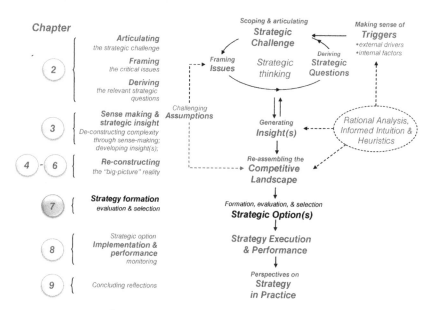

Figure 7.1 Strategic options; formation, evaluation, and selection

Too often, managers feel inclined to side-step the strategic think-ing process by jumping to "solutions" prematurely. Responses thus formed are seldom if ever "strategic"; critically, they lack rigor and compelling *"reason to believe."* There is no substitute for diligent sense making. Any attempt to circumvent such an approach jeopardizes the quality of decision making and thereby ultimately the prospects of coming up with a successful response to the strategic challenge.

STRATEGY IN PRACTICE: STRATEGY FORMULATION IN ORGANIZATIONS

Even under the most favorable circumstances, the formation of strategic options is not a trivial managerial task. Strategy formation is subject to at least three complicating factors:

- *Circumstances of incomplete knowledge:* Organizations are complex. Knowledge within organizations is continu-ally evolving and changing and is asymmetrically distrib-uted; strategy formation therefore necessarily occurs under conditions of incomplete knowledge.
- *Organizational power structures and conflicting inter-ests:* Organizations embody political systems that feature actors of differing interests, differing power relations, and legitimacy of claim to decision making. These may be conflicting and contradictory – and as often as not, inher-ently irrational.
- *Organizational complexity and ambiguity:* As a result of the foregoing factors, organizations feature varying degrees of ambiguity, some of which may be circumstantial, some of which may be deliberate. Irrational behavior on the part of some organizational players contributes a major part of the ambiguity typically found in organizations.

As might be expected, the three factors are not independent of one another. This adds to the complexity of strategic option

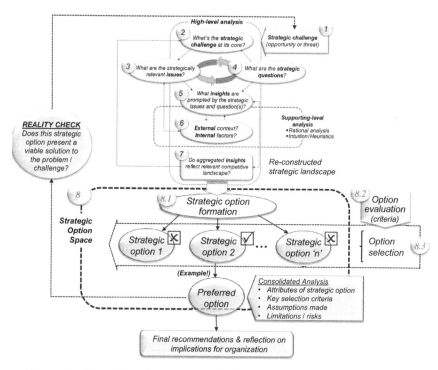

Figure 7.2 Strategic option space: option formation, evaluation, and selection

formulation. This complexity notwithstanding, insights generated by suitable supporting-level analyses (stage "6" in Figure 7.2) are nonetheless consolidated in a reconstructed strategic landscape.

The reconstructed strategic landscape represents a high-level, "big-picture" mapping of the firm's competitive position (indicated as "7" in Figure 7.2). Importantly, this is the strategic landscape relevant to the strategic challenge that prompted the exercise to begin with. The reconstructed landscape will never be complete, for reasons argued in the foregoing section. Nonetheless, when a consolidation of insights enables a sufficiently discernible "bigger picture" relevant to the strategic challenge at stake, we are in a position to proceed to strategic option space (indicated by "8" in Figure 7.2).

In this chapter we explore the three key elements of the strategic option space: strategic option *formation*, option *evaluation*, and *selection* of a most suitable response. In the first section, we examine how strategic options are formed. The second section examines techniques for evaluating suitability of strategic options, and in the last section we investigate approaches for narrowing the range of potentially suitable options to a single response representing the preferred way forward.

There is no such thing as a single "right" strategic option. Every option features liabilities of some sort or another. Hence, the objective of the selection stage is to narrow the choice of strategic options to the one option that for a given context and point in time represents the most suitable response to the strategic challenge in question.

Formation of Strategic Options

We find little consensus in the management literature on how strategic options are formed in management practice. There is certainly no "silver bullet" to strategizing. Neither are there any scientific or theoretical methods to strategy formation. Conceptual approaches such as Ansoff's[1] "growth matrix" and Porter's[2] "generic strategies," or Johnson, Scholes and Whittington's[3] "strategic clock," though often invoked for strategy formation, more correctly suggest option outcomes. They don't shed any light on the formation of strategic option. Moreover, they invariably fail to do justice to the dynamism and complexity inherent to real business environments. Rooted in traditional approaches to strategy that assumed stable and predictable competitive environments, these and similar approaches are overly simplistic and therefore limited in their applicability.

Not surprisingly, the strategic management literature on strategy formation has been criticized for these reasons. Mintzberg[4] has challenged the extant strategic management thinking on strategy formation, arguing that the strategy formation process in practice is likely far more devolved and nuanced than suggested in the current literature. Bingham *et al.*[5] point out that the changing nature of competition has led to a number of consequences for strategy formation, an important one of which is that many traditionally held assumptions are no longer valid. Moreover, given the range of variables involved in strategizing, the "right" strategy for an organization is ultimately determined by its particular circumstances, available resources, and suitable permutations of these in response to the challenge at hand.

Congruent with the line of argumentation explored in previous chapters of this book, a firm's competitive position is reflected by its *unique competing space* for a given value offering. In particular, we examined how triggers with potential impact on its unique competing space are typically sensed as perturbations at one, two, or all three of the strategic boundaries forming the perimeter of the unique competing space (Figure 7.3). Strategic challenges resulting from these either represent opportunities for expanding the firm's unique competing space, or they represent threats to the firm's competitive position. Threats to the firm's unique competing space prompt *defensive* responses; opportunities prompt strategic responses aimed at expanding its boundaries. The response in either case may involve, in simple terms, one of two types of strategic options: (1) a *make* option represents internally focused, "go it alone" effort on the part of the firm to come up with an appropriate response to the strategic challenge; or (2) a *buy* option, which represents a response that includes the involvement of external parties. This might range from partnering arrangements between the firm and other enterprises to outright acquisition of an enterprise by the firm.

Strategic options represent responses by the firm to specific strategic challenges facing the firm. The term *strategic* in this context reminds us that the challenge in question has implications for the firm's competitive position, which is reflected by its potential impact on its unique competing space. Hence, it stands

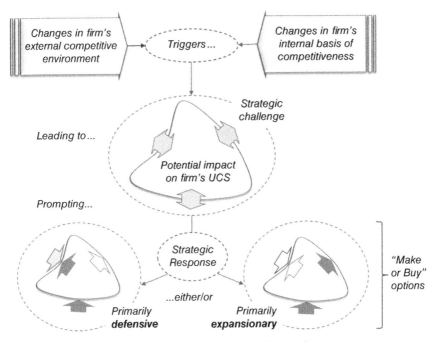

Figure 7.3 Emergence and formation of strategic responses

to reason that *strategically* appropriate responses are intrinsically linked to the firm's unique competing space. More to the point, we would expect to find appropriate strategic responses to be positioned within the perimeter of the unique competing space as shown in Figure 7.4. Strategic options therefore reflect specific elements of the strategic challenge in question; hence, a strategic response can reasonably be expected to comprise three vectors as indicated in Figure 7.4, each of which is directed at one of the unique competing space's three boundaries. The nature of the strategic challenge determines the relevance and magnitude of the contribution of any individual vector to the composition of the strategic option.

For example, an appropriate response to a *threat* to the firm's competitive position (with reference to option "n" in Figure 7.4) comprises three components, each of which is directed at one of

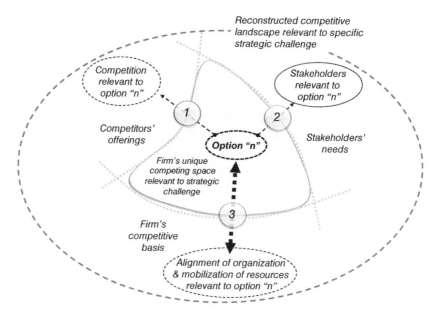

Figure 7.4 Components of a strategic option; unique competing space perspective

the three boundaries. However, given the ("threat") nature of the challenge, the option in this particular case would be expected to feature measures on the part of the firm aimed at mitigating the threat.

Strategic responses embody action deliberately instigated by the firm. Strategic responses require suitable alignment of resources and activities, and the organization's mobilization of these across boundary "3" (Figure 7.4) in a manner that suitably addresses the challenge. Hence, the "third boundary" plays a pivotal role in any strategic response. This shouldn't surprise; empirical findings presented in Chapter 5 (Box 5.5) suggest as much. Depending on the nature of the challenge, the thrust of the strategic option may be either directed to the competition (boundary "1") or to the stakeholders (boundary "2"); however, the firm's orchestration of whatever response it undertakes is rooted in its ability to mobilize activity and resources across boundary "3."

Take, for example, the case in which a firm is unexpectedly challenged by a competitor's introduction of a new competitive product offering to a market space in which the firm has an established position of competitive advantage – in other words, a market space within which the firm has legitimate claim to a relatively clearly defined unique competing space. The competitor's new value offering in that market space now poses a threat to the firm's competitive position. Its strategic challenge broadly revolves around how it might appropriately counter that threat. The firm engages in strategic thinking; it frames issues relevant to the challenge and derives a few key strategic questions, which it then purposefully sets out to explore through sense making. The thrust of the strategic options that emerge from the reconstructed strategic landscape relevant to the strategic challenge are primarily focused on a suitable response to the competitor's actions. For sake of illustration, these might involve:

1. Undertaking no immediate action, rather monitoring the market's reaction to the competitor's new offering (perhaps because of uncertainties in the market, which might evolve rapidly);
2. Mitigating or neutralizing the market impact of the competitor's offering with a comparable "me-too" offering; or
3. Accelerating the development of a viable alternative product offering that is superior to the competitor's offering, and rapidly launching it in the market.

Strategic options such as the ones outlined in the preceding example are generally composed of three elements that reflect the three boundaries of the unique competing space in question. On decomposing any such option, we find one of the elements reflecting the firm's deliberate orchestration of resources and activity in assembling a suitable response, and its mobilization across boundary "3" (Figure 7.4); the remaining two elements capture the intended impact at each of the two boundaries "1" and "2."

Strategic challenges are highly context dependent; no two situations are ever alike. Hence, we would expect no two responses to a strategic challenge to be alike either. For this reason there is no one-size-fits-all approach to the formation of strategic options. However, we would expect to find some commonality in the basic attributes of strategic options – and on the basis of the foregoing illustration, we conclude that a strategic option broadly comprises the following three components:

1. A component that encompasses the deliberate activity of the firm in orchestrating resources and activities within the firm, and their coordinated mobilization across boundary "3" of the firm's unique competing space;
2. A component representing an intended effect directed at boundary "1," the interface of the firm's unique competing space to its competition; and
3. A component representing an intended impact directed at boundary "2," the interface to the firm's markets, or stakeholders in a broader sense.

The nature of the strategic challenge ultimately determines the weighting between the three components.

Box 7.1 Nokia's Decision Revisited

Nokia's bid for Alcatel-Lucent in April 2015 appears to be an important milestone in yet another reinvention of the Finnish multinational. Few companies have gone through as many fundamental transformations; rubber boots and automobile tires, gas masks, and television sets have all been part of Nokia's history. It is now repositioning itself as a mobile internet player following its near-collapse and subsequent selling off of its mobile handset division to Microsoft in 2013.

Was Nokia's recent near-demise due to poor decision making? Was Nokia's decision to opt for Microsoft's Windows Phone operating system a "wrong choice" as Google's CEO

Schmidt claimed in its aftermath? While the debate will likely never lead to absolute closure, key decision points do lend themselves to closer scrutiny. At stake was Nokia's choice of operating system for its mobile phone handsets – and arguably, hinging on this decision, the future of its embattled mobile phone division. Nokia's rejection of Google's Android smartphone operating system in favor of Microsoft's Windows Phone system in February 2011 has been much debated. The decision was made by Stephen Elsop, Nokia's CEO at the time, and former Microsoft manager. Elsop's time at Nokia was controversial; the company's shares dropped by 85% during his tenure.

Did Nokia really have a choice? If so, what were the possible options? Arguably, there were several options: (1) moving from its dated Symbian operating system to an open-source Linux-based platform (Maemo/MeeGo); (2) Google's Android; and (3) Windows Phone.

At stake was the ecosystem associated with the choice of operating system. Nokia's choice of Windows Phone suggests a miscalculation of its growth potential with an Android operating system despite Elsop's claim at the time of the decision that Nokia would have run the risk of commoditization if it opted for Google's Android appears unfounded in retrospect. Global market shares by operating system in 2014 show Microsoft Windows Phone with 3.0% against Android's 81.2%.

Viewed from Nokia's smartphone-relevant unique competing space – or rather, what was left of it in 2011 – would suggest a misjudgment of its boundaries to its competition and its markets when in the process of forming its decision. Nokia's decision to launch its "X" model using Google's Android after all in 2014 would appear to support that view. Not that any of this matters much any longer anyway; since

February 2014 Nokia's mobile handset division has a new home within Microsoft. Indeed, rumors floated already early in Elsop's tenure at Nokia that his appointment to head the Finnish multinational was actually a Trojan horse strategy by Microsoft all along now appear prescient.

Sources: Milne, R. (2015) Finns Wary as Opportunity Knocks for Nokia, *Financial Times* (April 18/19, 2015); Parker, A., Taylor, P. and Watkins, M. (2011) Nokia "Made Wrong Choice", says Schmidt, *Financial Times* (February 15, 2011); *The Economist* (2013) Schumpeter: Microsoft and Nokia – Phone Home (September 3, 2013); Thomas, D. (2015) Smartphone Makers Battle for the Limelight, *Financial Times* (February 28, 2015); Thomas, D. (2014) Nokia Launches Google Android Phone, *Financial Times* (February 24, 2015).

Strategic options invariably fall into categories that reflect the firm's competitive context and strategic intent. Context reflects a number of important factors for strategic decision making; some of these include:

1. The *stage of maturity of the firm*; which may (though not necessarily) be further linked to the size of the firm and the dynamics of its competitive environment.
2. The *stage of maturity of the industry and market environment*, within which the firm chooses to compete, which in turn has an impact on the nature of the competition.
3. The *societal, political and regulatory environments* of the firm, which may harbor opportunities, alternatively barriers that need to be overcome by the firm.
4. The *attributes of the firm's greater economic context*, which may also provide opportunities for growth as much as they may present hindrances.

No doubt there are numerous other factors that influence how firms go about their strategic decision making. Mintzberg[4] proposes a

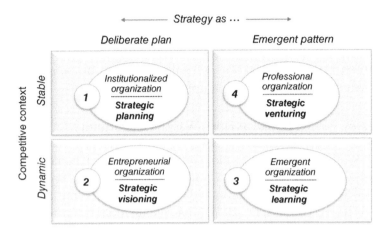

Figure 7.5 Strategy formation; configuration and primary strategic mechanisms

classification scheme for strategy formation that involves four basic organizational types:

1. Institutionalized, mature organization
2. Entrepreneurial organization
3. Emergent and adaptive organization
4. Professional organization

Associated with these organizational types are organizational attributes or configurations that determine the primary mechanism for the strategy process in the respective organization. Mintzberg categorizes firms in one of four distinct groupings or configurations suggested in Figure 7.5:

1. *Institutionalized* (or "machine-type") organizations that rely primarily on a *strategic planning process*.
2. *Entrepreneurial*-type firms that rely on a strategic visioning process.
3. Firms in *highly dynamic, emerging* contexts (or "adhocracy-type" organizations) in which strategy formation is based on the *strategic learning* process.
4. *Professional*-type organizations that deploy *strategic venturing* processes for their strategy making.

The attributes and mechanisms of strategy formation of each configuration are now examined in turn.

Strategy Formation in the Institutionalized Organization

These organizations are typically large, mature, and are first and foremost focused on preserving the status quo, stability, and predictability. Organizations of this form exhibit high levels of organizational inertia and are therefore typically resistant to internal change. They may even, if large, exert a stabilizing effect on their competitive environment. Internal stability is derived from a focus on standardized processes and efficiency of operations. With a strategic focus set on preservation, strategy formation is highly formalized and essentially consists of a strategic planning exercise that seeks to consolidate, institutionalize, and modulate the strategic direction of the organization, an activity that is often more controlling than strategic in nature. Events prompting substantial change in strategy are interspersed with long periods of stability. Even in the event of change, it is less the organization as such than the form of the organization that changes. When facing a crisis, the institutionalized configuration may suspend its machine form and revert temporarily to the entrepreneurial form, enabling a strong leader to impose the required changes. This is what happened at ABB, the Swiss-Swedish engineering multinational, under Juergen Dormann, who was brought in as CEO between September 2002 and December 2004 to get ABB back on track following its near collapse in late 2001. Once a new strategic direction has taken hold, however, the "turned around" organization reverts once more to its institutionalized form.

Strategy Formation in the Entrepreneurial Organization

Strategy formation in the entrepreneurial organization is dominated by its leadership. This might be an individual, often the founder, though it might be a small team around the founder. The competitive context of the enterprise is more often than not highly dynamic. The enterprise typically is a small start-up or new entrant to an established market with a compelling new value offering. Often, the entrepreneurial enterprise is a disruptor more intent on "imperfectly seizing the unknown" than intent on "perfecting the known."[6] However, as argued in the previous configuration, even a large institutionalized enterprise may go through punctuated periods or retrenchment or turnaround in which it most closely resembles the entrepreneurial configuration. The strategy process in this configuration therefore tends to be highly centralized and deliberately emergent in nature, reflecting on one hand the dynamic nature of the competitive environment and on the other the need for a clear strategy. This is often based on a novel vision for bringing the unique value offering to market – often product or service bound, but possibly via an innovative delivery mode. The entrepreneurial organization's leadership plays a central and direct role in the definition and enactment of its strategy.

Strategy Formation in Emerging, Dynamic Contexts

These organizations are typically organized around teams of experts that are involved in project-type work. Often on the cutting edge of highly dynamic environments found in emerging technology or market contexts, strategy formation rests collectively with the teams of experts in these organizations. Their approach to strategy making might most appropriately be described as "flying by the seat of their pants." Strategy formation has a strongly emergent component; single projects – each representing a learning platform – establish precedents that nudge the organization toward new strategies through learning. The strategy process features a strongly collective learning-based component. This organization interacts closely with its competitive environment, alternatively taking the lead and receiving direction from the changing needs of its competitive environment. Periods of strategy convergence may follow on longer periods of divergence during which there is no apparent strategy due to the high degree of uncertainty in the external competitive environment. Indeed, the competitive environment tends to be more influential in strategy formation than any leadership role within the organization.

Strategy Formation in the Professional Organization

The strategy formation process in the professional organization is driven predominantly by its highly skilled members. The strategy process is influenced by the autonomous mode in which these individuals tend to interact; it is based on *strategic venturing*. Professional organizations consist of individuals loosely associated through a common organization. Individuals in these organizations are intent on pursuing their own professional interests, however, so that the strategy process tends to serve the needs of individuals more than it does those of the organization. The individuals' professional organizations have an important if indirect role in the strategy process as well; professional organizations are subject to standard practices and norms that are set by their respective professional governing bodies (e.g. medical boards or legal bar associations). Strategy process outcomes serve to ensure the continuity within relatively narrow limits of change in the value offerings of these organizations. Typically, these organizations provide professional standardized services in stable settings. The overall leadership impact on strategy formation in this configuration is weak relative to the other three configurations. Mintzberg compares the individual professionals in this configuration to "cats after their own prey, not easily herded." This pattern extends to the learning we find in the professional organization; we also find a dependence on learning. However, learning in the context of this organizational configuration focuses primarily on the learning of *individuals* in that organization, much as the loyalty of these individuals lies more with their professional peer group than with their organization.

Despite this breakdown of the organizational types into four distinct configurations, Mintzberg's research suggests that in reality, more complex situations might occur, with instances of overlap and even infiltration of one configuration into another at certain points over the course of an organization's life-cycle.

Box 7.2 Europe's Hidden Champions

Modern theory of the firm has been dominated by a number of factors that are increasingly being viewed as out of date. For one, it is based on the theory of the public firm – and thereby limited primarily to the Anglo-Saxon world. A further limitation is its focus on transaction costs and short-term gain. The current theory of the firm makes far less sense outside of the Anglo-Saxon public company-dominated sphere if one considers that family businesses constitute more than 90% of the world's companies. Family businesses differ from public companies in a number of important ways. One of them is their ownership structure, which enables them to circumvent two of the most serious defects of modern capitalism – the obsession with short-term returns, and the *agency problem* (conflicts of interest that may arise between owners and managers). According to *The Economist,* family businesses make up a large portion of business outside of the Anglo-Saxon sphere; for example, approximately 40% of top companies in Germany and France are in this category.

Family-owned firms in Europe have traditionally been safe havens in times of crisis. Many, after all, have legacies that span two world wars and numerous waves of nationalization. Family-owned or *Mittelstand* firms particularly dominate in Germany; a number of these have been described as *hidden champions*[7] by the German economist Hermann Simon. They exhibit traits of both institutional and entrepreneurial configurations. On the one hand they tend to be conservative and cautious; this expresses itself in their wariness of debt, easy money, and speculation. On the other, family-owned firms intensely value honesty, careful work, and nurturing close customer relations. They instill great loyalty in their workers. And they are largely successful: according to an index compiled by the Swiss bank Credit Suisse, family-owned firms have outperformed the MSCI World Index by 4.8% since its launch in 2007.

So, what is it that makes this hybrid configuration different? Europe's family-owned firms appear to succeed in combining the best of both the institutional and the entrepreneurial configuration attributes. Their low leverage, long-term approach and loyalty to their employees have not gone unnoticed in the wake of the current economic crisis. Most importantly, many firms in this sector are not subjected to the tyranny of quarterly reporting.

However, some weaknesses have become apparent even in this sector. The first is that one of its strengths – the alignment of firm ownership and its management – can quickly become a liability when control is passed on to the next generation. Family-owned businesses also tend to lose caution when they get bigger. It seems that the less desirable attributes of the institutional configuration tend to hamper the performance of these firms, particularly as they are passed onto the following generation. Volker Beissenhirtz of Schultze & Braun, a German law firm, described the succession challenge facing these firms in the following way: *"Sometimes they [the next generation management] are arrogant, sometimes they are naïve, sometimes they are really good, but they are never the original entrepreneur."*

Sources: Simon, H. (1996) *Hidden Champions*, Boston: Harvard Business School Press; *The Economist* (2009) Dynasty and Durability (September 26, 2009); *The Economist* (2015) Special Report: Family Companies (April 18, 2015).

Strategy Formation and Ambidexterity

The notion of ambidexterity in the context of strategic options prompts a dynamic view of strategy formation that positions configurations at various stages along the organizational life-cycle curve. Ambidexterity, a notion based on organizational design, reflects the ability of a firm to adapt in the face of change by simultaneous exploitation of its existing competitive position and exploration of new business opportunities; as such it represents a dynamic capability in the firm's portfolio of resources.[7] Shown in Figure 7.6, we find two main curves – one solid curve representing the current business ("a"), and a second dotted one ("b") representing the "next curve," or emergent business opportunity. Each curve represents a unique configuration consisting of a value proposition, business model, and organizational attributes such as the organization's culture, paradigm, and configuration of resources and capabilities. While the solid curve ("a") representing current, ongoing business is focused mostly on exploitation of current competitive opportunities that present themselves to the

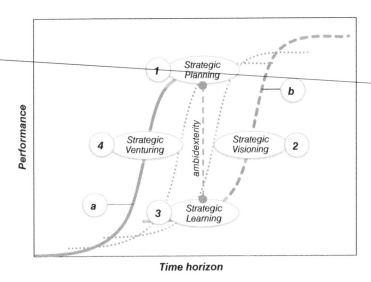

Figure 7.6 Primary mechanisms of strategy formation

firm, the dotted curve ("b") represents an exploratory competitive stance on the part of the firm.

We find the four configurations proposed by Mintzberg[4] distributed between the two curves as depicted in Figure 7.6. The *strategic planning* focus of the institutionalized organizational configuration positions this organization at the top of the curve "a" at point "1" representing an organization in a mature stage of growth of its industry.

Positioned at point "2" on curve "b" we find the entrepreneurial configuration with its *strategic visioning* focus, while the *strategic learning* focus of the emerging, ad hoc-type configuration at point "3" is consistent with an early stage of growth of an industry or business opportunity. Finally, the *strategic venturing* focus of the professional firm at point "4" is again positioned on curve "a" consistent with the stable environment typically associated with this configuration.

Arguably, the greatest polarity exists between configurations "1" and "3", spanning the two curves. Why is this so? The two configurations represent two diametrically opposing organizational types. The institutionalized configuration represents an entrenched position intent on preservation and exploitation of the current business. The emergent, ad hoc configuration, on the other hand, seeks to explore beyond the present. This often leads to disruption of established competitive structures and patterns. In Kelly's[6] terminology, the former is set on *"perfecting the known"* while the latter's mandate focuses on *"imperfectly seizing the unknown."* The two configurations represent potentially contradictory organizational mindsets, cultures, processes, and leadership challenges. Moreover, the two configurations have immense implications for the mode and nature of innovation pursued in the respective organizations. While the institutional configuration relies chiefly on incremental innovation, the emergent form immerses itself in radical, frame-breaking innovation.

Few companies to date have demonstrated the ability to operate both forms of configuration successfully under one roof; to reconcile and balance the *exploitative* with the *exploratory* within the same company. Organizations that succeed in doing so exhibit *ambidexterity*. The ultimate objective of ambidexterity is to derive competitive advantage from the current business (curve "a" in Figure 7.6) while pioneering radical innovation to position the firm on the "next curve" (curve "b") to ensure future competitiveness.

O'Reilly and Tushman[7] argue that an ambidextrous organization need not escape its past in order to renew itself for the future. The differences, however, are far from purely theoretical. Companies across all industry sectors are facing the challenges of bringing the two configurations under one hat. In the recent past, this has often resulted in failure. ABB, the Swiss-Swedish engineering multinational, for example, in seeking to reposition itself from a purely "bricks and mortar" company to a globally competitive "clicks and mortar" player established a corporate New Ventures Group in 2000 that was to forge closer links between "new economy" ventures (curve "b"-type business) and its traditional (curve "a") enterprise activities. The initiative, which was intended to serve as an innovation incubator to new, revolutionary business ideas, folded within only about a year of its establishment. The newly established group proved to be incompatible with the established corporate environment; presumably, ABB's management decided that differences in culture, objectives, and the means to achieve these were insurmountable.

Today's global news media industry is facing similar challenges. Most daily newspapers around the world are engaged in a fight for their existence. A number of established newspapers were forced to close down their operations; the list of recent closures includes the *Baltimore Examiner*, *Cincinnati Post*, and the *Halifax Daily News*. Expectations of free online content, a disruptive change to the traditional advertising business model, and changes in the way people are accessing news have sent traditional newspapers around the world scrambling to experiment with ambidextrous business configurations that include traditional printed media alongside online editions. No newspaper appears to have cracked the problem successfully. Many are seeking organizational configurations that successfully bridge the gap between the traditional institutionalized and emergent business configurations. While the former delivers editorial comment, depth of analysis, printed content – and ever decreasing advertising revenues – the latter demands an entirely new business model that would ensure new streams of online advertising revenues. Needless to point out, the organizational demands, competencies, and wherewithal of the two configurations couldn't be more different.

Strategy Formation: An Opportunity–Response Perspective

The *opportunity–response* analysis framework introduced in the previous chapter provides an alternative dynamic perspective that helps visualize the outcome of a deliberate and purposeful response of the firm. Figure 7.7 indicates an accelerated learning

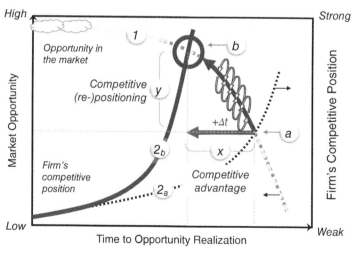

Figure 7.7   Strategic repositioning in response to market opportunity

trajectory ("2_b") representing the firm's deliberate learning efforts. This trajectory intersects the *market opportunity* curve ("1") at point "b" rather than at point "a." The accelerated learning trajectory results in both a lateral and vertical shift of the organization's competitive position relative to its original trajectory (curve "2_a," indicated with a broken line). The lateral shift depicted by a horizontal vector (with origin at "a") represents the competitive advantage gained by the firm's ability to deliver on the market opportunity sooner than originally targeted. The resulting competitive advantage (indicated by "x") is sometimes referred to as a *time-to-market* or *early-mover* advantage.

This advantage is measurable by the rewards early-movers stand to reap, such as a first-mover advantage in a given market. Importantly, however, there are exceptions to the rule. Notably, neither Apple nor Samsung – two dominant players in the current smartphone market – were first to the market with their smartphones.

Therefore, achieving a time-to-market advantage *can*, but does not necessarily need to, lead to competitive advantage. However, there is a second and arguably more important (though often overlooked) factor at play associated with first-mover advantage. This is indicated by the vertical shift (indicated by "y"). Inherent to the shift to an early-mover position is an internal repositioning of the organization's basis of competitiveness. An accelerated organizational learning curve that results in achieving early-mover advantage reflects deliberate effort on the part of the organization. This effort on the part of the firm is directed at transforming its *basis of competitiveness* – the configuration and exploitation of its strategic resources, capabilities, organizational culture, and leadership.

Lastly, the transition along the market opportunity curve ("1") from points ("a") to ("b") (Figure 7.7) represents the range of strategic options deployed by the organization to achieve its accelerated competitive position. This might include internally focused organic growth, external growth through strategic partnering or perhaps even a combination of the two options.

The formation of strategy, as we have seen, requires a complex interplay of intuition and insight derived from experience, reflection and analysis, learning and visioning. Moreover, as we have seen in this section, the configuration of the organization reflecting its stage of growth and the competitive nature of its external competitive environment provide the specific context within which strategy formation occurs. What we have done in this section is to broadly scope the space within which strategy formation takes place. This field of study is still evolving. Indeed, as Mintzberg[7] suggests, many questions about how strategy formation happens in practice remain to be addressed. What is the role of strategic planning in strategy formation – is it at the core of strategic thinking or is it simply an oxymoron? What about situations in which the chief executive views himself or herself as "chief strategist" – does this make the strategy formation process any less valid? There are many questions that demand to be addressed. In this section we have only scratched the surface. Hence, without any pretense of having dealt with the topic exhaustively, we will leave the topic of strategy formation on this note and move on to the final section in this chapter in which we examine how strategic options, once formulated, are appropriately evaluated and selected.

STRATEGY IN PRACTICE: STRATEGY FORMULATION – WHY BOTHER AT ALL?

The purpose of strategic analysis is to help the organization formulate strategic options for improving its competitive position through the creation and delivery of superior value to its stakeholders. Consequently, a lot of strategy is indeed formulated. The sobering fact, however, is that relatively little of the strategy formulated in organizations is actually put into practice. Estimates in the informal strategy practice grapevine suggest figures possibly as low as 20%; that is to say, only about a fifth of the strategies formulated are actually put into practice. Now, there might be good reasons for this low estimation of strategies implemented: some of the strategies formulated in organizations are simply not good; they miss the mark, are unrealistic and therefore do not merit implementation in the first place. Rapidly changing competitive conditions make other strategies, possibly even good ones, prematurely obsolete. Alternatively, organizations find themselves incapable of putting potentially good strategies into practice due to internal factors that hinder their implementation.

Of course, very few CEOs would have the courage to stand up in front of their shareholders and the financial community and admit that only a fifth of their companies' formulated strategy has been put into practice.

That is, until the recent economic crisis. The current economic climate has changed many things, including the attitudes of CEOs with regard to their strategies. More and more CEOs are showing a willingness to admit the inadequacy of their strategy in the current economic climate. Jamie Dimon, CEO of J.P. Morgan Chase & Co., admitted as much in late 2008 when suggesting that he had abandoned the organization's strategy projected for 2009 in view of the prevailing economic uncertainty.

Source: Colvin, G. (2009) How to Manage Your Business in a Recession, *FORTUNE European Edition* (January 26, 2009).

Where does this leave strategy formulation? If anything, it suggests that increasingly, even organizations of the *institutional* configuration are reverting to *adhocracy*-type strategy formation –

strategy making of the type most suitable in dynamic and emerging competitive environments, and which draws heavily on organizational learning. Perhaps this is only a transitional phenomenon that we are observing. Perhaps not, though. There are indications suggesting that we are in the midst of an irreversible and cross-board shift in the approach to strategy formation; that strategy formation will increasingly rely on an adhocracy-type approach, even in established enterprises.

Evaluation of Strategic Options

We have examined in the previous sections how strategizing leads to the formation of a limited number of potentially suitable strategic options. We have argued that, conceptually, we would expect to find these within the bounds of the unique competing space. This implies that a suitable strategic option represents an orchestration of the firm's resources and actions that appropriately addresses stakeholders' needs in a way that the competition cannot within a given context and point in time – in response to a particular strategic challenge. Strategic options inevitably represent trade-offs and compromises – this is no more than a reflection of reality, which is complex and changing even as responses are being formulated. Astute sense making and strategizing narrow the choice of options down to a manageable minimum number. Further evaluation of these then enables the selection of one option that represents the most suitable response to the strategic challenge in question.

So, how is this evaluation of strategic options best approached in practice? Several methods have been developed in the past. Systematic and structured approaches to strategy option evaluation have been proposed by Johnson, Scholes and Whittington,[2] Thompson and Martin,[8] Haberberg and Rieple,[9] and Mintzberg, Quinn and Ghoshal.[10] The rationale underpinning these approaches generally revolves around evaluating strategic options on the basis of specific criteria that scrutinize the option in question for its suitability.

STRATEGY IN PRACTICE: DISCRIMINATING BETWEEN STRATEGIC OPTIONS

Approaches to evaluating strategic options typically found in the management literature challenge the suitability of an option on the basis of three key criteria:

- Is the strategic option *appropriate?* Is the option consistent with the organization's available and needed resources, skills and competences, values and culture; is it simple and understandable?
- Is it *desirable?* Does the option satisfy the objectives of the organization in terms of level of expected returns, synergies to be expected, level of risk it entails, and stakeholder needs and expectations?
- Is it *feasible?* Is the strategic option feasible in terms of the change that will be required; its ability to fulfill *key success factors;* the competitive advantage it promises to deliver and the demands on the organization for achieving this; its timing in relation to the opportunity it seeks to address?

The three criteria, while arguably conceptually legitimate, often lack incisiveness in practice. Therefore, despite their token validity, application of these criteria in practice often leads to less than meaningful outcomes.

The alternative approach to the evaluation of strategic options developed in the following builds on the fundamental building blocks of strategy introduced in Chapter 1 (Box 1.2) and is consistent with the strategic thinking process discussed at length in the preceding chapters of this book.

A Strategic Thinking Approach to Strategy Evaluation

The five building blocks of strategy, we argued in Chapter 1, capture the essence of a firm's strategy. They comprehensively cover those elements of a firm's competitive reality that are relevant to its competitiveness. Strategic challenges, if and when they arise, are inevitably rooted in one or several of the firm's five strategy building blocks. For this reason, they help guide the strategy thinking process triggered by a strategic challenge facing the firm; that is, they support the framing of the relevant issues, the derivation of strategic questions from these, and ultimately the purposeful and targeted generation of insights relevant to the strategic challenge in question.

For this reason, it stands to reason that the firm's five building blocks constitute an appropriate framework for evaluating the outcome of the strategic thinking that has led to the formation of possible strategic responses, as suggested in Figure 7.8.

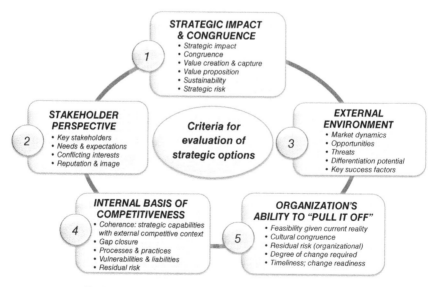

Figure 7.8 Evaluation of strategic options; framework derived from strategy building blocks

The evaluation framework derived from the five strategy building blocks comprises five corresponding evaluation criteria and subcriteria (Table 7.1).

Table 7.1 Strategic option evaluation: key criteria and associated subcriteria

Criteria	Subcriteria	Elaboration
1 Strategic impact and congruence with unique competing space	Strategic impact	Impact/enhancement of unique competing space
	Congruence	Alignment and congruence with overall business objectives
	Value creation/ capture	Enabling of maximization of value creation
	Value proposition	Enhancement of value proposition
	Sustainability	Potential for sustainability of competitive advantage
	Strategic risk	Level of strategic risk associated with option
2 Stakeholder perspective	Key stakeholders	Alignment with key stakeholder interests
	Needs and expectations	Fulfillment of key stakeholders' needs
	Conflict of interests	Reconciliation of potential conflicts of interest
	Reputation and image	Enhancement of reputation, image, and brand
3 External competitive factors	Market dynamics	Alignment with key drivers of change in external environment
	Opportunity potential	Potential for capture of opportunities
	Defensive potential	Effectiveness of defense against potential threat

		Differentiation potential	Potential for competitive differentiation
		Key success factors	Alignment with/delivery on key success factors
4	Internal basis of competitiveness	Resource utilization	Utilization of existing resources and capabilities
		Resource enhancement	Enhancement of current portfolio of resources/ capabilities
		Gap closure	Extent to which options help close current gaps
		Processes and practices	Compatibility/enhancement of processes and practices
		Vulnerabilities/ liabilities	Alleviation of vulnerabilities and liabilities
		Residual risk	Level of operational and financial risk
		Coherence	Alignment of internal differentiating capabilities with right external market position
		Synergies	Potential synergies associated with option
5	Organization's ability to "pull it off"	Feasibility	Alignment with organization's current reality
		Cultural congruence	Alignment with current culture, mindset, and mental models
		Timeliness	Appropriateness in terms of timing
		Residual risk	Probability that organization will not be able to "pull it off"
		Organizational change	Amount of organizational change associated with option

The subcriteria suggested in Table 7.1 are, of course, representative and not to be viewed as exhaustive. Moreover, in a given situation, not all subcriteria listed will necessarily be relevant. Additional subcriteria suitable to the evaluation task may be appropriately defined. The nature of the strategic challenge ultimately determines which subcriteria are applicable. For example, an evaluation of strategic options related to capturing an *opportunity* for business growth places the emphasis on different criteria than an evaluation of defensive strategic options geared toward thwarting a *threat*.

This inevitably results in a different weighting of evaluation criteria and associated subcriteria. Weightings reflect the relative importance of any single criterion and associated subcriteria; they thereby allow a greater degree of granularity to be introduced to the evaluation. However, they are often subjective and context dependent, and therefore need to be continually challenged for validity.

Once relevant and appropriate subcriteria have been identified for each of the key evaluation criteria, strategic options are evaluated in a comparative analysis, such as the one shown illustratively in Figure 7.9.

Indicated in Figure 7.9 are the five key criteria associated with the five strategy building blocks. For illustration purposes only a single subcriterion for each of the key criteria. In practice, of course, we would expect any number of suitable subcriteria associated with each of the key criteria. For the evaluation, each option is scored against the set of relevant subcriteria. Next, each of the subcriterion scores is multiplied by the respective weighting; these are subsequently summed for each of the options. When setting up the evaluation, it is of course important to use a consistent scoring scheme. For example, in Figure 7.9, a *high* score for subcriterion "5.n" (amount of organizational change associated with the option in question) implies *little* change required. Organizational change always entails risk of

Illustrative!		Strategic Option 1	Strategic Option 2
Evaluation criteria and selected sub-criteria	*Weighting (1-5)*	*Scoring (1-5)*	*Scoring (1-5)*
1. STRATEGIC IMPACT & CONGRUENCE			
1.n. Congruence with overall strategic objectives	4	5	3
2. STAKEHOLDER PERSPECTIVE			
2.n. Key stakeholders' needs addressed	3	4	4
3. EXTERNAL COMPETITIVE CONTEXT			
3.n. Delivery on Key Success Factors	4	5	3
4. INTERNAL BASIS OF COMPETITIVENESS			
4.n. Maximisation of resource utilisation	3	4	2
5. ORGANIZATIONAL ABILITY TO "PULL IT OFF"			
5.n. Amount of organizational change associated with option	5	4	1
Σ *(Scores*		84	47

Preferred option!

Figure 7.9 Illustrative evaluation of strategic options: comparative analysis

failure; little change implies low risk, and hence a high (that is to say, favorable) score.

Finally, Some Caveats

The purpose of the option evaluation process is to narrow the choice of options from a selected set of potentially suitable ones to a single preferred option. The evaluation process is based on a systematic and comprehensive scrutiny of criteria comprised of both objective and subjective components. The purpose of the evaluation frameworks is to provide structure to the thinking on which the evaluation is based, not to replace the thinking. The outcome of the evaluation exercise is only as good as the quality of the thinking effort that has gone into it. This begins with the choice of the appropriate subcriteria for evaluation. The choice of balance between qualitative and quantitative subcriteria and their validity are further important factors; often reliable quantitative data simply isn't available, much as we tend to prefer "hard facts" for the sake of argumentation. Strategy is inherently about the future – any projection or extrapolation of data reflecting the organization's current situation into the future has a subjective character, even if semi-quantitatively determined. Finally, when the evaluation has been completed, when a preferred option has been identified, we need to step back and critically review the outcome by asking ourselves:

1. Have the options been subjected to valid scrutiny; have appropriate subcriteria been used in the evaluation?
2. What assumptions have gone into the evaluation; which of them are the most critical for the analysis?
3. How rigorous is the outcome; what residual risk remains?
4. Given that even the most favorable strategic response features potential liabilities, what are the potential "killer issues" associated with the preferred strategic option? Do the criteria clearly highlight these; have they been appropriately weighted in the analysis?

SUMMARIZING THE CHAPTER . . .

- Strategy formation occurs within a complex organizational context characterized by incomplete information, political interests and power, and ambiguity; there is neither scientific method nor "silver bullet" for strategy formation.
- Likewise, there is no such thing as a "perfect" strategic response; real business contexts are complex, ambiguous, and constantly changing; hence, even the most suitable strategic response in a given situation exhibits liabilities and risk.
- Strategies take shape in organizations on the basis of the firm's "bigger picture" relevant to the immediate strategic challenge that emerges from strategic sense making and analysis.
- Strategic responses are linked conceptually to the firm's unique competing space; suitable strategic options involve deliberate mobilization of an appropriate response across

the firm's third boundary; the response aligns with appropriate action directed at the remaining two boundaries of the unique competing space.

- Competitive contexts vary, and hence there is no "one-size-fits-all" approach to strategizing. However, we do recognize broad parameters relevant to strategy formation that relate to the maturity of the enterprise and the dynamics of its competitive context.
- Strategic options, once derived, are scrutinized and evaluated for their suitability; the strategy building blocks suggest suitable criteria. Corresponding subcriteria may include both objective as well as subjective factors that ultimately enable selection of a preferred strategic response.
- Finally, we have seen that strategic options must be critically challenged on their underlying assumptions, their validity, and suitability. It goes without saying that a suitable strategic option, once identified, has a shelf life the duration of which is determined largely by the dynamics of the organization's competitive environment.

Notes

1. Ansoff, I. (1957) Strategies for Diversification, *Harvard Business Review*, September–October Issue, pp. 113–124.
2. Porter, M.E. (1980) *Competitive Strategy*, New York: Free Press.
3. Johnson, G., Scholes, K. and Whittington, R. (2008) *Exploring Corporate Strategy*, 8th edition, Harlow: FT–Prentice Hall.
4. Mintzberg, H. (2009) *Tracking Strategies – Toward a General Theory*, Oxford: Oxford University Press.
5. Bingham, C.B., Eisenhardt, M. and Furr, N.R. (2011) Which Strategy When? *MIT Sloan Management Review*, Fall 2012 Issue, pp. 71–78.
6. Kelly, K. (1998) *New Rules for the New Economy*, New York: Viking.
7. O'Reilly, C.A. and Tushman, M.L. (2013) Organizational Ambidexterity: Past, Present, and Future, *Academy of Management Perspectives*, Vol. 27, No. 4, pp. 324–338.

8. Thompson, J. and Martin, F. (2005) *Strategic Management*, 5th edition, London: Thomson.
9. Haberberg, A. and Rieple, A. (2008) *Strategic Management*, Oxford: Oxford University Press.
10. Mintzberg, H., Quinn, J.B. and Ghoshal, S. (1995) *The Strategy Process*, European edition, London: Prentice Hall.

CHAPTER 8

Strategy Execution and Performance Appraisal

No strategy survives contact with the enemy.
        —(Prussian) Field Marshal Helmuth Graf von Moltke

IN THIS CHAPTER, WE:

- introduce and discuss key elements of strategy execution and its link to the preceding strategy formation stage;
- reflect on critical issues related to the execution of strategic responses in practice; in particular, why many fail;
- develop and elaborate on a "third boundary" perspective on strategy execution that builds on the unique competing space concept;
- introduce three basic approaches to strategic performance appraisal and elaborate on their application in practice;
- reflect on limitations of strategic performance appraisal in the practice field.

Strategy, we argued at the outset of this book, is about winning. Winning is achieved on the basis of a differentiated value offering with which the firm or organization sets itself apart from its competitors. In previous chapters the basic principles of the strategic thinking process that the firm engages in when faced with a strategic challenge were examined; sense making and strategic analysis were shown to contribute to the building of an understanding of how the firm might respond appropriately to that challenge. While there is no such thing as a single "right" response, a preferred option exhibits the most suitable attributes and least amount of risk under the circumstances defined by the strategic challenge in question.

This leaves the final stage of the strategy process: that of strategy execution. Strategy execution is difficult; it is a highly complex management task that draws on a number of management disciplines that lie outside the realm of mainstream strategy. For example, execution invariably involves organizational change – which may include anything from restructuring of the firm to transformation of the organization culture. Particularly for this reason, organizational change is intrinsically linked to organizational leadership. The rollout of a strategy thus might make specific demands on the leadership charged with the associated transformation of the organization. Strategy also requires astute project management. Often, this involves simultaneous management of multiple parallel initiatives.

All of these (and numerous more) topics associated with strategy execution are dealt with extensively in their own right in the management literature. One can therefore hardly expect to do justice to the range of topics relevant to strategy execution in a single chapter of a book. Hence, the focus of this chapter is restricted to some of the practice-relevant aspects of strategy execution. In particular, the emphasis of the chapter is on establishing a link between concepts and thinking dealt with in earlier chapters of the book on strategy execution. The chapter therefore begins with a perspective on strategy execution that builds on the *unique competing space* concept. In particular, we examine the relevance of the "third boundary" of the unique competing space for strategy execution; this being the boundary that most aptly captures critical aspects of a strategy's deployment. A "third boundary" perspective is thus used to establish a conceptual link between strategy execution and the strategic thinking theme introduced at the very outset.

Strategy execution very often is the point at which the strategy process breaks down in practice. Many strategies put to paper are never actually realized. The numbers are debatable, but estimates suggest that roughly only about half of strategies conceived are subsequently successfully implemented. Why?

There are a number of possible reasons:

1. *Sense making gone wrong*: managers sometimes get side-tracked at the very outset; they fail to register triggers signaling change in their competitive environment altogether. Even when they do recognize triggers, managers sometimes interpret them incorrectly, or they jump to premature conclusions rather than engaging in appropriate strategic thinking – elucidating the strategic challenge through framing of issues and derivation of strategic questions. Flawed sense making leads to a breakdown of the strategy process at the outset.
2. *Failed strategizing*: good sense making is an important prerequisite to strategy formulation; however, sense making, even if appropriately done, doesn't necessarily result in the "right" decisions being made. Inferences reached on the basis of conjectures, speculation, biases and irrational reasoning, and faulty assumptions lead to flawed strategic options. Strategic options derived on this basis are bound to lead to a failed execution effort.
3. *Organization unable to "pull it off"*: managers may correctly identify a compelling strategic challenge; they may have drawn the right conclusions, and perhaps even come up with a strategic response that may be appropriate. However,

the organization is not in a position to execute the response within the time period required. Organizational inertia may prevent the organization from responding quickly; this might possibly be for reasons not anticipated (or neglected) during the evaluation of the strategic options. Hence, the strategy process breaks down due to inability of the firm to execute.

4. *Changing circumstances*: Finally, in some cases the strategic response derived on the basis of sense making and strategizing is appropriate, the firm has the ability to execute the strategy – and yet, conditions have changed to the extent that key assumptions underpinning the strategic rationale on which the strategic response relies are no longer valid. Needless to point out, the firm would be ill-advised to proceed with the execution of a particular strategic option under such circumstances.

The strategic management literature has relatively little to say about strategy execution from a strategy practice perspective. This doesn't really surprise. Much of the strategic management literature focuses on strategic analysis and strategy formation, both of which are much more tractable and amenable to conceptual thought and theory than a strategy's execution. Strategy execution, on the other hand, is "where the rubber hits the road"; this is where "conceptual" meets "reality" in the practice field. Strategy execution, we have pointed out earlier, inevitably involves organizational change. Change is complex even under the most favorable circumstances; it is highly context dependent, typically messy, difficult, and prone to failure. The strategic management literature offers little guidance on how to deal with these and other difficulties typically encountered when executing a strategy in real business situations.

The popular management literature does, of course, attempt to address strategy execution. But what we typically find in "the airport management genre" are highly prescriptive approaches to implementing strategy – as if executing a strategy successfully is as easy as following a seven or eight-step list of "this is what you need to do to succeed"! There is no "silver bullet" for strategy execution because each situation is different. This is one of the reasons why little consensus exists in the management literature on how best to approach it: just as no two strategic challenges are alike, no two approaches to the execution of strategic responses are alike.

Hence, what we explore in this chapter are some basic principles related to strategic execution that draw on *strategic thinking* approaches introduced and elaborated on in earlier chapters. The absence of a "theoretical" approach to strategy execution does not preclude the need for astute and incisive strategic thinking. Indeed, we will see how strategic thinking forms the basis for effective, practice-relevant approaches to strategy execution.

Thematically, the topics of strategy execution and performance examined in this chapter are shown to follow the stages of strategy formation and evaluation as indicated in Figure 8.1; in practice, however, as will be explicated further on in this chapter, there is some degree of overlap between the two activities.

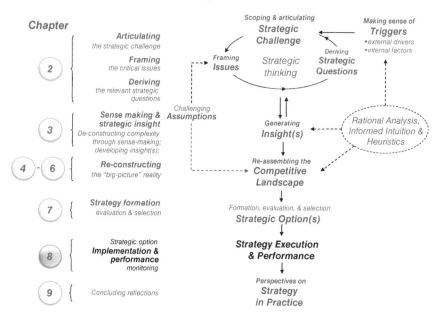

Figure 8.1 Strategic execution and performance

Strategy Execution: A "Third Boundary" Perspective

In the previous chapter the formation of strategic options was examined from a *unique competing space* perspective. A strategic option was shown in the previous chapter to comprise three components (Figure 7.4) directed at each of the three boundaries of the unique competing space in question. Therefore, strategic responses are formed within the organization (space representing the firm's competitive basis) with a view to their impact at the two boundaries representing the external interfaces (boundaries "1" and "2"). However, the realization of the strategic response is entirely contingent on the alignment and orchestration of internal effort. Therefore, as suggested in Figure 8.2, strategy execution, viewed conceptually, is highly dependent on the ability of

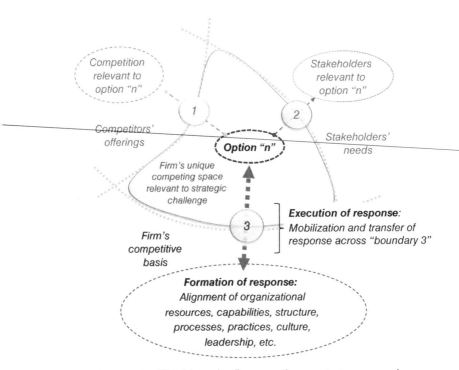

Figure 8.2 "Third boundary" perspective on strategy execution

the firm to mobilize a suitable response across the "third boundary."

The "third boundary" of the unique competing space represents the organizational threshold across which a firm must mobilize its response to a strategic challenge. Conceptually, the threshold represents the difference between a firm simply *owning* potentially strategic capabilities and the firm's actual *exploitation* of these for competitive advantage. A firm's strategic resources become *strategically relevant* only when the firm succeeds in mobilizing these across its "third boundary." It is only when that happens that the response becomes strategically relevant. Conversely, strategy execution breaks down when the firm fails to mobilize across its "third boundary," typical reasons for which are examined in the next section.

Link between Strategy Formation and Strategy Execution

A tight linkage between the formation of a strategy and its execution is critical. The *executability* of a strategic response needs to be a consideration from the very outset of its formation stage. In practice, this is often ignored. Strategy execution is too often viewed as merely "operational" and detached from the strategic rationale and purpose at the root of the strategic challenge. A recent finding reported by The Economist Intelligence Unit[1] suggests that only 17% of C-suite respondents viewed their company's strategy execution as "strategic." In reality, strategy *formation* and its *execution*, form a continuum, as suggested in Figure 8.3. This means that at any point in time, certain elements of strategy formation and strategy execution occur simultaneously. This may sound paradoxical at first glance; it doesn't however, when one considers the purposeful sequencing of activities between these two strategy stages. Key execution-related activities need to be initiated already during the strategy's formation stage; activities such as bringing "on board"

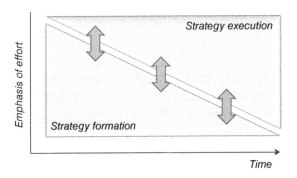

Figure 8.3 Overlap of strategy formation and strategy execution

the line management that will be implementing the strategy early on, building commitment and buy-in, initiating and putting in place appropriate communication channels and developing appropriate performance measures at the outset.

Another often overlooked cross-stage activity involves establishing and using effective feedback mechanisms between the formation and execution stages. While the majority of executives (72% according to a recent *Economist* study[1]) claim to recognize the value of learning from experience and channeling learning appropriately between formation and execution, only 40% of these executives affirmed that their companies were "good" or "excellent" at the task. Thirty-three percent claimed to have no such mechanisms in place at all.

Elaborating on a point argued earlier in this section: a strategic option – assuming it is appropriate to the task to begin with – is ultimately only as good as its execution. In the formation stage of a strategic response an option selected for execution will (or rather, should) necessarily have been subjected to careful scrutiny in the course of its evaluation and selection in the manner introduced in the previous chapter. Hence, the *executability* of a strategic option constitutes an important selection criterion. Circumstances relevant to the strategic option in question, however, may change; assumptions underpinning a particular option may no longer be valid when it comes to the execution stage of a strategic response. Thus, all selection criteria relevant to a strategic option must be continually monitored right up to, and of course during, its execution. Any changes to the executions are reflected by appropriate adjustment of relevant activities associated with the "third boundary."

In this chapter we examine some basic aspects of strategy execution from a "third boundary" perspective. We begin with a critical reflection of where and why execution typically breaks down. We then proceed to examine some key dimensions of strategy execution in the practice field. Any consideration of strategy execution is incomplete without some thought on how its outcome is to be assessed. The maxim attributed to Peter Drucker *"what gets measured gets done"* generally holds for strategy execution as well – albeit with nuances. The problem is that not everything we would like to measure is readily measurable. Therefore, a recurring theme in strategic performance revolves around how to capture the relevant insights that really matter. We explore the notion of strategic performance measurement and metrics in the second part of this chapter.

Strategy Execution: Where and Why it Typically Fails

Strategy execution ranks high on the list of challenges facing corporate leaders. A recent survey of 400 global chief executive officers placed it at the top in a list of 80 issues.[2] The majority of companies struggle with strategy execution; the failure rate is, not surprisingly, proportionately high.

So, where does strategy execution break down; why does it fail so often?

Some reasons why many strategies do not make it to successful realization were identified in the earlier section of this chapter; potential reasons and sources of failure were identified along the strategy process. A number of other reasons for failed strategy execution exist; a number of these are explored in this section.

Great Aspirations – but Where's the Strategy?

No doubt, aspirations are important in strategy; however, they are only one part of a strategy. Many managers focus on the vision of their company, their strategic intentions and aspirations – and mistakenly believe they have a strategy. Aspirational elements such as the firm's vision, mission, and goals are not to be denigrated. They are important for energizing and inspiring the organization. But none of these elements constitutes a strategy. Lou Gerstner, who as CEO of IBM led the multinational through a difficult turnaround in the early 1990s, famously declared[3]: *"The last thing IBM needs right now is a vision."* He went on to explain: *"Vision is easy. It's just so easy to point to the bleachers and say 'I'm going to hit it over there.' What's hard is saying, 'OK, but how do I do that? What are the specific programs, what are the commitments, what are the resources, what are the processes in play that we need to go implement the vision, to turn it into a working model that people follow every day in the enterprise?' That's hard work."*

The questions raised by Gerstner address the foundation and the context for making the requisite choices, building commitment and trust, allocating and aligning the resources, and ensuring appropriate orchestration of these to achieve the vision. These, not the aspirations, are critical for strategy execution.

Unrealistic Targets and Expectations

"Our strategy is to achieve top-line growth of [often double-digit] percent over the next [typically very short] period." Statements such as this are not infrequently heard at the senior executive level. There are several problems with this sort of statement: first, such a statement is at best an aspiration and not a strategy. Second, managers sometimes get carried away with aspirations

that are clearly unrealistic for a firm given its current reality and competitive context. Strategies are sometimes doomed to failure from the outset simply on account of unrealistic target setting. Targets may be unrealistic in terms of preconceived targeted outcomes, bottom-line impact, and scheduling. Managers sometimes succeed in setting a potentially viable strategic direction for their firm, but then jeopardize the successful execution of that strategy by setting targets that are unrealistic in light of the organization's ability to deliver. Some managers pride themselves on "raising the bar" intentionally high. While their objective is to positively influence the performance culture of their organization the real impact is often quite the opposite. Mismatches between strategic targets and the firm's reality might be rooted in cultural incongruities, lack of coherence, and alignment of the firm's capabilities with the task to be accomplished. Targets may therefore simply be "over the top" in view of the firm's current reality. A flip side to this problem is that managers solely intent on hitting their numbers invariably resort to conservative performance commitments, which may jeopardize the strategy's execution. Alternatively, targets may not reflect the reality of the firm's competitive context. For example, targeting a 15% growth of the business in a market environment that is currently growing at a rate of only 8% is very likely to lead to failed delivery; whereby the detrimental effect on the organization of being held to an impossible target is arguably reason for even greater concern.

Targets, when tied inappropriately to performance measurement, may be simply unsuitable for the task at hand. Attempts to measure the success or failure of a strategy execution on the basis of inappropriate metrics can be misleading at best, and lead to disastrous interventions at worst. For example, emphasis on short-term financial outcomes in a situation in which the execution of the strategy involves a major turnaround of the organization is bound to lead to a perception of execution failure. Much more appropriate would be longer-term measures that reflect attainment of milestones along the transformation, whereby suitable milestones are typically of a qualitative nature – at least during the critical periods of the transformation. Measurement and performance management are revisited and explored in greater depth in the latter part of the chapter.

Lack of Cross-Organizational Alignment and Commitment

Strategy execution typically breaks down not for lack of coordination and alignment within a given organizational unit, but when it is dependent on cross-organizational collaborative effort. Recent research[2] indicates that alignment of effort and commitment to that effort is generally not an issue – as long as this remains within an organizational unit involving direct reports. The situation is quite different, however, when commitment is required from colleagues in neighboring organizational units or functions, or external partners in the value chain. Only 9% of managers reported that they can rely on colleagues in other functions to deliver all of the time. These findings suggest that the problem in strategy execution is not so much vertical alignment, but much more horizontal performance: although 80% of companies report having formal systems for managing commitments across organizational silos, only 20% of managers polled were of the opinion that this effort works well.

Obstruction by Strategic Planning

Strategic planning, despite the criticism that has (justifiably) been leveled at it, is still widely used in strategy execution – in more organizations than their managers would likely want to admit. Strategic planning is used to create detailed schedules and implementation roadmaps that set out who does what, with which resources, and when. When things don't go to plan, as they inevitably are prone to in strategy execution, deviations from the plan are viewed as failed effort. Helmuth Graf von Moltke (1800–1891), a German field marshal and chief of staff of the Prussian Army for 30 years, is said to have stated that *"no strategy survives contact with the enemy."*[4] His system of directives, which became a fundamental tenet of all German military theory, comprised a general framework of a military mission that spelled out intentions, rather than detailed orders. Deviations from a directive were accepted, provided these were within the general framework of the mission. Von Moltke viewed the execution of a military strategy as a system of options since only the beginning of a military operation was plannable.

Business managers often fail to appreciate the parallels to strategy execution to be drawn from the military analogy. They ignore the fact that no execution planning, no matter how prescient, survives contact with reality. Hence, strategy execution must adapt to reality as it evolves and presents itself "on the ground"; hurdles must be overcome as they arise. More than that, good strategy execution must take advantage of unanticipated opportunities that might emerge in the course of its deployment; the integration of these, of course, needs to be coordinated and aligned with the overall thrust of the intended strategic directive.

Lack of Agility

Flexibility to make required adjustments in response to unanticipated changes on the ground requires agility on the part of the organization. Many companies do ultimately adapt in most situations; the problem is that they do not adapt quickly enough to capture opportunities that present themselves, or to ward off threats that emerge. Companies, when they react, often either do so too slowly or they react quickly but get distracted from the strategy to be executed. Effective execution demands a balance of disciplined yet fluid allocation of funds and people; above all, however, these must be aligned with the strategic objectives in question. Speed of execution is crucial to strategy; it has been suggested (The Economist Intelligence Unit[1]) that in this day and age of rapidly changing contexts and transparency of information, achieving differentiation on the basis of superior insights may be secondary to a firm's ability to execute quickly.

Lack of Shared Understanding and Buy-In

Strategy execution must be supported by effective communication; this is widely recognized. However, communication alone is not sufficient, it is simply an input. More important are the outcomes of communication. Outcomes should include shared understanding of the strategic objectives and the organization's buy-in to these. Executives often only measure communication effort and neglect managing what really counts: how well the message being communicated is *understood* by its recipient stakeholders. Not only are strategic priorities not widely understood, it is often not clear how strategic objectives are linked, and how they fit into the bigger picture. Failure to achieve shared understanding typically leads to a further problem, that of failed buy-in by the organization. Buy-in needs to be at all levels of the organization, whereby the focus in the management literature is often on the importance of buy-in at the grass-roots level. Research findings recently reported by The Economist Intelligence Unit[1] suggest, however, that buy-in by senior executives is also an issue. The study indicates that almost a third of all execution effort fails to find adequate C-suite sponsorship. Strategy execution thus often proceeds only in a piecemeal manner. The fragments often fail to converge; this then leads to a breakdown of the overall effort.

Strategy Execution: Basic Principles

Strategy execution invariably entails organizational change and transformation. Strategy execution involves a deliberate response, an action or reaction, on the part of the organization. The orchestration and delivery of such action more often than not requires transformation within the organization. The underlying premise, of course, is that the firm has engaged in astute strategic thinking and the basis of this has identified a suitable strategic response. Once this is in place, however, the execution of that response is essentially about the transformation required of the organization as it seeks to realize that response.

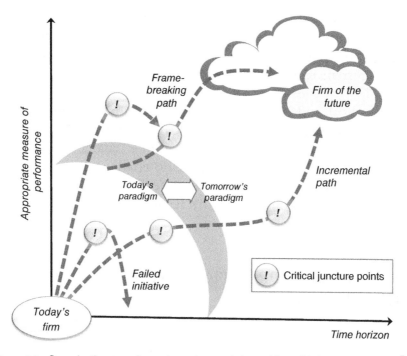

Figure 8.4 Organization transformation schemes (adapted from Birchall and Tovstiga[5])

Figure 8.4 indicates two broad types of transformation trajectory. The lower curve represents incremental transformation. This approach is typical for situations in which the urgency for change is not great, or when the amount of transformation required is not substantial. The upper curve, on the other hand, signifies radical change that might include "curve-jumping" or "frame-breaking" transformation. This approach is used when there is a major need for change in any important aspect of a firm. Often, this is the case in turnaround situations. The transformation required for achieving the execution of the strategy may be radically frame-breaking, which may require step-changes and "jumping the curve." Alternatively, the transformation may be incremental, as indicated in Figure 8.4. The objective, either way, is to take the organization through a transformation that takes it from its current paradigm through to some future state that features a different paradigm. A change of paradigm implies a change of mindset, organizational culture, and strategic orientation. Regardless of whether the transformation follows a radical path or an incremental transformation, the objective is to close the gap between the organization's current reality and its aspired state.

Both radical and incremental transformations feature *critical juncture points* along the paths. Critical juncture points represent key stations along the firm's change trajectory; these stations are marked by specific challenges that require deliberate effort at a given point in time. Failure to resolve these critical juncture points typically leads to a breakdown of the transformation.

STRATEGY IN PRACTICE: CRITICAL JUNCTURE POINTS

Critical juncture points can be thought of as *sand traps* on a golf course. They represent potential hazards to be resolved as an organization progresses with transformation initiative. Critical juncture points are often associated with difficult decision making; decisions that possibly affect people's jobs and livelihoods. This might be a necessary headcount reduction at a given point during the post-merger integration phase following the merging of two companies. Managers are generally loath to take decisions of this type. Hence, difficult decisions are often postponed indefinitely, or not taken at all. Failure to deal with critical juncture points appropriately leads to a setback in the execution of the strategy, if not its failure altogether.

While Figure 8.4 indicates two major categories of transformation, Figure 8.5 indicates a more detailed breakdown of transformation types on the basis of two criteria – strategic relevance of an organizational component requiring change and the urgency of that change.

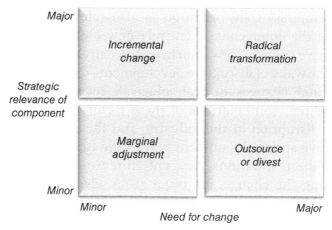

Source: D. Birchall & G. Tovstiga (2002). Future Proofing, John Wiley & Sons

Figure 8.5   Transformation as a function of "need for change" (adapted from Birchall and Tovstiga[5])

Strategic relevance (ordinate in Figure 8.5) refers to the importance of the component in question to the organization's ability to create and deliver a differentiated value offering, whereby the component may include processes, structure of the firm, and capability clusters; perhaps even entire organizational units. A component of minor strategic relevance requiring substantial transformation should be considered for outsourcing, possibly even for divestment. Components typically found in this category are ones that make only marginal contributions to the business's bottom line. This might be due to their competitive obsolescence, on the one hand, often coupled with a high cost of maintenance on the other. The last category, those components of minor strategic relevance and in minor need of change, constitute the least critical group. Components in this category need to be monitored, of course, but as a rule require only marginal adjustment from time to time.

Jumping the Curve

Radical or "frame-breaking" transformation is often associated with transformation in strategic turnaround situations demanding radical intervention. However, frame-breaking or "curve-jumping" transformation is also relevant in situations involving the emergence of entirely new industries in the face of disruptive change. New industries typically make their appearance in the wake of disruptive developments that can be traced to fundamental changes in technological, economic, or societal factors. Often, combinations of these factors lead to the emergence of disruption in the industry, and the emergence of new competitive spaces. Incumbent players are frequently caught off guard in these situations; new entrants, usually the disruptors propagating the change, are often at an advantage. Disruption typically nurtures opportunities for new players; the competitive position of incumbents, on the other hand, is often under threat.

The situation is shown schematically in Figure 8.6: Curve "1" represents the industry (or market) trajectory relevant to the current, ongoing business. Over time, performance growth – which might reflect profitability, returns on investment, or similar measures – gradually stagnates as the market matures and gradually becomes saturated. The competitive focus, particularly

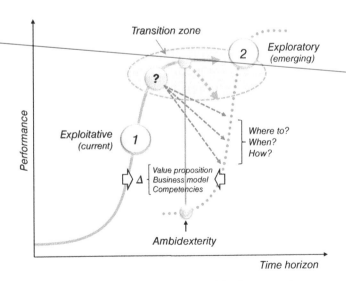

Figure 8.6 Frame-breaking transition from exploitative to exploratory modes

as markets reach maturity, is on exploitation of the current business opportunity. Exploitation manifests itself in a number of ways, as discussed in Chapter 7; most critically, it reflects the prevailing mindset of the players in the respective markets. The accompanying legacy-oriented thinking of these incumbents seeks to nurture preservation of the status quo, established routines and thereby perpetuate predictability.

All the while, extant firms face increasing competition and commoditization of their value offering. From a competitive perspective, this is important for several reasons: as competition increases, it becomes increasingly *price-based*; opportunities for creating a *differentiated* value offering gradually diminish to the point where competition reduces to pricing alone – and price is dictated by the market place, not by any single player in that market. Decreasing prices, resulting in shrinking margins, further lead to diminishing bottom-line outcomes, which leave firms with even less to reinvest in their business. This instigates a vicious cycle, in which firms find themselves increasingly locked into a situation from which it becomes difficult to break free.

In Chapter 4 we argued that a firm's competitive position is closely tied to its ability to create a value premium. One of the attractive features associated with value premiums is that if positioned to create a differentiated value offering, the firm can basically set the price of its offering. As a rule, value premiums are very difficult if not impossible to create in commoditized, price-driven markets. However, there are exceptions. Apple's ability to command a sizeable above-market average margin in the pricing of its iPhone comes to mind. Although the global smartphone is rapidly becoming commoditized, Apple has managed to hold on to a formidable premium position with its iPhone.

Curve "2" in Figure 8.6 depicts an emerging industry. The emergence of new industries is often driven by factors external to the immediate industry they threaten to replace (curve "1" in Figure 8.6). The eradication of the typewriter industry and its replacement with word processor software is a case in point; the two representing very different industries. Trajectories of this type indicated by curve "2" encompass exploration of new opportunity. They demand a mindset that is comfortable with destabilizing existing structures, business models, and modes of competition. They introduce disruption and discontinuity to the ongoing business. Moreover, they usher in entirely new rules of competition, which invariably threaten incumbents.

Disruptive trajectories customarily introduce fundamental change in three key dimensions:

1. *New value proposition*: the new opportunities introduced through disruption are accompanied by entirely new value constructs. Though perhaps lacking in maturity in their early versions, they are fundamentally superior to existing forms of value generated in the current business, and typically evolve rapidly to the point where they replace the existing value offering. An example is the replacement of 35 mm photographic film based on silver halide chemistry with digital formats, which have now essentially replaced the former in the consumer mass markets.
2. *New competencies*: disruption draws on entirely new sets of competencies, capabilities, and skill sets. Disruption has thus been referred to as "competence destroying." As new industry trajectories evolve and grow, traditional competencies gradually become obsolete. This frequently leaves incumbents saddled with legacy assets, which rapidly become liabilities rather than the source of competitive advantage they represented in the past. Highly developed skill sets required for building typewriters are of very limited use in developing new word processing software.
3. *New business models*: Both value propositions and competencies are integral parts of a firm's business model. Hence, it stands to reason that discontinuities also introduce entirely

new business models. Business models delineate how an organization creates, delivers, and captures value. As such, they represent a blueprint of a firm's strategy. Hence, new business models introduced by discontinuities reflect a shift in the way firms need to compete in order to derive competitive advantage from the new opportunities. Disruptive trajectories demand new strategies for competing; corresponding business models reflect the operationalization of these new strategies.

All three factors explain why incumbents are often at a distinct disadvantage when discontinuity occurs in their industry. Incumbents are often hampered by legacy thinking. Kodak is a case in point: it need not have been sidelined by the new digital formats that threatened its ongoing photographic film business. The company, in fact, owned the early patents on digital photo processes. Yet it chose to ignore developments in the evolving digital market place so as not to jeopardize substantial profits generated from its traditional photographic film business. New disruptive players moved in to capture the opportunities presented by the new digital formats while Kodak ignored these. This is frequently the case: new disruptive players are typically better positioned to capture the new opportunities. An important reason is that disruptors frequently are not saddled with the legacy liabilities assets that typically hamper incumbents.

However, there are notable exceptions. Companies such as IBM, Intel, Berkshire Hathaway, and Nokia are examples of companies that have successfully reinvented themselves; in some cases, several times in the course of their firm history. Reinventing requires successful transition from an existing industry trajectory to one representing an entirely different business. Transitioning is fraught with danger. Exploratory trajectories present multiple risks. At the point of their emergence, new trajectories are often not clearly distinguishable. In fact, new opportunities are often associated with multiple competing trajectories, some of which disappear altogether at some point in time. Hence, selecting an appropriate new trajectory is typically associated with a high degree of risk. Even when a viable target trajectory has been identified, migration to the new curve may take incumbents through an ambidextrous transition phase in which they compete simultaneously in both the existing business and the new business. As discussed in Chapter 7, operating both business configurations at the same time presents the company with a formidable strategic challenge. Generally, incumbents facing a transition to a new opportunity trajectory face a number of questions that demand to be addressed; questions such as which trajectory to transition to (given the uncertainty of emerging markets), when to initiate the transition, and how to ultimately pull it off. Adobe Systems, a computer software company, is currently undergoing a transition between two business trajectories and offers some useful insights.

Box 8.1 Adobe

The transition from traditional software services to cloud-based solutions illustrates well the challenge numerous technology companies are currently facing in seeking to position themselves on the latter, exploratory curve. Not many have succeeded. Adobe is one of the few that is currently exciting investors with a radical transformation of its value offering and business model. Its new Creative Cloud service represents a dramatic repositioning as a cloud-based service provider. The transition represents a curve-jumping departure from its traditional, exploitative Creative Suites business as a vendor of expensive, shrink-wrapped software on discs to an exploratory mode business that offers online cloud-based services to its users for a monthly subscription fee.

Adobe's traditional flagship Creative Suite is a package of software discs that sells for up to $2,600. The software is updated once every 18 months or so; making it vulnerable to slumps in revenue if customers eschewed an update. Its

Creative Cloud, featuring the same applications, is offered for $50 per month on a 12-month subscription, or $75 on a month-by-month fee basis. Notably, the online cloud service package is updated seamlessly, with customers barely noticing. The cloud service offers other advantages, such as allowing Adobe more opportunity to customize its offering to specific customers' needs. For example, a package targeting photographers that sells for $10 a month combines Adobe's software with an online community where photographers can post their photos.

The impact of Adobe's transition has been notable in a number of ways. Financially, the transition presents a paradox that is nothing short of intriguing: over the period spanning 2012 to 2014, Adobe's net profits have been in decline (Figure 8.7); a situation that in most listed companies would trigger a crisis.

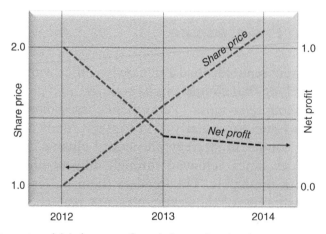

Figure 8.7 Adobe's net profit and share price development over the period 2012 to 2014 (adjusted and normalized; period ending end of November in respective year/data)
(*Source:* Finance.yahoo.com/q?s=ADBE; accessed April 20, 2015)

Notably, Adobe's share price has soared in the same period. Adobe's current profit decline reflects the phasing out of its old value offering and business model. Investment interest, on the other hand, has been driven by investors' optimistic expectations that profits will rebound over time as the new subscription model attracts many new customers with its more attractive features – and for Adobe, much more predictable revenue streams. The transition has meant juggling competing business models and has been a challenge; but in the words of a senior Adobe executive: "*It gets to the point where you have to burn your boats to signal there is no going back to the old way of doing things.*" This step was taken in May 2013 when Adobe announced that it would no longer release future disc versions of its Creative Suite software. This triggered outrage in some customer circles. For Adobe, however, it marked an important milestone in the transition to its future business trajectory.

Source: The Economist (2014) Adobe: Super Subs (March 22, 2014).

Strategic Performance

Albert Einstein reputedly had a sign on his office wall that stated: "*Not everything that counts can be counted, and not everything that can be counted counts.*" Performance assessment is always a contentious issue, particularly so in strategy. Many of the parameters "that count" in strategy are indeed elusive. Many of the important outcomes achieved through diligent and deliberate effort remain intangible. This renders them no less important; their "measurement," however, presents real challenges. We have encountered this already in the context of sense making and analysis. This challenge carries over into strategy during its execution phase. Strategy is about achieving a future state of competitiveness; this begs the question of what insight is required at what point in time along a strategy's rollout to ensure the success of the endeavor. A lack of appropriate means of monitoring the rollout of a strategy as it is enacted threatens to impede its progress once initiated.

Quantitative and Semi-Quantifiable Measures of Strategic Performance

Strategic performance appraisal serves multiple possible purposes. It can focus on assessing outcomes; that is, it can be used to monitor the degree to which a firm's strategy fulfills its objectives over a given period of time. Typically, this is a retrospective view on strategic performance, such as a measure of annual returns on investment, as shown in Figure 8.8, which indicates total one-year returns for a selection of multinational companies for the one-year period ending February 5, 2014. The firm's performance is measured in terms of a return to respective investors over the period of time in question. The performance of individual companies is compared with the average return achieved across the Standard & Poor's 500 (S&P 500) stock market index, which happened to be 18.4% during the period in question. A measure such as a return on investment is an objective, quantifiable metric. It is, however, a measure of past, historical performance. Exceptional performance in the past is no

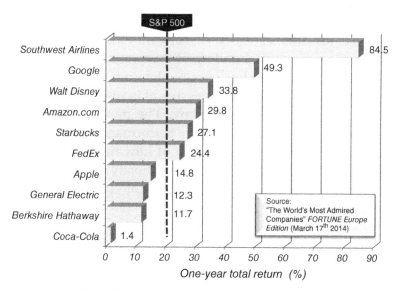

Figure 8.8 Strategic performance reporting in terms of one-year return; comparison to S&P 500 performance during same period.[6] (Note: returns indicated are for period ending February 5, 2014)

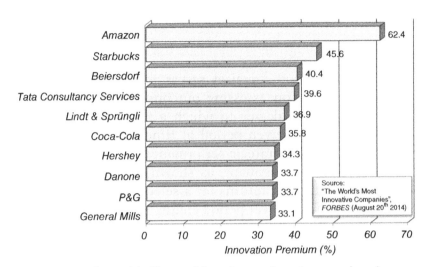

Figure 8.9   Forward-looking, anticipated strategic performance based on "innovation premium"[7]

guarantee of performance in the future. Any projection of historical outcomes into the future is speculative.

Attempts to predict performance in the future exist, of course. However, these are subjective and therefore inherently risky. Exemplary for this category of forward-looking performance "measures" is the annual polling of investors that is conducted by *Forbes*, an American business publication. *Forbes'* "innovation premium" (Figure 8.9) is a measure of investors' expectations of future performance of a company. The method relies on the respondent's ability to predict future performance expressed as an "innovation premium" – a measure of how much investors are prepared to bid up the stock price of a company above the value of its current business in anticipation of future innovative performance.

Companies are ranked by their "innovation premium," a measure that takes into account the difference between a company's market capitalization and a net present value of cash flows from existing businesses. This difference provides the basis for prediction of profitable future growth of the company.

Both retrospective and forward-looking measures of strategic performance reflect the degree to which a firm succeeds in creating and delivering a value premium. A measure of the value premium reflects the extent to which the firm's performance is relative to a market average – for example, the S&P 500 index. Investors tend to choose investment targets that outperform the market average, although the respective investment horizon may also play an important role in investment decision making, as the Adobe example illustrates.

Qualitative Measures of Strategic Performance

Strategic performance measurement has thus far been considered from an investment viewpoint. No doubt, this outcomes-focused perspective is important, but it addresses the needs of only one group of stakeholders – the potential investors.

The tracking of the progress of a strategy's implementation is another important motivation for performance appraisal. This raises questions regarding *which* determinants are to be monitored in the course of a strategy's execution, and *how* this is best accomplished and *when*; that is, at what intervals. To address these questions, we begin by examining some of the basic principles introduced earlier in this book for their applicability for the task.

"Strategy Building Blocks" Performance Framework

The strategy building blocks introduced in Chapter 1 provide a befitting approach not only for sense making and strategy formation; the building blocks can also be used as a basis for monitoring and assessing the progress of a strategy as it is being rolled out. The five building blocks, we argued in Chapter 1, comprise five key dimensions of a strategy; those key elements of a strategy that cannot be ignored. These five elements comprise the basic constructs of a strategy score card-type appraisal framework (Figure 8.10) for assessing and monitoring a strategy from its

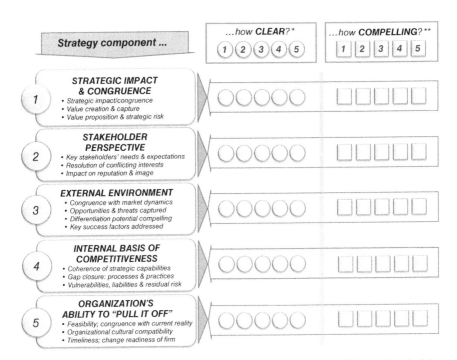

Figure 8.10 Strategy appraisal based on basic blocks of strategy. (Notes: "clarity" is appraised on a scale of "1" (poor) to "5" ("very clear"); likewise, "compellingness" is appraised on a scale of "1" ("not at all") to "5" ("highly compelling"))

inception and through to its execution. The appraisal is typically carried out with key stakeholders. For the appraisal, the strategy is subject to two key criteria, degree of *clarity* and extent to which the strategy is *compelling*:

1. *How clear is the strategy?* This probes the strategy for how *clearly* its addresses each of the five building block components, each of which is described by several subcriteria, as indicated in Figure 8.6. Each of the strategy components are scored on a scale of "5" (excellent) to "1" (poor). Clearly, if any of the components isn't addressed at all by the strategy, the score will be a "1."

2. *How compelling is the strategy?* This criterion probes the extent to which the strategy is compelling in each of its components. The degree to which a strategy is compelling

correlates with the extent to which it achieves buy-in; hence, a low score for this criterion would suggest a low degree of buy-in on the part of the respondent; this would typically be a stakeholder.

The appraisal is used to track and capture a number of important insights relevant to a strategy option's implementation. First, it can be used to challenge a proposed strategic response on its key components right at the outset when it is first proposed. Used this way, the building blocks approach can be used to identify any apparent gaps in the strategy. The "clarity scores" indicate which components the strategy is clear on, which it isn't clear on, and which components may be missing altogether.

Second, the appraisal is then used to probe the level of stakeholder buy-in on the basis of how compelling the strategy is as a response to the strategic challenge at hand. Both clarity and *compelling-ness* of the strategic option are critical factors for building and nurturing buy-in for a strategy, which in turn is crucial for its success.

Third, appraisal can be used to identify discrepancies between the strategy's clarity and the extent to which it is compelling. For example, the appraisal may indicate that a particular aspect of a strategy is relatively clear – and yet, that it fails to convince. This situation typically prompts a review of the aspect in question and appropriate rework of the aspect in question.

The appraisal framework can be purposefully applied at the very outset, as pointed out earlier. It can be subsequently applied at intervals during the strategy's rollout to monitor progress and to flag issues as they arise. Importantly, for successful strategy execution, progress needs to be consistent across all five building blocks. Major lags in any one or two of the building blocks invariably jeopardize progress in the remaining ones. The framework is simple enough to be used as a "back of the napkin" type of assessment, for example, when in a meeting listening to an executive present their organization's strategy. Questions prompted by the framework include: which of the framework's "boxes" does the strategy "tick"; which elements are not addressed (what's missing?); how clear is the strategy; and how convincing is it?

Strategic Maturity Continuum

The *strategic maturity continuum* is another useful way of visualizing the progress of an organization as it seeks to reposition itself strategically over time. The continuum can be viewed as a set of structured levels that reflect the state of an organization, whereby *maturity* refers to the degree of competitive excellence achieved at any point in time. The approach can be used to monitor the progress of an organization along a strategic performance trajectory; it can also be used to benchmark that organization against competitors. The trajectory comprises five levels of strategic maturity, ranging from an initial ad hoc phase to a final stage of maturity characterized by a high-performing manner. Each of the five stages is characterized by appropriate criteria. The concept underpinning for the maturity continuum is based on the *Capability Maturity Model (CMM)*, which has its origins in a development model introduced by the US Department of Defense for objectively assessing the work of government contractors, primarily in the field of software development.

The five phases of the strategic maturity continuum framework are indicated in Table 8.1 along with defining characteristics for each of the phases. Progress is indicated as a position along a trajectory comprising the five maturity stages defined in the table. The strategy maturity continuum suggests a growth of the strategy's competitive impact with increasing degree of maturity as shown in Figure 8.11. Maturity can be viewed from various perspectives. Strategic maturity relates to the organization's overall competitive effectiveness. Competitive

Table 8.1 Strategic maturity continuum framework

Level	Phase	Characteristics
1	*Ad hoc*	• Lack of focus, shared objectives, alignment, and structure • Strategic thinking non-existent; decision making largely short term, opportunistic and chaotic; tasks defined on an ad hoc basis • Fragmented knowledge about stakeholders and their needs • Lack of performance orientation
2	*Nascent*	• Emergence of basic constituents of a value proposition • Elementary sense making; decision making irregular and inconsistent • Emergence of shared understanding; though values inconsistent • Focus largely operational; rudimentary performance metrics defined
3	*Reactive*	• Value premium defined; value proposition articulated • Strategic direction aligned with value premium and stakeholder insight • Strategy process in place, but with gaps; intermittently operationalized • Performance metrics in place for most strategic objectives
4	*Pre-emptive*	• Focused, aligned, and deliberate creation, delivery and capture of value • Strategy process is strategic thinking oriented and ongoing • Key capabilities, resources, and processes, organizational structure coherent with strategic objectives and aligned with external context • Purposeful strategic performance measures in place; consistently tracked and used for decision making
5	*Superior*	• Clearly established unique competing space; full alignment of structures and systems with premium-oriented value proposition • Strategy process aligned with continual, internal challenging of basis of differentiation and competitive advantage • Consistent, coherent, and purposeful orchestration of resources across "third boundary" (unique competing space) • Widely recognized as industry leader

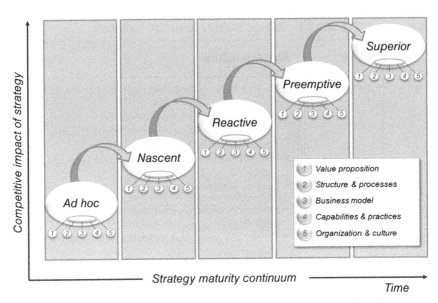

Figure 8.11 Strategy maturity continuum as a function of competitive impact

effectiveness, in turn, is inextricably tied to multiple factors that characterize an organization. Strategic maturity is thus intrinsically linked to the overall growth of the organization. Table 8.1 indicates this by suggesting dependence of strategic maturity on a number of characteristics of an organization. As an organization matures, its growth can be viewed from any number of dimensions, a few of which might include its organizational structure, its processes and practices, its portfolio of resources and capabilities, its culture, and, of course, its leadership. The point to note here is that stagnation of growth in any single dimension adversely affects progress in the remaining dimensions. For example, failure to suitably develop the organizational culture will hamper the organization in its effort to build appropriate processes, capabilities, and practices. In order to achieve overall growth, therefore, progress needs to be consistent across all relevant organization dimensions.

Steady growth of strategic maturity along the continuum is therefore dependent on consistency of effort across multiple organization dimensions; indicated in Figure 8.8 as *value proposition, structure and processes, business model, capabilities and practices,* and *organization and culture.*

The strategic maturity continuum notion raises the issue of goal setting and its management. The problem has long been contentious as it has been an obsession by management theorists. Peter Drucker's "management by objectives" theory, introduced in 1954, decreed that management goals should be SMART – that is specific, measurable, actionable, realistic, and time sensitive. Despite criticisms leveled at this approach – one of which is that the approach is too bureaucratic – extensive research indicates that there is merit in using the approach, particularly when applied more frequently than once per year.

Research findings released by Deloitte, a consulting firm, indicate that firms that set goals on a quarterly basis are four times more likely to be in the top quartile of performers.[8] Other studies suggest, though, that objectives need to be appropriately chosen. Objectives need to be aligned and congruent with the organization's stage of growth. Further, they should include *all* relevant and important performance facets; too often, employees tend to focus only on those matters relevant to their goals, all the while neglecting other potentially important tasks.

Stakeholder Engagement: Monitoring and Management

Stakeholders, we have argued earlier in this book, assume a central position in strategy. Not only are they the recipients of the value created by the organization, they are also important players in the enactment of a strategy. They can play variable roles; they might play a passive role – for example, as a sponsor with a keen and vested interest in the strategy's successful implementation. Alternatively, they may be directly involved in the rollout of the strategy. Whatever the case, key stakeholders need to remain engaged throughout a strategy's execution.

Engagement typically begins with effective communication and development of a relationship between key agents representing the firm and its stakeholders. However, engagement ultimately demands a plausible basis of "reason to believe" to be established and nurtured along the change trajectory.

Using an approach attributed to Gleicher,[9] strategic change can be envisaged as a function of some key variables of change that collectively comprise the requisite "reason to believe."

The strategic change formula can be envisaged to comprise five elements as shown in Figure 8.12:

1. *Amount change (Δ)*: Dependent variable, indicating amount of change that can be expected; it is a function of the further three factor variables.
2. *Degree of urgency (U)*: A variable reflecting perceived degree of dissatisfaction on the part of active stakeholders and within the organization with its current state; hence, an indicator of the degree of urgency to change within the organization.

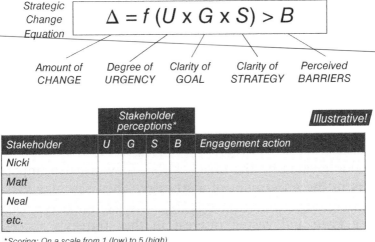

Strategic Change Equation

$$\Delta = f\,(U \times G \times S) > B$$

| Amount of CHANGE | Degree of URGENCY | Clarity of GOAL | Clarity of STRATEGY | Perceived BARRIERS |

| Stakeholder | Stakeholder perceptions* | | | | Illustrative! |
	U	G	S	B	Engagement action
Nicki					
Matt					
Neal					
etc.					

*Scoring: On a scale from 1 (low) to 5 (high)

Figure 8.12 Strategic change equation and stakeholder engagement monitoring and planning

3. *Clarity of goal (G)*: This variable reflects stakeholders' perceptions regarding clarity of the overall goals, objectives, and aspired direction and vision of the proposed strategy.
4. *Clarity of strategy (S)*: A perception of the clarity of the strategic roadmap for achieving the goals and aspirations delineated by the previous variable.
5. *Perceived barriers (B)*: Barriers reflecting the perceived cost on the part of any individual stakeholder of achieving the targeted strategic objectives.

The four independent factor variables (U, G, S, and B) are subjective, of course. The approach can be used effectively to both capture and calibrate perceptions of key stakeholders relevant to the change initiative. Values of the change variables are derived (semi-quantitatively) on the basis of perceptions that might be captured on a five-point Likert-type scale, with a value of "1" representing a low (that is, undesirable) score, and a value of "5" reflect a high (that is, "excellent") score. The strategic change equation shown in Figure 8.12 suggests a multiplicative relationship between factor variables U, G, and S. This implies that Δ, the amount of strategic change to be expected, is directly correlated with the product of the three factor variables.

Equally, the tendency of any of the three factor variables U, G, or S toward low scores results in a breakdown of the strategic change initiative.

Factor variable B, reflecting perceived barriers, provides a measure of the degree of "buy-in" on the part of an individual stakeholder. The inequality sign suggests that the perceived "cost" of the strategy to the individual stakeholder must be less than the benefit of the strategic initiative. Put differently, the degree of "buy-in" on the part of the stakeholder in question must be greater than the combined effect represented by overall strategic initiative for any effective change to occur.

On the basis of the strategic change equation one can easily derive an effective practitioner instrument for gauging and monitoring stakeholder engagement. The instrument, shown illustratively in Figure 8.12, is applied with individual stakeholders. Stakeholders are asked to score their perceived perceptions on a scale of "1" to "5" on each of the three factor variables U, G, and S.

Factor variable B is approached somewhat differently; its purpose is to directly gauge engagement of the individual stakeholder. Hence, stakeholder respondents are asked a simple question: "are you 'on' board (*yes*), or 'off' (*no*)"?

The outcomes of the gauging of factors U, G, and S are then appraised with a view to the corresponding B outcome. The three former factor variables typically point to deficiencies in the strategy; indeed, they may provide an explanation for a negative B outcome. Insights derived from careful analysis and reflection on the outcomes of the exercise are subsequently used to derive appropriate interventions in response to issues raised by the analysis.

Clearly, in order for this sort of approach to work, assurance of discretion and confidentiality of individual stakeholder respondents is absolutely crucial. If discretion and confidentiality are assured, this approach can be a very effective means of ensuring that a strategic initiative remains on track.

STRATEGY IN PRACTICE: THE PERFORMANCE METRICS DILEMMA

Strategy is inherently about the future; a future state of competitiveness the organization aspires to achieve. Moreover, many insights deemed critical to an outcome are not readily available or accessible. The dilemma this presents to firms already at the sense making and analysis stage of strategy carries over to its execution stage. Many, if not most, of the really critical performance insights required for guiding a strategy's rollout and monitoring its execution are neither quantifiable nor readily accessible. As a rule these measures are subjective and only indirectly accessible. This, of course, presents limitations to traditional approaches to performance measurement. On the other hand, it challenges the strategy practitioner with new opportunities; for example, to seek and explore alternative approaches to resolving the performance measurement dilemma on the basis of thinking outside of the traditional strategy field.

SUMMARIZING THE CHAPTER . . .

- Strategy execution constitutes the third and final stage of the strategy process.
- There are no established "theoretical" approaches to strategy execution; strategic thinking nonetheless provides a suitable basis for developing tenable practice-relevant approaches.
- When strategies fail, it is most often during this stage; many formulated strategies are never realized in practice.
- Conceptually, strategy execution can be viewed as the mobilization of a firm's response to a strategic challenge across the "third boundary" of its unique competing space.
- Timing and sequencing of strategy execution and strategy formation exhibit some degree of overlap, though with variable emphasis.
- Strategy execution failure has numerous possible explanations: some important ones include setting unrealistic targets, lack of organizational alignment with the strategy, dysfunctional organizational cultures, and lack of agility on the part of the organization.
- Strategy execution invariably involves organizational change and transformation; change can vary from incremental to radical, frame-breaking modes.
- Strategy performance appraisal presents a critical challenge because many critical performance insights are neither quantifiable nor directly "measurable" by traditional means.

- Strategy performance appraisal is used in response to variable stakeholder needs; quantifiable measures are invariably based on historical data. Forward-looking measures are invariably of a qualitative sort.
- Three approaches to strategic performance appraisal relevant to monitoring progress of a strategy's rollout practice include: (1) an approach based on the strategy building blocks, (2) a strategy maturity continuum-based approach, and (3) a method that monitors stakeholder engagement.
- The chapter closes with a critical reflection on the limitations of the strategic performance appraisal.

Notes

1. The Economist Intelligence Unit (2013) Why Good Strategies Fail: Lessons for the C-Suite (research sponsored by: Project Management Institute).
2. Sull, D., Homkes, R. and Sull. C. (2015) Why Strategy Execution Unravels – and What to Do About It, *Harvard Business Review*, March 2015 Issue, pp. 58–66.
3. Favaro, K. (2013) How Leaders Mistake Execution for Strategy (and Why that Damages Both), *Strategy + Business*, February 2013.
4. Von Moltke, H. Graf (1996) *Moltke on the Art of War: Selected Writings* (Editor/translator: Hughes, D.J.; Translator: Bell, H.), New York: Presidio Press.
5. Birchall, D.W. and Tovstiga, G. (2002) *Future Proofing*, Oxford: Capstone/John Wiley & Sons.
6. *Fortune Europe Edition* (2014) The World's Most Admired Companies (March 17, 2014).
7. *Forbes* (2014) The World's Most Innovative Companies (August 20, 2014).
8. *The Economist* (2015) "Schumpeter – The Quantified Serf" (March 7, 2015).
9. Cady, S.H., Jacobs, J., Koller, R. and Spalding, J. (2014) The Change Formula: Myth, Legend, or Lore? *OD Practitioner*, Vol. 46(3), pp. 32–39.

CHAPTER 9

Insight-Driven Strategy in Perspective

There are those who make things happen; . . . there are those who watch things happen; . . . and then there are those who wonder what happened.

—Anonymous

IN THIS CHAPTER, WE:

- examine strategic thinking and insight-driven strategy from two practice perspectives:
  - a perspective set against the backdrop of complexity, uncertainty, and multiple possible futures,
  - an organizational learning perspective;
- explore the implications of these perspectives in the context of how strategy is formulated and enacted in practice;
- examine strategy as a pretext for action and the creation of meaning in organizations;

- revisit the notion of organizational configuration introduced in the previous chapter and examine the implications of an organization's predisposition for how its
strategy plays out in practice;
- conclude with a reflection on the purpose and implications of strategic thinking for strategy in practice.

So far in this book we have examined how strategic thinking
evolves from the articulation of a strategic challenge, the formulation of compelling strategic questions, and a subsequent
deconstruction of the reality prompted by the questions. This
is followed by a reconstruction of the competitive context relevant to the strategic challenge on the basis of insights generated
through sense making based on analysis and intuition (Figure 9.1).
Strategic thinking, we have argued all along, serves ultimately to
help us identify a viable strategy in response to the strategic
challenge triggered by events with potential impact on the firm's
unique competing space.

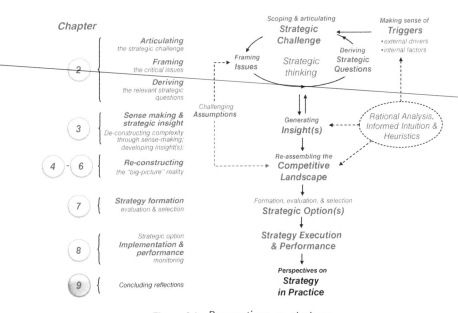

Figure 9.1 Perspectives on strategy

The underlying premise throughout has been that a firm needs a strategy. But is that unequivocally so?

Some strategy thinkers have challenged this notion. De Bono's[1] assertion that *"strategy is good luck rationalized in hindsight,"* or Burgelman's[2] claim that *"strategy is a theory about the reasons for past and current success of the firm"* come to mind. These statements suggest that what we call "strategy" is often really only a retrospective view on events and activities that lie in the past. The bias we exhibit in hindsight, the apparent coherence and rationality of the strategy in question, might therefore result in misleading conclusions in respect of what we can do now and what we need to do in the future.[3] Indeed, Mintzberg *et al.*[4] have argued that a lack of strategy altogether is sometimes even desirable, especially when in transition between an outdated one and a new, more viable one – or when environments are so dynamic that it makes sense to temporarily suspend all pretense of a strategy until the environment settles down somewhat. J.P. Morgan Chase & Co. CEO Jamie Dimon's statement in late 2008: *"I am shocked by the number of people who are still worrying about their strategic plan for 2009. We cancelled all that stuff – all of it"*[5] exemplifies a situation in which it was deemed preferable not to claim to have a strategy in view of the turbulent markets circumstances in the US financial sector at the time.

Where does this leave strategic thinking? Do the foregoing views build a case against the need for strategic thinking in practice?

Not at all. Complex and turbulent competitive contexts do not preclude the need for strategic thinking. Indeed, astute strategic thinking under these circumstances may, indeed, even lead to a temporary suspension of a strategy as in the case of J.P. Morgan Chase.

The recent economic crisis has been a major contributing factor as business failure and uncertainty have become the new business norms. Success in today's business environment has become more volatile and transient than ever before. Business strategists have coped with changing competitive environments in the past. The recent economic crisis, however, has contributed to the formation of entirely new "game changing" rules that are at the root of an emerging "new normal." This "new normal" has introduced new factors of competition that has radically changed the nature of competition.

Companies are competing in an increasingly borderless world, whether in a geographic or market sense. Once distinct boundaries between industry sectors are rapidly dissipating. Players that have seemingly appeared from nowhere (think Facebook) are redefining new spheres of competition that represent opportunities for some players – and formidable threats to many incumbents. In this emerging "new normal," many traditional firms are struggling more than ever to find a viable strategy – if not to achieve strategic growth, then at the very least to counter threats with more effective defensive strategies. The changing rules of competition are forcing business leaders to think differently about where they compete and how they compete.

These changes have two major implications for firms. First, firms are being forced to fundamentally rethink the notion of "competitiveness." Viewed traditionally in terms of a firm's "right to win," firms are no longer guaranteed a better-than-average chance of achieving success by means that in the past endowed them with competitive advantage. This is being exacerbated by dramatically shrinking strategic time horizons. Firms are finding that playing by the conventional rules of the game no longer suffices; the game itself has changed.

The second important implication touches on firms' understanding of the notion of *sustainability* of competitive advantage. The notion is being challenged as never before. Traditionally considered something akin to the "holy grail" of strategy, the notion of sustainability is being challenged as never before. Increasingly firms are finding themselves pursuing not "sustainable" competitive advantage, but sporadic, temporary positions of "unsustainable" advantage.

Thus, if at all, circumstances currently experienced by business leaders demand *more* strategic thinking as traditional approaches to strategizing that worked under circumstances characterized by conditions of relative of stability and certainty are essentially obsolete.

In the previous chapter we examined strategy formation in a variety of contexts determined by the dynamics in the enterprise's external competitive environment and its stage of maturity. In this closing chapter we extend this view to explore strategy and strategic thinking as such in an evolving environment that is increasingly unpredictable and complex. We close the chapter with a look at emerging organizational practices that are supportive of strategy and the strategic thinking in today's complex though nonetheless real competitive business environment.

Strategy in practice – the way strategy plays out in the reality of an organization's context – can be examined from multiple perspectives. We will restrict ourselves to examining only two. We begin with an external perspective. In view of the current global economic recession such a perspective is rather timely. Many companies are currently struggling to come to grips with the implications of the crisis for their strategy. The external perspective we will examine is one prompted by multiple possible futures.

For the second perspective we then delve into the organization and explore strategy practice from an internal organizational perspective. Specifically, we look at the learning organization. Why these two perspectives? They represent two different views – one externally instigated; the other relating to internal determinants. Arguably, these two perspectives aptly reflect many of the key factors that are prompting changes in management thinking in the field of strategy today.

Multiple Possible Futures Perspective

As our emerging global economy is expanding in the wake of unprecedented technological and socio-economic change, it is increasingly ushering in its own new rules and distinct opportunities. All the while, it is relegating to obsolescence traditional and existing approaches to management theory that view the world as predictable, linear, measurable, and controllable.

The emerging competitive landscape is complex; it is comprised of a context involving emerging patterns of behavior of organizations, market places, economies, and political infrastructures.[6] One of the implications for organizations emerging from this reality is that of multiple possible futures with varying degrees of uncertainty. Courtney[7] has suggested four possible futures and implications for strategy under the respective circumstances:

- *Level one: Single view of the future* – emerging from a relatively stable environment with a high degree of predictability and little uncertainty.
- *Level two: Limited set of possible futures* – one of which can be expected to occur with high probability.
- *Level three: Range of possible future outcomes* – with increasing uncertainty as to the outcome most likely to occur.
- *Level four: Limitless range of possible future outcomes* – with any outcome possible.

Courtney argues that while all four situations have always existed, it is only now that the realization has set in that a lot more of these are of the level three and level four types than would previously have been admitted.

What does this situation entail for strategy and strategic thinking? Level one through level three situations can be bounded in terms of possible outcomes; with uncertainty obviously increasing with each level. Nonetheless, in all three cases some analysis is possible. Key drivers and triggers can be identified; some analysis of the external environment and the internal context are possible, though with each increasing level the dynamics of the external environment renders this ever more difficult. While a precise forecast may not be possible, approximate bounds of the possible outcomes can be staked out.

Level four situations, on the other hand, represent those for which the range of possible outcomes cannot be bounded. The distant future is fundamentally "unknowable"; it's a situation in which anyone's guess goes. Does this mean that none of what we have examined in previous chapters can be applied? Are companies in these circumstances left simply with the option to "wing it"?

Not at all. Level four situations do not at all eliminate the need for incisive strategic thinking. In fact, given the futility of any attempt at planning in this context, strategic thinking is the only viable approach left to the strategy practitioner under these circumstances. Importantly, level four circumstances require an exploratory mindset of the type encountered in the emergent, *adhocracy*-type organizational configuration examined in Chapter 7. We also saw that strategic learning served a primary supporting role in the strategy process in this type of an organization.

Indeed, strategic learning is not only called for in level four situations; in view of the evolving dynamics of change in global competitive environments, strategic learning is indispensable for the strategy process at all levels.

So, what insights does this perspective lend to our discussion? First, it suggests plausible boundaries to the type of strategy making firms are likely to be engaging in. Very few firms today enjoy the "luxury" of level one and two contexts; most firms compete in level three and level four-type contexts. Therefore, while this doesn't mean that strategy can be approached any less rigorously, it does mean that strategizing needs to be approached *differently*. Embedding and putting to practice a strategic learning perspective is one way of achieving this objective.

Organizational Learning Perspective

The strategic thinking process features all the components of a classic learning process. Hence, it is appropriate that we close the final chapter of this book with a brief reflection on the learning perspective in strategy. It is not by chance that the strategic learning perspective has attained disproportionate attention in recent years. It is arguably the most amenable to building a position of sustainable competitive advantage in today's turbulent business environment. In practice it finds expression in the learning organization and integrates elements of the emergent strategy school. However, as Mintzberg[8] points out, in reality strategy necessarily combines emergent learning with some degree of deliberate control on the part of the firm's management. Strategy in this context has been described in various ways – as encouraging open communication, with a bias for experimentation and reflection, whereby learning through trial and error is tolerated, perhaps even deliberately fostered by management. Indeed, the learning organization is in many ways the antithesis of the traditional, bureaucratic institutionalized organization,[9] which would be operating primarily in a controlling mode.

STRATEGY IN PRACTICE: STRATEGY AND ORGANIZATIONAL LEARNING

It is difficult to imagine an organization devoid of any learning. Senge[10] describes two types of organizational learning, both of which are critical for the strategy process, albeit in different ways:

- *Adaptive reactive learning*: This entails reacting to impulses from the external competitive environment.
- *Generative learning*: This form of organizational learning is pre-emptive and geared towards anticipating the future environment.

The two learning modes are positioned between two extremes of the spectrum of management styles. These have been described in Chapter 7 as the two diametrically opposed organizational configurations – the *institutionalized* configuration and the *emerging, adaptive configuration*. *Adaptive learning* is typically found in institutionalized organizational configurations while *generative learning* is the mode most amenable to an emerging, adhocracy-type configuration.[11] It is to be assumed that increasingly, generative learning will be the preferred mode of learning adopted by organizations.

The two extreme organizational learning styles (*adaptive* versus *generative*) are aptly described in the following quotation, which has been attributed to Ralph Stacey[12]:

> **Ordinary management** is practiced when most of the managers in an organization share the same mental models or paradigm. Cognitive feedback loops then operate in a negative feedback manner so that shared mental models are not questioned; ordinary management is about rational processes to secure harmony, fit, or convergence to a configuration, and it proceeds in an incremental manner.

> **Extraordinary management** involves questioning and shattering paradigms, and then creating new ones. It is a process which depends critically upon contradiction and tension . . . Extraordinary management, then, is the use of intuitive, political, group learning modes of decision making and self organizing forms of control in open-ended change situations. It is the form of management that managers must use if they are to change strategic direction and innovate.

We have already argued in Chapter 7 that the two management styles and associated organizational configurations have important implications for the strategy process. The predispositions have a direct bearing on the approach to strategy taken by these very different configurations. Their respective predisposition is embedded in their fundamental organizational configuration – their structure, processes, culture, and leadership. Increasingly, Stacey's notion of *extraordinary management* is becoming the predisposition of firms focused on achieving a sustainable position of competitive advantage.

Box 9.1 Strategic Dissonance and Strategic Inflection Points

Former Intel chairman and CEO Andy Grove's account of Intel's transition from memory to chip producers exemplifies the notion of *extraordinary management* (or was it, in fact, Intel's *extraordinary organization* at the time?). In reflecting on Intel's exodus from the memory chip business in the mid-1980s, in which it had at one point held practically a 100% share of the market, to the microprocessor business, Grove refers to the *strategic dissonance* and *strategic inflection points* Intel experienced in the critical years in which it abandoned the memory chip business and established itself as market leader in the microprocessor business.[13]

What had happened? Intel as first mover had developed and introduced memory chips or "memories" to the nascent computer industry soon after its start-up in 1968. Competitors, mostly American and small in size, followed in the early 1970s. Throughout the 1970s competition for the next generation of memory chips was largely among American companies. During this period, Intel kept its leadership position. Then, in the early 1980s, the Japanese made their appearance in force in the memory chip market. Not only did they rapidly build an awesome capacity base in memory chip manufacturing, but the quality levels of Japanese memories were consistently and substantially better than those produced by American companies. In fact, Japanese quality levels were superior to what was thought possible by Intel.

What exacerbated the situation for Intel was not only that the Japanese offered superior quality, but that they did so at market dumping price levels. All the while Intel continued to spend heavily on research and development. It focused mostly on improving its memory chips, but some R&D effort was also devoted to a new technology for another device that had been invented in the early 1970s: microprocessors. Both microprocessors and memories are built with a similar silicon chip technology, but their design is different. Microprocessors calculate; they are the brains of the computer, while memory chips merely store information. Because they represented a slower-growing and smaller-volume market than memory chips their technology development was not considered a priority.

That changed after 1984 when memory chip sales virtually collapsed. Intel lost its bearings and was floundering. Its priorities and identity were clearly still focused on memories. In fact, the importance of memories to Intel was firmly embedded in its very beliefs and corporate dogma. Yet memories had become a worldwide commodity. Intel was at a loss as to what to do. In Grove's words, Intel entered into a period of *strategic dissonance* – a period marked by divergence between an organization's actions and its statements. This was a critical three-year period in which Intel's middle management were already in the process of positioning the company in the emerging microprocessor market while its senior management was still engaging in heated strategy debates on how to recapture its former leading position in the memory chip market.

Grove recalls asking Intel's chairman and CEO, Gordon Moore, in a meeting sometime in mid-1985: *"If we got kicked out and the board brought in a new CEO, what do you think he would do?"* To which Gordon responded without hesitation: *"He would get out of memories."* In response, Grove, staring at him numbly, countered: *"Why shouldn't you and I walk out the door, come back and do it ourselves?"*

The rest, as they say, is Intel history. Fortunately, the adjustment of Intel's strategic posture from manufacturer of memories to manufacturer of microprocessors had already begun some time before Intel's senior management caught on. While its senior management was still looking for clever memory strategies, men and women lower in Intel's organization were already initiating the change in direction. Increasingly, production resources were being directed to the emerging microprocessor business – not as a result of senior management direction, but rather as a result of daily decisions by middle managers close to the business front in the face of declining demand for memories and increasing opportunities for business profitability from microprocessors. By the time that Intel's senior management made the formal decision to exit the memory business, only one out of eight silicon fabrication plants were producing memories. The change in strategic direction – in Grove's terminology, Intel's *strategic inflection point* – took a total of three years. It turned out that the exit decision had a significantly less drastic market impact than anticipated and feared by Intel's senior management. A typical reaction of Intel's customers on being informed about Intel's decision to exit memories was: *"It sure took you a long time."*

Grove draws a number of important lessons from Intel's strategic transition period relevant to the strategic learning perspective:

One of these lessons concerns the immensely immobilizing effect that a firm's identity can have. In Intel's case, its legacy and identification with memories formed one of its deep corporate beliefs that, by Grove's admission, were as strong as religious dogma. These blocked the way for an open-minded and rational discussion during the crucial period in which Intel's memory chip markets were rapidly eroding. Interestingly, Intel's customers, having no emotional stake in Intel's decision-making process, had far less difficulty in realizing much sooner what Intel should have been doing. New managers are also often much less encumbered by *legacy thinking* – the emotional involvement experienced by people who have devoted long periods of their life to a company, and who are typically incapable of applying impersonal logic to a situation that calls for detached reasoning.

Finally, it is usually the "people in the trenches" who are in touch with impending changes and the need for strategic adjustment much earlier than senior management. Grove emphasizes this by pointing out that:

> *While management was kept from responding by beliefs that were shaped by our earlier successes, our production planners and financial analysts dealt with allocations and numbers in an objective world. For us senior managers, it took the crisis of an economic cycle and the sight of unrelenting red ink before we could summon up the gumption needed to execute a dramatic departure from our past.*

Intel's strategy shift is remarkable for several reasons. First, it is an example of a successful organizational transformation that was primarily grassroots driven. Second, it resonates with what has always distinguished great strategy in military contexts: the ability, when necessary, to drop preconceived notions and adapt action in accordance with present circumstances. Greene[14] argues that the greatest generals stand out not because they have more knowledge but because of their ability to change a course of action in the face of changing circumstances. Greene elaborates on this point; he explains that knowledge, experience, and theory have limitations in that no amount of advance thinking can prepare you for the ambiguity and countless possibilities often presented in critical circumstances. The Prussian military theorist Carl von Clausewitz referred to the difference between plan and actual happening as *friction*; it is what Grove refers to as *strategic dissonance*. Since friction or strategic dissonance are inevitable in reality, the better we are at adapting our thinking to changing and new circumstances, the more appropriate our responses to those changes will be. Conversely, the more we cling to obsolete and legacy thinking, the more inappropriate the response.

In many ways, Intel's experience confirms what was alluded to in the previous chapter; that is, that strategy formulation and execution occur simultaneously. Weick[3] takes the point further, asserting that *"execution is [strategic] analysis and implementation is [strategy] formulation."*

Indeed, organizational configuration often plays an important factor in determining the approach taken by firms in "finding their strategy." As the Intel case suggests, companies may straddle diametrically opposed organizational configurations when positioned at a *strategic inflection point*. On the one hand, we find the institutionalized configuration representing an entrenched position intent on preservation and exploitation of the current business ("perfecting the known"); on the other hand, the emergent and ad hoc configuration that is at ease with "imperfectly seizing the unknown."[15] Intel's period of *strategic dissonance* illustrates the tension organizations experience when positioned between the two configurations. Not all organizations, however, succeed in resolving the dilemma as well as Intel did. The list of companies that struggled until their final demise to "perfect the known" is long. One needs only to look at companies that have been bumped off the Fortune 100 list over the years for evidence of this.

Weick[3] argues that what is more important than an *a priori* deliberate strategy is a mechanism for channeling and stimulating focused and intense action. This in turn creates meaning and provides the requisite stability and structure for the organization to "get on with it" in the absence of a strategic rationale. Even a vague plan, map, or explanation can serve the purpose. More important than the coherence and accuracy of the plan is the response and attention it receives from the organization. Meaning and validation of the emerging strategic direction then often only take shape *ex tempore.*

To illustrate this point Weick cites the example of the Naskapi natives of Labrador. The Naskapi employ an unusual approach to deciding where they should hunt. A shoulder bone of a caribou is held over a fire until it begins to fracture. The natives take direction on where to hunt from the cracks in the fractured caribou shoulder. Surprisingly, this approach appears to work well for the Naskapi; they almost always succeed in finding game.

Weick offers possible explanations for why this approach appears to work for the Naskapi: the natives end up spending most of each day hunting once they have taken direction from the fractures in the caribou bone. They don't sit around the fire debating on where they should be hunting. On those rare days on which they do fail to find game there is no individual to blame. The failed effort is attributed to the gods testing their faith. The fractured caribou bone keeps the Naskapi moving; by their very action the amount of insight multiplies the data from which meaning can be derived.

Strategy thus often becomes apparent only through retrospective reflection. The coherence and rationality of strategy often become inflated by bias introduced in hindsight. This can lead to misleading conclusions on what needs to be done currently and what appropriate action should be taken in future.

This does not invalidate the strategic thinking approach promulgated in this book in any way. Strategic thinking is as much a mindset as it encompasses an activity, of which the outcome might vary considerably. Critical to good strategic thinking is a clear understanding of the limitations of the insights generated at any point in time. Situations requiring thinking evolve even as we are required to act. Hence, the centrality of the learning process in strategy; learning in the guise of action from which experience and meaning are derived. This is the essence of strategy in practice.

Organizational learning and strategic thinking are inextricably linked. At the core of an organizational culture adept at both learning and strategic thinking is a deeply embedded pre-disposition to challenge assumptions and behaviors. It goes without saying that not all organizations are endowed with these attributes. The following case provides an amusing illustration of how deeply embedded drill routines can long outlive their once logical purpose.

Box 9.2 Holding the Horses

A story (apparently true) that goes back to the early days of the Second World War relates the experiences of a British gun crew of veterans that was training on an aging piece of field artillery. Particularly in the days following the fall of France armaments of all sorts were in short supply. Ancient field artillery units dating back as far back as the Boer War were dusted off, mustered, and redeployed. Hitched to lorries they were used as mobile units in building Britain's coastal defense. One particular gun crew consisting of five veterans appeared to reach a plateau when trying to increase the rapidity of fire. A time-motion expert, brought in to advise the crew on how to improve their performance, watched carefully as the soldiers went through their routines of loading, aiming, and firing. Puzzled by what he observed, the expert took slow-motion pictures of the crew in action. Something appeared odd. It appeared that a moment before firing two members of the gun crew came to a complete standstill and stood at attention for the three-second interval during which the gun discharged. The time-motion expert, at loss for an explanation, sent for an old colonel of the artillery and pointed out the puzzling inactivity of the two crew members. The colonel, too, was puzzled at first. Then, on reexamination of the pictures he exclaimed, *"Ah, I have it. They are holding the horses."*

Source: Morison, E. (1997) Gunfire at Sea: A Case Study of Innovation (Chapter 9 in Tushman, M.L. and Anderson, P. (1997) *Managing Strategic Innovation and Change – A Collection of Readings,* Oxford: Oxford University Press).

Sutton[16] has looked at how organizations can promote learning cultures. He suggests encouraging approaches and practices that run counter current to the prevailing business logic in order to maximize the learning essential for survival in today's relentlessly changing competitive environments. In essence his approach might be seen as a modern business version of the Naskapi caribou bone technique.

An extract from Sutton's list of suggestions for breaking the stranglehold of institutionalized logic is presented in the following summary.

STRATEGY IN PRACTICE: BREAKING THE STRANGLEHOLD OF INSTITUTIONALIZED LOGIC

- In approaching a problem or a new situation emerging from changing circumstances, don't study how a problem of this kind has been approached in the company, industry, or field where you are working – learn to forget by discarding old ways and bringing in people who never knew about the good old days.
- If you do happen to know a lot about how a problem of the type has been resolved previously, bring people on board who are ignorant of it to study it and help resolve it – include a few crackpots, heretics, and dreamers, especially if they are wildly optimistic about their ideas.

- Go outside of your industry for fresh ideas; study how analogous problems have been resolved elsewhere.
- To remind people about the dangers of taken-for-granted assumptions, revisit ideas that were proposed in your company and elsewhere that were once thought to be absurd, but are now widely accepted.
- Identify the most absurd things that companies in other industries are doing (or have done), and develop arguments about why your company ought to do them.
- Use a devil's advocate and dialectical inquiry: assign people to challenge your group's assumptions and decisions and to develop arguments that the opposite assumptions and decisions are actually superior.
- Encourage people to be agnostic about the best business models, business practices, and technologies.
- Hire and retain slow learners of the organizational code.
- Recall the past in your company and others, but interpret it as a cautionary tale about all the blunders and failures suffered by those who become snared in success traps.
- Encourage people to keep fighting over whether established practices are obsolete.

In essence, we conclude that insight-driven strategy is most aptly practiced and most likely to yield strategically relevant insights in an organizational context most closely resembling that of a learning organization. It is in this context that we find organizations capable of the cumulative learning and continual self-renewal required for sustainable competitive positioning.

STRATEGY IN PRACTICE: ADOPTING AN APPROPRIATE LEARNING MINDSET

Lampel[9] describes learning organizations as those that:

- Can learn as much, if not more, from failure as from success;

- Reject the adage *"if it ain't broke, don't fix it"*;
- Assume that the managers and workers closest to the core of the business, whether this be in design, manufacturing, distribution, or the sale of the product, often know more about these activities than their superiors;
- Actively seek to move knowledge from one part of the organization to another, to ensure that relevant knowledge ends up in the organization where it is most needed;
- Invest a lot of effort looking outside their own organization for knowledge.

A Closing Reflection on Insight-Driven Strategy in Practice

In previous discussions we have examined perspectives on how strategy plays out in practice. The choice of the term "plays out" is deliberate, since we might justifiably ask ourselves how much of strategy is deliberately decision driven and how much of strategy is recognizable as a pattern only after the fact. And in light of this, one might ask: where does strategic thinking fit into all of this?

It would appear that increasingly strategy thinkers are reluctant to view strategy as deliberate decision making, as intended by the plan. Increasingly, strategy is seen as a *"pattern in a stream of decisions"* manifested, though, in concrete actions.[8] Decisions, though implied by the actions, are much more elusive. If decision does indeed precede action then the evidence of its realization might range from a statement of intent to nothing at all. Viewing strategy as a stream of actions challenges earlier implicit assumptions made in the literature of organizational theory, which suggests that decision precedes action. Mintzberg's view of strategy, positioned along the continuum between deliberate and emergent – though with an important learning component that resonates more strongly with the emergent view – is consistent with that of Weick,[3] one of the few organizational thinkers to have suggested this early on and, moreover, to have suggested that this need not necessarily be a cause for managerial concern. In fact, he argues that deliberate "strategy" can hurt an organization, possibly leading to paralysis, and that strategy-like outcomes can originate from sources other than deliberate strategy. Weick proposes three themes that suggest how strategy plays out in practice: (1) that action gives rise to, and clarifies, meaning; (2) that the pretext for action is of secondary importance; and (3) that deliberate strategic planning is only one of many pretexts for the generation of meaning in organizations. Weick recounts the anecdote in Box 9.3, an incident that allegedly happened in the Great War, to illustrate his interpretation of strategy.

Box 9.3 Alpine Excursion

A small Hungarian military unit on a reconnaissance mission in the Swiss Alps lost their way in an intense snow storm that lasted for two days. The young lieutenant who had sent out the unit, fearing that he had dispatched the unit to their certain death, was devastated after the unit failed to show up by the second day. However, on the third day the unit returned unscathed and in good spirits. What had transpired? How had they found their way back? Members of the unit recounted how they had indeed considered themselves lost until one of the soldiers in the unit found a map in his pocket. That inspired confidence and prompted the unit to pitch camp and to sit out the storm in the relative safety of their tents. After the storm had broken, they had determined their bearings with the help of the map and proceeded to make their way back to the base camp.

The lieutenant asked to borrow the map and closely examined it. To his astonishment he realized that it was not a map of the Alps at all, but of the Pyrenees!

Did it matter to the lost reconnaissance unit? Not at all, as it turned out. Conceivably, though, it might well have – though detrimentally – had they realized that it was map of the Pyrenees. As it happened, the discovery of the map strengthened their resolve to survive, mobilized clarity of thinking, and prompted focused action. Thereby, irrational though it might seem in hindsight, an entirely irrelevant map saved the unit from almost certain death in the icy alpine wilderness.

Is the insight-driven approach to strategy, indeed is *strategic thinking*, inconsistent in view of the positions argued by Mintzberg and Weick? Not at all. Savvy strategic thinking, by virtue of its facility to animate and orient people in organizations, is entirely consistent with Weick's notion of strategy in practice: people acting, learning, and thereby creating meaning, even if in the absence of a rigorous rationale. These are what enable an appropriate strategic response. Weick's anecdote about the lost alpine reconnaissance unit underscores this point. The map, despite its factual irrelevance, achieved the following: its discovery restored the unit's confidence; it prompted action that enabled the soldiers to survive the storm. And when that had broken, it got them moving in some general direction. Once on the move, iterative observation and reflection enabled the unit to assess where they were in relation to where they wanted to go. Meaning was thereby derived from the circumstances as they evolved – these ultimately led the unit back to their base camp.

What then were the elements of the "strategy" that brought the reconnaissance unit safely back to their base camp, what were its elements? First, it was the action that gave rise to meaning; second, the map as pretext for that action was only of secondary importance; and third, deliberate "strategic planning" as such might be argued to have been inapplicable in this case altogether considering that the map was factually irrelevant to the circumstances.

Strategy as a pretext under which people act and generate meaning in response to changing circumstances is often only recognized as such in retrospect. Given the nature of the complex and fast-changing context of our competitive environments today, regardless of industry, this is a realistic assessment. In a way, this perspective on strategy should not surprise. It is intrinsically Darwinian. Already Darwin understood why adaptation is often so much more powerful than the setting of deliberate direction in the face of evolutionary change. Business environments resemble evolving ecosystems much more than they do the static and predictable settings often assumed in strategic analysis.

This take on reality, however, need not imply chaos and infer helplessness. However, strategic pretexts for action do need to derive contributions from a balance of clear intentions and action based on the best analysis available *and* from action and occurrences that were entirely unplanned for. Further, allowance must be for the fact that plans may not result in outcomes in the way originally intended. Strategic intent and evolving reality thus become much more entwined as action is taken and the firm observes and reflects on what works and what doesn't – and from this derives further appropriate action to be taken.

Strategic thinking might be viewed as an integral component in the strategy process in practice that underpins this activity; it serves as a guiding mechanism for analysis, intuition, and interpretation in the creation of meaning, thereby enabling the derivation of insight required for appropriate strategic action.

SUMMARIZING THE CHAPTER . . .

- Strategy, though often instigated by external factors, is ultimately a pretext for organizational action in the form of an appropriate response.
- Strategy as a pretext for response on the part of the organization in practice occurs along a continuum of

activities positioned between those that are a result of deliberate control and those that are purely emergent in nature.

- Strategy more often than not is recognizable only in hindsight; its coherence and rationality discernible only *a posteriori*; strategy in practice is therefore perhaps most aptly viewed as a pretext for action, from which meaning is derived only after the fact.
- Strategy in practice derives direction from deliberate, intended action as much as it does from unintended occurrences and actions.
- Whether through its contributions to rational analysis, intuition, or interpretation, thereby leading to the ascription of meaning in retrospect, strategic thinking plays a critical role regardless of where we are along the strategy continuum.

Notes

1. De Bono, E. (1984) *Tactics: The Art and Science of Success*, Boston: Little, Brown.
2. Burgelman, R.A. (1983) A Model of the Interaction of Strategic Behaviour, Corporate Context, and the Concept of Strategy, *Academy of Management Review*, Vol. 8, pp. 61–70.
3. Weick, K. (2001) *Making Sense of the Organization*, Oxford: Blackwell Publishing.
4. Mintzberg, H., Ahlstrand, B. and Lampel, J. (2005) *Strategy Bites Back*, Harlow: FT Prentice Hall.
5. This quotation was taken from *Fortune European Edition*: Colvin, G. *How to Manage Your Business in a Recession*, January 26, 2009, p. 68.
6. Boulton, J. and Allen, P. (2007) Complexity Perspective, in Jenkins, M., Ambrosini, V. and Collier, N. (eds) *Advanced Strategic Management*, 2nd edn, Basingstoke: Palgrave Macmillan.
7. Courtney, H. (2008) A Fresh Look at Strategy under Uncertainty: An Interview, *The McKinsey Quarterly*, December 2008.

8. Mintzberg, H. (2009) *Tracking Strategies*, Oxford: Oxford University Press.
9. Lampel, J. (1998) Towards the Learning Organization, in Mintzberg, H., Ahlstrand, B. and Lampel, J. (eds) *The Strategy Safari*, New York: The Free Press.
10. Senge, P.M. (1990) The Leader's New Work: Building Learning Organisations, *Sloan Management Review*, Fall, pp. 7–23.
11. Hall, R. (1997) Complex Systems, Complex Learning, and Competence Building, in Sanchez, R. and Heene, A. (eds) *Strategic Learning and Knowledge Management*, Chichester: John Wiley & Sons Ltd, p. 53.
12. Hall, R. (1997) Note that this quotation is taken from Hall (1997) – which attributes the quotation to Stacey (1993); (Stacey, R.D. (1993) *Strategic Management and Organisational Dynamics*, Pitman) – although the quotation appears not to have made it into R.D. Stacey's 4th edition (2003) of the book.
13. Grove, A. (1996) *Only the Paranoid Survive*, New York: Currency Doubleday.
14. Greene, R. (2006) *The 33 Strategies of War*, London: Profile Books, pp. 21–22.
15. Kelly, K. (1998) *New Rules for the New Economy*, New York: Viking.
16. Sutton, R.I. (2002) *Weird Ideas that Work*, New York: The Free Press.

Putting Strategy to Practice

Probing the Strategic Boundaries of the Firm's Unique Competing Space

IN APPENDIX A, WE:

- derive practical guidance for putting questions for reflecting on the dynamics and their strategic implications at the boundaries of the firm's unique competing space;
- provide templates for summarizing the analyses at the three boundaries;
- extend this analysis to examine interdependencies between the firm's strategic boundaries and their strategic implications.

Strategic issues relevant to the firm's competitive position, we argued in Chapter 5, invariably present themselves at the boundaries of its *unique competing space*. The firm's unique competing space, after all, represents the core of what really matters to the firm in competitive terms. Firms therefore need to continually monitor and scrutinize conditions as they evolve for their potential impact on the boundaries of their unique competing space. The need for strategic thinking arises as a result of events that trigger potential strategic challenges. Strategic thinking, as elaborated on in Chapter 2, then provides systematic guidance on how to proceed with a framing of the relevant issues, the derivation of strategic questions, and, ultimately, clarification regarding the insights required for reconstruction of the relevant "bigger picture." Real business contexts, however, are complex. As has been argued in Chapter 5, issues emerging at one boundary are often coupled to issues that present themselves at one or both of the other two boundaries. Hence, managers also need to look beyond any single boundary of their firm's unique competing space; they need to probe interactions evolving between boundaries.

Consequently, a purposeful exploration of the firm's strategic boundaries enables managers to "cut to the chase" in terms of what really matters to the firm.

The following exercise provides guidance on how to approach the exploration of the firm's strategic boundaries. The method builds on a strategic thinking approach to identifying relevant issues at each of the firm's three strategic boundaries. Relevant strategic issues are prompted by a series of questions that probe the dynamics and strategic implications of change evolving at individual boundaries of the firm's unique competing space as well as interactions between issues arising at more than one of the firm's strategic boundaries.

The three sets of questions presented in the following section pertain to the boundaries indicated in Figure A1.

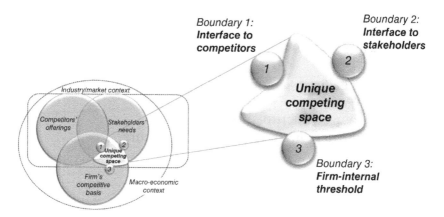

Figure A1   Strategic boundaries of the firm's unique competing space

IMPORTANT: the analysis approach described in this section focuses on a *singular* value offering and its associated unique competing space within a firm. As we argued in Chapter 4, firms usually have more than a single value offering; consequently, their business activities typically extend beyond a single unique competing space and associated value proposition. Hence, the exercise described in the following might be viewed to represent the first of a possible number of such analyses; to cover the extent of a firm's portfolio of value offerings, the exercise would need to be repeated for each value offering (in practice, beginning with the 20% of the business activities that constitute 80% of its competitive impact is a meaningful starting point). A unique competing space and associated value proposition, we argued in Chapter 4, can be defined for any value offering that (1) addresses specific stakeholder (customer) needs; (2) draws on dedicated resources and capability within the firm; and potentially (3) competes against competitors' offerings. Consolidated findings across the firm's portfolio of unique competing spaces provide a comprehensive perspective of the firm's competitive position.

Boundary "1": The Interface to Competitors' Offerings and the Competition

Questions specific to competitors and their value offering(s):

- Who are our competitors today?
- Who might they be in the foreseeable future?
- What do we know about them?
- What don't we know about them?
- What is their competitive offering?
- What do we know about their competitive offering?
- What do we know about customers' perception of our competitors' offering?
- What makes our competitors' value offering inferior (possibly superior?) to ours?
- How is our competitors' offering changing – and in response to what?

More questions, but with a view to the greater competitive implications:

- What critical threats are emerging from our competitors?
- How quickly are these evolving?
- Which key factors are driving changes in our competitor space?
- Which are the really critical ones; the ones requiring prioritized attention?
- How are we protecting ourselves?
- Where are we most vulnerable in view of our competitors' offering(s)?
- What new, potential opportunities are there relative to our competitors?
- How are we exploiting these?

Having addressed these (and possibly other) questions relevant to boundary "1," the most critical issues, threats, and opportunities are summarized in the manner suggested in Table A1.

Table A1 Summary: competitor interface

1. *THE COMPETITOR INTERFACE*		
1. *Three most critical ISSUES at this interface (ranked)*	1.	
	2.	
	3.	
2. *Three critical THREATS emanating from the competition*	1.	
	2.	
	3.	
3. *Three critical OPPORTUNITIES emerging at this interface*	1.	
	2.	
	3.	

Boundary "2": The Interface to Stakeholders' and/or Markets' Needs

Questions specific to our stakeholders and/or markets:

- Who are our key stakeholders?
- What are their needs?
- How well do our stakeholders understand their (own) needs?
- How well do *we* understand our stakeholders and their needs?
- How are stakeholders and their needs changing?
- What makes us special (preferred) in the eyes of our stakeholders?
- Where have we failed in meeting stakeholders' needs?

More questions, but with a view to potential implications:

- What makes us the supplier of choice in our stakeholders' eyes?
- What is the nature of the relationship we are nurturing with our stakeholders?

Table A2 Summary: customer interface

2. THE STAKEHOLDER/MARKET INTERFACE		
1. Three most CRITICAL ISSUES at this interface (ranked)	1.	
	2.	
	3.	
2. Three CRITICAL THREATS evolving at the stakeholder interface	1.	
	2.	
	3.	
3. Three CRITICAL OPPORTUNITIES emerging at the interface to our stakeholders and/or markets	1.	
	2.	
	3.	

- What would we need to do to strengthen our stakeholders' preference for our value offering?
- What new opportunities are emerging in our markets?
- What entirely new, emerging stakeholder/market segments might we be targeting?
- How are we positioned to exploit these new opportunities?

Boundary "3": The Firm-Internal Threshold

Questions specific to the firm's internal threshold:

- What are our most critical resources/capabilities?
- To what extent are these enabling us to achieve a position of competitive advantage?

Table A3 Summary: firm-internal threshold

3. THE FIRM-INTERNAL THRESHOLD		
1. Three most CRITICAL ISSUES at this interface (ranked)	1.	
	2.	
	3.	
2. Three CRITICAL THREATS that present themselves at this interface	1.	
	2.	
	3.	
3. Three IMPORTANT OPPORTUNITIES that present themselves at this interface	1.	
	2.	
	3.	

- To what extent is the organization set up to exploit the organization's resources and capabilities; i.e. mobilize them across the "third boundary"?
- What critical organizational factors enable us most towards achieving competitive advantage?
- Which hinder us most?

More questions, but with a view to greater potential implications:

- How do we orchestrate our strengths most effectively for maximum impact; which factors are most relevant for "getting our act together"?
- Which critical few issues, if resolved in the way we mobilize our resources, would make a substantial difference to our competitiveness?
- What's hindering us from resolving these?
- What are the critical internal hurdles to ensure the optimal transfer of strategic resources into our unique competing space?

- How do we remove these and nurture a smooth running organization?

Consolidation of Analysis Findings with a Critical Reflection on Implications for the Firm's Unique Competing Space

Finally, we pull the outcomes of the preceding boundary analyses together and present these in Table A4, which summarizes the most critical issues, threats, and opportunities for the organization's unique competing space.

Key findings from the preceding analyses that scope the dynamics at the boundaries of the firm's unique competing space are now taken forward and consolidated. Table A5 suggests a structured approach for capturing and presenting the consolidated outcomes.

Table A4 Summary analysis: the unique competing space

4. SUMMARY FINDINGS: UNIQUE COMPETING SPACE	
1. Three most CRITICAL ISSUES challenging our firm's unique competing space	1.
	2.
	3.
2. Three CRITICAL THREATS to our firm's unique competing space?	1.
	2.
	3.
3. Three most IMPORTANT OPPORTUNITIES presenting themselves in our firm's unique competing space?	1.
	2.
	3.

Table A5 Consolidation of analysis findings; derivation of implications for the firm's unique competing space

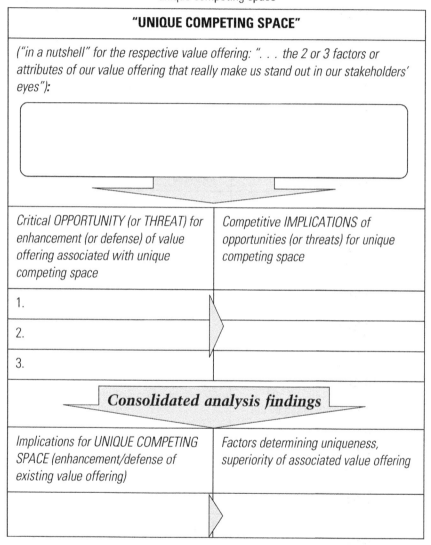

"UNIQUE COMPETING SPACE"
("in a nutshell" for the respective value offering: ". . . the 2 or 3 factors or attributes of our value offering that really make us stand out in our stakeholders' eyes"):

Critical OPPORTUNITY (or THREAT) for enhancement (or defense) of value offering associated with unique competing space	Competitive IMPLICATIONS of opportunities (or threats) for unique competing space
1.	
2.	
3.	

Consolidated analysis findings

Implications for UNIQUE COMPETING SPACE (enhancement/defense of existing value offering)	Factors determining uniqueness, superiority of associated value offering

Inter-Boundary Analysis: Scoping Linked Issues

In the preceding analysis, we have focused on individual boundaries. This is always a good starting point; however, in reality, issues, threats, and opportunities arising at the boundaries of the firm's unique competing space are typically cross-boundary spanning. Questions arising as a result may address interdependencies between any two of the boundaries, as suggested in Table A6.

Table A6 Boundary spanning issues and implications

Implications for . . .

Perspective from . . .	Boundary 1 Competitor interface	Boundary 2 Stakeholder interface	Boundary 3 Internal threshold
Boundary 1 Competitor interface		New entrant competitors with disruptive value offerings positioning themselves in market	Sensing and interpretation of changing nature and intensity of competition; translation of insights into appropriate responsive action
Boundary 2 Stakeholder interface	Customer needs picked up and addressed by the competition; new entrants with disruptive value offerings that fulfill stakeholder needs		Sensing and interpretation of changing customers' needs; translation of these into appropriate responsive action
Boundary 3 Internal threshold	Identification of new opportunities to sustain competitive edge on competitors; alternatively, to catch up	Mobilization of internal capability to improve responsiveness to stakeholders'/ markets' needs	

Often, issues arising at one of the boundaries of the unique competing space have implications for the remaining two boundaries. Hence, the analysis needs to extend to include interdependencies between the boundaries. This quickly becomes a complex task, although one that tends to reflect reality. In real business environments we do often find interrelationships that involve all three boundaries. As a case in point, let's examine the impact that Apple's introduction of its iPhone in 2007 had in the smartphone market. In particular, let's take the perspective of an incumbent player in that market, say, BlackBerry, a leading player in the global smartphone market. Let's assume the perspective of Black-Berry's unique competing space related to its smartphone offering. Although initially dismissive of the new entrant (BlackBerry belittled the iPhone's touchscreen) when the iPhone made its appearance at boundary "1" the iPhone quickly emerged as an offering that addressed customers' needs in a way that Black-Berry's comparative offering in smartphones failed to address (boundary "2"). BlackBerry's inability to respond in a way that protected its incumbent position in the smartphone market points to issues at its internal threshold boundary. Issues at each of the three boundaries were compounded at the other two boundaries (see Box 5.4 in Chapter 5). This ultimately led to BlackBerry's loss of its position in the smartphone market.

Strategy Mapping and Narrative (based on Analysis of the Relevant Strategy Building Blocks)

IN APPENDIX B, WE:
- derive a practical approach for mapping the firm's strategy on the basis of an analysis of its relevant strategy building blocks;
- extend the strategy mapping outcome to include an accompanying narrative that seeks to articulate the firm's strategy;
- provide guidance on deriving an appropriate "three-minute elevator pitch" that captures and expresses the essence of the firm's strategy "in a nutshell."

Strategy Mapping

A number of approaches exist for mapping the firm's strategy.[1] Often these appear in conjunction with strategic performance measurement and monitoring. In this section we develop an approach for distilling and consolidating the essence of the firm's strategy in a way that can be easily understood and communicated. It builds on the outcomes of the preceding analysis (Appendix A) to the extent that it elaborates on and extends the outcomes of the analysis of the firm's *unique competing space*. The approach examined in this section enhances the foregoing analysis with an appropriate "reason to believe"; moreover, it derives an accompanying narrative that enables a clear statement of the firm's strategy. The approach developed in this section draws on the strategy building blocks introduced in Chapter 1.

Strategy mapping and the accompanying narrative are critically important for strategic thinking. They are particularly important for communicating the essence of the firm's strategy to its multiple stakeholders. Relatively few executives can summarize the essence of their firm's strategy in an articulate, concise, and brief statement.[2] In this section we show how the concepts and analysis approaches derived and presented throughout this book can be applied to do just that.

Figure B1 presents the general scheme involved in developing the strategy map and accompanying narrative. The strategy building blocks in Chapter 1 serve to prompt the inputs to the underlying analysis.

---

[1] See Marr, B. (2006) *Strategic Performance Management*, Oxford: Butterworth-Heinemann/Elsevier; or Kaplan, R.S. and Norton, D.P. (2004) *Strategy Maps*, Boston: Harvard Business School Press.
[2] Collis, D.J. and Rukstad, M.G. (2008) Can You Say What Your Strategy Is? *Harvard Business Review*, April 2008, pp. 82–90.

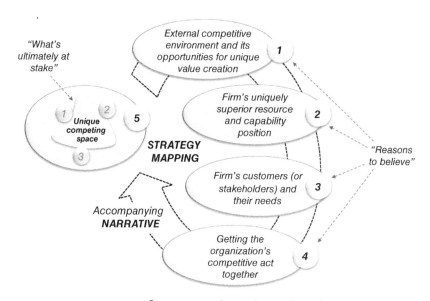

Figure B1   Strategy mapping and narrative scheme

Four of the building blocks probe the external context, internal basis of competitiveness, customers' needs, and the organization's ability to orchestrate mobilization of its resources and capabilities in a way that makes them strategically relevant and converge on the expression of a fifth building block, the firm's unique competing space.

The following templates provide a structured approach to the analysis that culminates in summary of the firm's relevant strategy on a single page.

1. Assessing the External Competitive Context

The first building block probes the firm's external competitive context; in particular changes at all levels of analysis – including macro-economic, industry, and market levels. Factors affecting change in the firm's external context cannot be influenced by the firm; a good understanding of them nonetheless provides critical insight into existing and emerging opportunities and threats.

Building block 1: *EXTERNAL COMPETITIVE CONTEXT*		
Which MACRO-ECONOMIC factors are driving changes; how are these changing the nature of competition?		
What INDUSTRY- and MARKET- level factors are changing; how are these changing the nature of competition in the relevant markets?		
Who are the COMPETITORS; what are they doing?		
What are the order-winning KEY SUCCESS FACTORS – and how are these changing? What are the implications?		
What are the key OPPORTUNITIES that emerge from these?		
What are the key THREATS that emerge from these?		

2. Assessing the Firm's Internal Basis of Competitiveness

The second building block probes the firm's internal basis of competitiveness. These are mainly the firm's (ideally uniquely superior) resources and capabilities, and therefore those factors that the firm controls.

Building block 2: *INTERNAL BASIS OF COMPETITIVENESS*		
What are our UNIQUE RESOURCES AND CAPABILITIES; what makes them "unique"?		
How do our resources and capabilities compare with our competitors?		
To what extent are we exploiting our unique resources and capabilities?		
What key OPPORTUNITIES exist exploiting these even more?		
What THREATS exist with respect to our resources/capabilities?		
What are the key THREATS that emerge from these?		

3. Assessing the Firm's Customers' Needs

The third building block probes the firm's internal basis of competitiveness. These are mainly the firm's (ideally uniquely superior) resources and capabilities, and therefore those factors that the firm controls.

Building block 3: STAKEHOLDERS' NEEDS ASSESSMENT		
Who are our CUSTOMERS (and key stakeholders)?		
What are our CUSTOMERS' NEEDS and how are these changing?		
What is enabling us to understand our customers' needs better than our competitors?		
What new OPPORTUNITIES are emerging with respect to our customers?		
What THREATS are emerging?		

4. Assessing the Firm's Organizational Wherewithal

The fourth building block probes the firm's ability to orchestrate its (ideally uniquely superior) resources and capabilities in a way that makes them competitively relevant. Essentially this task focuses on the mobilization of the firm's strategic resources and capabilities into its unique competing space. Resources and capabilities in the firm are strategically relevant only when this is accomplished.

Building block 4: "GETTING THE ACT TOGETHER"		
What are our greatest PERFORMANCE STRENGTHS?		
What are our greatest WEAKNESSES/ VULNERABILITIES?		
Which few improvements would have a significant impact on our competitive performance?		
What are the key OPPORTUNITIES emerging for the organization?		
What are the key THREATS facing the organization?		

5. Pulling it all Together: The Firm's Unique Competing Space, Associated Elements, and Strategy

This final template pulls together key elements of the preceding analyses.

UNIQUE COMPETING SPACE AND ELEMENTS OF THE STRATEGY MAP		
Our unique VALUE PROPOSITION		
	Our external OPPORTUNITIES (possibly, THREATS)	
Reasons to believe	Our unique RESOURCES AND CAPABILITIES	
	Our CUSTOMERS' NEEDS addressed	
	Our ORGANIZATIONAL WHEREWITHAL	
Our uniquely differentiated STRATEGY "in a nutshell"		

Strategy Narrative

The strategy narrative is the final piece of this exercise. It goes hand in hand with the strategy derived in the previous section. The strategy narrative summarizes the essence of the strategy derived in the preceding part; it does this in the form of a concise articulation of the key elements of the strategy encompassed by the respective unique competing space; importantly, it also provides a compelling rationale, the "reasons to believe" that underpin the firm's claim to its unique competing space. This rationale is based on arguments derived from the constituent four building blocks (Figure B1).

While there is no prescribed format and style, the strategy narrative is normally no longer than about 500 words. Its storyline needs to be clear, readable, and geared towards communicating the essence of the strategy in the most effective manner possible. It needs to be leveled at the relevant stakeholders. Its ultimate version is the "three-minute elevator pitch," in which the essence of the strategy and its underlying rationale are credibly and effectively delivered in a time-limited briefing.

The potential power of compelling and well-scripted strategy narratives cannot be emphasized enough; they are the means by which firms optimally communicate and achieve buy-in with both external and internal key stakeholders.

INDEX

Printed and bound by CPI Group (UK) Ltd, Croydon, CR0 4YY

16/04/2025